BEST OF THE JOURNALS IN
RHETORIC AND COMPOSITION

Best of the Journals in Rhetoric and Composition
SERIES EDITORS: STEVE PARKS, JESSICA PAUSZEK, KRISTI GIRDHARRY, AND CHARLES LESH

The Best of the Journals in Rhetoric and Composition series represents an attempt to foster a nationwide conversation—beginning with journal editors, but expanding to teachers, scholars and workers across the discipline of Rhetoric and Composition—to select essays that showcase the innovative and transformative work now being published in the field's journals. Representing both print and digital journals in the field, the essays in each edition represent a snapshot of the traditional and emergent conversations occurring in our field—from classroom practice to writing in global and digital contexts, from border rhetorics to social justice research. Together, the essays provide readers with a rich understanding of the present and future direction of the field.

Essays included in the series undergo a rigorous review process. First, all essays must have already crossed the threshold to be published in an academic journal in the field. Then, out of all the essays published by a journal, the editor can only select two essays. Next, the series editors create reading groups across the country. These groups feature full-time faculty, adjunct faculty, and graduate students who teach in a range of institutions. In this way, all the nominated essays are assessed and ranked for how they speak to the interests of all those who work in our field—a review process that is unique to the series. The series editors, plus one guest editor, then assemble a final selection of essays that have the strongest support from the reading groups for inclusion in a particular volume.

In this way, the Best of the Journals in Rhetoric and Composition series includes the only publications in the field that can truly claim to represent the collective insight of students, teachers, and scholars into the pressing issues of the current moment. For this reason, authors selected for inclusion are celebrated at their home institutions and journals actively seek recognition for their work. The series provides the broadest conception of scholarship in our field and so each volume can find a home in introductory graduate courses and advanced undergraduate courses everywhere.

BEST OF THE JOURNALS IN RHETORIC AND COMPOSITION 2020

Edited by Jessica Pauszek, Kristi Girdharry, Charles Lesh, David Blakesley, and Steve Parks

Parlor Press
Anderson, South Carolina
www.parlorpress.com

Parlor Press LLC, Anderson, South Carolina, USA

© 2021 by Parlor Press. Individual essays in this book have been reprinted with permission of the respective copyright owners.
All rights reserved.
Printed in the United States of America

S A N: 2 5 4 - 8 8 7 9

ISSN 2327-4778 (print)
ISSN 2327-4786 (online)

978-1-64317-223-1 (paperback)
(978-1-64317-224-8 (pdf)
(978-1-64317-225-5 (ePub)

2 3 4 5

Cover design by David Blakesley.
Printed on acid-free paper.

Parlor Press, LLC is an independent publisher of scholarly and trade titles in print and multimedia formats. This book is available in paper and digital formats from Parlor Press on the World Wide Web at http://www.parlorpress.com or through online and brick-and-mortar bookstores. For submission information or to find out about Parlor Press publications, write to Parlor Press, 3015 Brackenberry Drive, Anderson, South Carolina, 29621, or email editor@parlorpress.com.

Contents

Transformational Change: Answering the Call of the Moment   *vii*
    Genesis Barco Medina, Berte Reyes, and Brian McShane

COLLEGE COMPOSITION AND COMMUNICATION
Reflection as Relationality: Rhetorical Alliances and Teaching Alternative Rhetorics   *3*
    V. Jo Hsu

COMMUNITY LITERACY JOURNAL
Decolonizing Community Writing with Community Listening: Story, Transrhetorical Resistance, and Indigenous Cultural Literacy Activism   *32*
    Rachel C. Jackson with Dorothy Whitehorse DeLaune

COMPOSITION STUDIES
Decolonial Potential in a Multilingual FYC   *58*
    Cruz Medina

THE JOURNAL OF MULTIMODAL RHETORICS
Powerful Marginality: Feminist Scholarship through Comics   *85*
    Rachel Rys

LITERACY IN COMPOSITION STUDIES
Making Citizens Behind Bars (and the Stories We Tell About It): Queering Approaches to Prison Literacy Programs   *105*
    Alexandra Cavallaro

PEDAGOGY
The Adaptive Cycle Resilience in the History of First-Year Composition   *132*
    Clancy Ratliff

REFLECTIONS
Learning to Value Cultural Wealth Through Service Learning: Farmworker Families' and Latina/o University Students' Mutual Empowerment via Freirean and Feminist Chicana/o- Latina/o Literature Reading Circles   *154*
    Georgina Guzmán

RHETORIC OF HEALTH & MEDICINE
"All Smell Is Disease": Miasma, Sensory Rhetoric, and the Sanitary-Bacteriologic of Visceral Public Health   *182*
   Emily Winderman, Robert Mejia, and Brandon Rogers

THE WAC JOURNAL
Building Sustainable WAC Programs: A Whole Systems Approach   *215*
   Michelle Cox, Jeffrey Galin, and Dan Melzer

WLN: A JOURNAL OF WRITING CENTER SCHOLARSHIP
The Role of New Media Expertise in Shaping Consultations   *245*
   Jessica Clements

Transformational Change: Answering the Call of the Moment

Genesis Barco Medina, Berte Reyes, and Brian McShane

Let's talk about a *transformation*.

Scholars in this collection call for radical positions, or what we identify as transformational change. We define transformational change as a recognition that past myths, systems, beliefs, and methods simply do not suffice in continuing to embody where the field is heading. Once transformational change is enacted, our perception changes. We no longer can return to seeing, doing, or being like past ways. A new foundation, new pillars to support our work, begs to be built. When will we consider that perhaps the existing pillars of our field cannot continue to hold the weight of our new work? The scholars here are interested in bridging gaps that have existed in the discipline and in our society for years now, allowing teachers and students to engage in the field of Rhetoric and Composition and communities without repeating older assumptions or reinforcing previously held biases. In other words, a great deal of this collection's work considers a move away from foundational practices, the pillars that built this field, towards a creation of something new that operates in a unique way.

This year's collection asks us to consider how we see, how we understand, and what we plan to do about the worlds we are a part of—in effect, providing some answers to questions of visibility, assessment, and transformational change. Scholars offer a variety of possibilities by way of student stories and pedagogical models that teachers on-the-ground can employ right now that add valuable resources to be integrated in today's realities and not our past histories. While Rhetoric and Composition has long held interest in changing pedagogies and shining a light on voices currently oppressed, scholars in this collection continue this work in innovative ways that are reflective of our current moment.

Visibility

Several works in this volume are interested in examining, expanding, and pushing against notions of *visibility*. Scholars such as Emily Winderman, Robert Mejia, Brandon Rogers, Rachel Jackson, Dorothy Whitehorse DeLaune, and Cruz Medina take opportunities to revisit and *re-see* certain knowledge our field has accepted to be true. As scholars in this edition questioned who we are seeing and how we are seeing them, they identified some areas in need of re-vision.

The focus and scope of scholarship is subject to change given the political, economic, and social realities of the moment. In the face of COVID-19, scholarship concerned with previous events of diseases or viruses will invariably be read through the lens of the current pandemic, but we can take lessons from this view. In "'All Smell is Disease': Miasma, Sensory Rhetoric, and the Sanitary-Bacteriologic of Visceral Public Health" Winderman et al. illustrate the ways in which a public can be shown a disease in a light that causes them to fear members of a certain group – be that cultural, gendered, or otherwise – and it raises questions we would all benefit from asking today about why this attitude persists. As Winderman et al. note, "[T]he metonymic transformation of Mallon into Typhoid Mary threatened to subsume the ethnic, gendered, and classed essence of Irish immigrants writ large, and it operated as a visceral public health pedagogy about corporeal and national boundaries."

Scholars in this volume address issues of colonization by implementing decolonial tactics into pedagogy and research. This work allows readers to see how bodies are systematically rendered invisible. Jackson and DeLaune's "Decolonizing Community Writing with Community Listening: Story, Transrhetorical Resistance, and Indigenous Cultural Literacy Activism" focuses on the systems of injustice that have been obscuring Native Americans and their rights for hundreds of years. Noting the "genocidal policies that included violence, militarism, containment, land theft, removal, relocation, and assimilation," Jackson and DeLaune are shining a harsh light on governmental practices that have attempted to erase a population from the national discussion and strip their culture from them through physical and legislative violence. To combat this history and strategies of injustice, Jackson and DeLaune offer a decolonial praxis: community listening. Extending the decolonial lens to the classroom, Medina's article "Decolonial Potential in Multilingual FYC" shines a pedagogical light on how to approach the often still-colonizing effect first-year composition can have on students who are non-native English speakers. Medina cites the writings of students who have encountered the FYC system's standardization and highlights words like "vulnerability," "assimilation," as well as the perceived superiority of English. Medina is clear to connect this attitude to today's xenophobia in politics and argues a bilingual approach as an antidote to the colonized classroom. Medina offers pedagogical tools that provide "space for students to discuss the spectrum of their languaging abilities," challenging perceptions of the composition classroom and (in)visibilities to language practices.

As the field expands, the ways in which we see the problems we have been grappling with has started to change. We are making visible the pillars of silence we've built around some and rebuilding and uncovering forgotten history. We are learning to shift from Western modes of listening, from the fearful attitudes of the past, but are still grappling with their vestiges. We are beginning to see these problems as indicative of broader, systemic deficiencies that need to be addressed.

Assessing Ecologies

The authors in this volume take up the need for addressing systemic deficiencies by adopting ecological approaches to their practices. The unique approaches towards *assessing ecologies* translates into practices that prioritize relationship building between various stakeholders--whether in the classroo, the university, or communities. Scholars demonstrate their receptivity towards another and recognize their position as accountable to another within their communities. This is beyond empty pledges to an ephemeral "social responsibility." Instead of acting as outsiders serving an Other, the authors position themselves and others as part of an interdependent ecology.

Clancy Ratliff takes on an ecological approach in "The Adaptive Cycle: Resilience in the History of First-Year Composition." Ratliff borrows from environmental studies to analyze the state of FYC by using various phases of ecological growth to explain the program's precarity. Ratliff provides ideas for reorganization, a way to bolster FYC into a program which can survive pressures, with such options as more involvement with the teaching and shaping of dual-credit composition classes, all the way to embracing translanguaging and worker solidarity, all with the aim of radically transforming the current structure for long term sustainability. With a similar emphasis on systemic examinations and sustainability, Michellle Cox, Jeffrey Galin, and Dan Melzer propose a new framework for designing WAC programs in "Building Sustainable WAC Programs: A Whole Systems Approach." The authors draw from complexity, systems, resilience, and sustainable development theory to construct the whole systems approach--a theoretical foundation for developing WAC programs which "creates an iterative and participatory cycle to establish institutional change that integrates ongoing assessment of sustainability."

Moving from the systemic to the interpersonal, V. Jo Hsu re-envisions the personal narrative as a relational practice in "Reflection as Relationality: Rhetorical Alliances and Teaching Alternative Rhetorics." Hsu looks to theories of alternative rhetorics as well as rhetorical alliance to develop a pedagogical practice which allows students to "see themselves forging alliances across disparate communities in order to change the conditions of our shared worlds." In this way, Hsu's pedagogical practice asks students to consider themselves as part of a living network, taking the ecological approach to their reflective writing. Similarly, Georgia Guzman's article, "Learning to Value Cultural Wealth Through Service Learning" examines social change through relationship-building. Here, Guzman presents a service-learning model that connects Latinx students at a Hispanic Serving Institute (HSI) with farmworkers in California. Guzman assesses an ecology based in inclusion that moves away from the Predominantly White Institution (PWI) serving a community they have no relation with, and rather focuses on the ecology created when similar identities between students and farmworkers are discovered through partnered reading circles.

It's that kind of relationship building, between community and academy, that is at the heart of assessing ecologies. Where visibility shows us the systemic issues within our communities, assessing ecologies allows us to understand the communities we are a part of, affecting others while being affected through our scholarly practices. From building these interdependent relationships, it becomes possible to make lasting structural change.

Transformational Change

Uncovering the (in)visibility of our work and assessing ecologies are radical exercises that lead towards transformational change. To be clear, transformational change is different than transitional change. Transitional change calls for ephemeral adjustments—it continues to work from the current foundational pillars for discussing assessment, teaching, and writing. Transitional change is simply a cover-up; a temporary fix rather than uncovering the roots to plant new ones. Transformational change has the potential to be a revolutionary solution that uproots systems of exclusion and replaces them with change that resists recreating practices that may be oppressive, outdated, or misaligned for the current moment. As we will witness in the coming pages, transformational change for 2020 scholars leaves the scholarship, for a moment, in pursuit of a politics of inclusivity, community, and equity. Once these three are met, the scholarship itself organically comes to unfold. In essence, our practices of research and knowledge-making is changing. Replacing the current foundation of Rhetoric and Composition's practices presents much expected contention and resistance. As it should, considering transformational change is disrupting years of knowledge and its making; however, as radical as a demand transformational change calls for, scholars of our field were found knocking down pillars of tradition and reconstructing new ones to revolutionize how we form our goals as writers, teachers, community organizers, and public citizens.

For this collection, scholars accredit transformational change in unique measures. Alexandra Cavallaro, Jessica Clements, and Rachel Rys reveal that transitioning from one method, practice, or way of knowing does not bring about change that is revolutionary or radical enough; rather, these scholars are interested in inventing and thinking of new ways of doing that builds a new foundation for the field. In "Making Citizens Behind Bars," Cavallaro is not interested in transforming the individual, but rather transforming the system in the institution. The study uproots and shifts the focus from a narrative that is usually focused on the individual to the system and its precedents. Similarly, Clements also focuses on how to change the assumed beliefs and narratives of an institute: the Writing Center. Clements argues writing centers need to transform training for student tutors to include multimodality. Clements transforms how to view Writing Center pedagogy that is inclusive to multimodality scholarship and creates an opening where students can contribute to the expertises of multimodality regardless of limitations on experience and knowledge. Finally, much like Clements creates openings for new ways of thinking, Rys also compels readers to become receptive of new writing forms. The work comes together by making visible the silenced voices, assessing the ecologies that lead to that marginalization, and transforming the systems by introducing spaces of empowerment through comics. Rhys transformationally changes the field's expectation of scholarly writing by encouraging audiences to take up other new, exploratory ways of presenting research and knowledge-making.

Politics of inclusivity, community, and equity can be guides towards transformational change and create opportunities to develop radical scholarship as seen in these three scholars. Transformational change provides the capacity to challenge the field to think outside our limitations and question how we view ourselves as instructors, mentors, and listeners. We become better advocates and missionaries to our disciplines of interest when we center a fight for change that reorients and questions our foundation, rather than falling victim to another set of temporary, older solutions.

Conclusion

The Best of the Journals in Rhetoric and Composition 2020 encourages us to contemplate the limitations of the structures the field has built and placed before us. Therefore, we are invited to ask ourselves some ambitious questions. Who are the voices we are silencing in the name of scholarship? What are the practices we fail to see? How do we better center the community rather than our own scholarly ambitions? Where are we falling short in creating radical solutions? How can we employ pedagogical changes to decolonize higher education? How do we consider the temporality of scholarship in our present and for the future? What *type* of change do we want to see? What *type* of change do we *need*?

To be clear, transformational change is not a fix-all-solution to provide equity across all mediums and peoples. In fact, transformational change can be dangerous for some depending on what values are replaced. However, the work of this collection provides news pillars of support for the work we need now. What we can conclude from their work is that the mission of writing studies, rhetoric, and composition cannot continue to be built on its current pillars. The above scholars have displayed that this much is true. In creating new pillars, we shift the apex of rhetoric and composition: the practice of writing. Our goals are reoriented, and we are reinventing the standards of our field and what we do. Suddenly, old practices do not suffice to complete the work we set out to do. Such radical change is our only option to now witness the assets of our investments in new practices and beliefs. This collection previews just a few scholars who are paving the way. Change is inevitable, but the type of change we choose to enact is worth considering. Transformational change becomes necessary if we look to revolutionize what and who others will remember us as. Otherwise, we risk the greater impact of what our work can do now, who we do it for, and those who will come after us.

A Note on the Selection Process

The ten articles selected for this volume represent important scholarship from journals in our field. Each selection was first nominated by the current editor(s) of the journal. From these nominations, graduate students and faculty of all ranks from a range of institutions read and ranked each article according to the following criteria:

- Article demonstrates a broad sense of the discipline, demonstrating the ability to explain how its specific focus in a sub-disciplinary area addresses broader concerns in the field.
- Article makes original contributions to the field, expanding or rearticulating central premises.
- Article is written in a style which, while based in the discipline, attempts to engage with a wider audience or concerns a wider audience.

Based on the recommendations from reading groups, the series editors selected the final list of essays. We hope that this selection illustrates the richness and diversity of our field and the possibilities that emerge when we are given the chance to read across journals and publishing platforms.

We are very grateful to all of the associate editors who organized and participated in reading groups that helped choose the selected essays. We are also grateful to our assistant editors who took the time to diligently read and discuss the nominated articles and offer their insights. We proudly list them here:

Associate Editors

Emily Artiano, University of Southern California
Genesis Barco Medina, Northeastern University
Erin Costello Wecker, University of Montana
Heather Falconer, Curry College
Kristen Getchell, Babson College
Brent Griffin, Northeastern University
Eva Latterner, University of Virginia
Brian McShane, Texas A&M University - Commerce
Michelle Niestepski, Lasell College
Maria Novotny, University of Wisconsin-Milwaukee
Berte Reyes, University of Arizona
David Riche, University of Denver

Assistant Editors

Curry College
Kellie Cannon (also Coastal Carolina Community College)
Lindsay Illich

Framingham State University
Colleen Coyne

Endicott College
John Fiske

Lasell University
Gregory Cass
Alex Cronis

Sara Large
Annie Ou

Massachusetts Institute of Technology
Mary Caulfield

Massasoit Community College
Katherine DiMarca

Northeastern University
Thomas Akbari
Laura Beerits
Bret Keeling
Matthew Noonan
Melissa Wolter-Gustafson

Northern Essex Community College
Patricia Portanova

Texas A&M University - Commerce
Miriam Akoto
Emily Bauer
Rachel Huddleston
Reza Panahi

University of Denver
April Chapman-Ludwig
Richard Colby
Pauline Reid
Keith Rhodes
Rebekah Shultz-Colby
Daniel Singer

University of Southern California
Stephanie Bower
Brent Chappelow
Rochelle Gold
Cory Nelson
Alisa Sánchez

University of Virginia
Anastatia Curley
Heidi Nobles
Emelye Keyser
Micah Holmes
Mary Chandler Philpott
Natalie Thompson
S. Fain Riopelle
Samuel Nicol
Karen Huang
Indu Ohri

University of Wisconsin-Milwaukee
Kristin DeMint Bailey
Daphne Daugherty
Angelyn Sommers
Trevor Sprague
Molly Ubbesen

Washington State University Tri-Cities
Patty Wilde

Best of the Journals
Rhetoric and Composition

COLLEGE COMPOSITION AND COMMUNICATION

College Composition and Communication is on the web at https://cccc.ncte.org/cccc/ccc

College Composition and Communication publishes research and scholarship in rhetoric and composition studies that supports college teachers in reflecting on and improving their practices in teaching writing and that reflects the most current scholarship and theory in the field. The field of composition studies draws on research and theories from a broad range of humanistic disciplines—English studies, rhetoric, cultural studies, LGBT studies, gender studies, critical theory, education, technology studies, race studies, communication, philosophy of language, anthropology, sociology, and others—and from within composition and rhetoric studies, where a number of subfields have also developed, such as technical communication, computers and composition, writing across the curriculum, research practices, and the history of these fields.

Reflection as Relationality: Rhetorical Alliances and Teaching Alternative Rhetorics[1]

V. Jo Hsu's "Reflection as Relationality: Rhetorical Alliances and Teaching Alternative Rhetorics" models how personal writing and a pedagogy attentive to it can increase students' sense of belonging while also exploring radical critique of identity politics and writing itself as personal practice.

---

1. *College Composition and Communication*, vol. 70, no. 2. © 2018 by NCTE.

Reflection as Relationality: Rhetorical Alliances and Teaching Alternative Rhetorics

V. Jo Hsu

Building on studies of alternative rhetorics, this article envisions personal writing pedagogy as a relational endeavor that fosters rhetorical alliances among disparate communities. I detail a particular course design through which "personal reflection" becomes a means of enacting more radical forms of belonging.

The mandate is to search for classroom practices that use, build upon, and enhance experiences and that permit the re-definition and reconfiguration of acceptable forms of expression, representation, and presentation.

—Jacqueline Jones Royster,
"Academic Discourses or Small Boats on a Big Sea"

Fifteen years ago, Christopher L. Schroeder et al.'s *ALT DIS: Alternative Discourses and the Academy* examined the emergence of "hybrid," "mixed," and "alternative" discourses within scholarly and student writing. These texts, wide-ranging and diverse, blend nonstandard discursive forms with academic conventions to explore new methods and reach broader publics (Bizzell, "Hybrid" 12). In Bizzell's words, they "have combined elements of traditional academic discourse with elements of other ways of using language, admitting personal experience as evidence, for example, or employing cultural allusions or language variants that do not match the cultural capital of the dominant white male group" ("Intellectual" 2). The book's introduction suggests that "these kinds of nontraditional academic discourse may soon make the debate over students' right to their own language moot" (Schroeder et al. ix). That debate, however, has a way of resurfacing. While most of composition's scholar-teachers acknowledge the tremendous contributions that have been made through strategic combinations of personal and academic traditions, many express concern that assignments based in personal experience would only encourage students to parrot dominant cultural values (Eldred and Mortensen; France; Williams, "Heroes," "Speak"). This essay begins by asking how we might reenvision personal writing assignments to encourage the sort of complicated, paradigm-shifting work with which we associate texts such as Victor Villanueva's *Bootstraps*, Min-Zhan Lu's "From Silence to Words," and Keith Gilyard's *Voices of the Self*. Like Gilyard, I remain aware that "whenever we participate in the dominant discourse, no matter how liberally we may tweak it, we help to maintain it" ("Literacy" 268). I share Gilyard's optimism, though, that these forms of participation might open "very real material possibilities" both for helping individual students engage the convoluted codes of the academy and for reexamining and gradually changing those codes.

To explore such possibilities, this essay proceeds in four parts. First, I bridge several disciplinary discussions to define alternative rhetorics as a relational endeavor that finds "connective possibilities" (Powell, "Down" 40) among disparate experiences. Second, I draw from Native theories of rhetoric to show how rhetorical alliance can direct personal writing assignments toward helping students examine and respond to the discursive practices that surround them—including those of the academy. Third, I describe a course in which students used personal writing to participate in alternative rhetorics. Particularly, by interrogating and clarifying one another's requests for more "reflection" in essay drafts, students were able to develop a wider repertoire of relational tactics for negotiating different rhetorical exigencies. Their stories demonstrate how personal writing as alliance building might enable more deliberate engagement with discourses of power and invite alternative ways of speaking and being in the world. In the spirit of relationality, I then conclude with insights from my students—who have taught me how our classes can help us reassess our own assumptions about language and writing.

Defining Alternative Rhetorics

> *"[W]e must be willing to go beyond the page upon which our scholarly essays are printed, we must be willing to forego the pretense that each story exists all by itself, that each essay provides all the knowledge that any reader would need."* (Powell, "Down" 57)

In her chapter in *ALT DIS*, Malea Powell rightfully questions the term "alternative," which risks reaffirming certain discourses as the "center" ("Listening" 15) but may also reflect a "genuine turn to embrace 'alternative assumptions about discourse'" (Royster, qtd. in "Listening" 15). As

I use it here, *alternative* does *not* signal any inherent quality of a text. Rather, it describes discursive practices that de-center normative worldviews. Toward that end, alternative rhetorics are a tireless process—vigilant in recognizing and responding to the appropriative tendencies of dominant narratives.

I build this working definition from David L. Wallace's *Compelled to Write*, which describes alternative rhetorics as negotiating among personal and collective identities in order to "bring the operation of culture into relief" (12).[1] Alternative rhetorics are inherently personal because they "[engage] the individual's subjectivity rather than attempting to erase it" (5), and they use those personal experiences to "unsettle problematic dominant cultural values and the discourses of power that support them" (15). These texts strategically combine personal and cultural narratives to expose structures of domination as well as how individuals move within—and can at times resist or change—those structures. In using the plural *rhetorics*, I align with Laura Gray-Rosendale and Sibylle Gruber's (2001) *Alternative Rhetorics*, which stresses the "multiplicity and fragmentation within and between different rhetorics" (5). Like Wallace, though, I focus on the deeply personal costs of disciplinary and social change and urge rhetoric and composition toward more reflexive pedagogical practices that address how individual students encounter these histories through different trajectories. In its study of alternative rhetorics, *Compelled to Write* focuses primarily on texts that have already achieved substantial recognition within the academy, exploring narratives by major figures such as Frederick Douglass and Gloria Anzaldúa. In fact, both Douglass's *Narrative* and Anzaldúa's *Borderlands* appear frequently in both composition textbooks and rhetoric anthologies as examples of how rhetoric "can be inhabited by those considered to be 'others'" (Glenn and Lunsford 9). Undoubtedly, rhetoricians have written and recovered a robust archive of materials that use personal narrative to intervene in and shift academic writing practices, and these "landmark" texts have been critical in those shifts. Alterity, however, is not a fixed state, but a relationship—an angle of approach that is continually recalibrated. In the words of Gayatri Spivak, it is an unglamorous "chipping away at the binary oppositions and continuities that emerge continuously in the supposed account of the real" (72). In this essay, then, I focus on alternative rhetorics as an ongoing pursuit rather than an endpoint.

For students to participate in this continual renegotiation of "the real," they need tools with which to understand and articulate the operations of power through which their realities have been built. They must be equipped to chart and mobilize their own positions within existing social configurations. Toward that end, writing assignments based in students' experiential knowledge have underexplored potential. While personal writing remains a staple in composition classes, these assignments are typically self-contained. Kimberly K. Gunter's 2011 "Braiding and Rhetorical Power Players" observes that personal writing in composition is more often relegated to the initial, easy "gimme" assignment (71)—a far cry from the intellectual exploration and cultural critique of alternative rhetorics. With this essay, I hope to extend alternative rhetorics into the composition classroom by reconceptualizing personal writing assignments as a means of rhetorical alliance.

Among Bizzell's, Wallace's, and Gunter's entreaties that we teach students to "connect the [course] materials with their own experience" (Bizzell, "Hybrid" 19), to "tell [their] story" (Wallace 207), and to "bring to bear a critical lens on their cultures, subjectivities, and rhetorics" (Gunter 77), there is little concrete guidance in terms of how to help students develop their critical lenses. In fact, Bizzell's "Hybrid Academic Discourses: What, Why, How" expressly advises against presenting students with the taxonomy of alternative rhetorics that she creates in her article. Instead, these hybrid forms should be a place of experimentation. In the absence of more explicit discussion, though, alternative rhetorics have remained inaccessible for many student writers.

Over a decade after Bizzell's foundational text, Gunter still describes academic writing (in composition classes) as the impersonal, thesis-driven, jargon-heavy and scientific essay that Bizzell contrasted with alternative rhetorics in 1999.[2] Meanwhile, personal writing assignments often replicate the "dominant narratives" that have shaped students' understandings of a topic, evoking David Bartholomae's memorable description of the student's first draft as "already written by the culture" with "certain predict-able" understandings of writing and identity (Bartholomae and Elbow 85). For example, studies of student literacy narratives found that a vast majority of essays traced the ("predictable") narrative of literacy as success (K. Alexander, "Successes"; Carpenter and Falbo; Williams, "Heroes").[3] Even as readers, students often lack the vocabulary and critical lens through which to navigate operations of power, and thus they often reinscribe the hegemonic viewpoints that created the conditions of marginalization (Miller; Murray; King). If alternative rhetorics are to "help [students] be in conversation with the discourses of power" (Wallace 19), we need further conversations about how to prepare students for such rhetorical challenges. Pedagogies of alternative rhetorics require more than placing the personal alongside the cultural; rather, they demand the more difficult work of situating the personal among competing cultural narratives and charting convergences and disjunctures.

Personal Writing and Pedagogies of Alliance

[T]he most important story the immigrants would hear from the Natives was how to make a united nation by combining people from various tribes. It is this eloquent act of unification that explains how America was created from a story. (Howe 30)

Alternative rhetorics have a natural bridge to rhetorical alliance in that the latter term is often attributed to Malea Powell—a contributor to *ALT DIS* and a scholar whose writing regularly "mixes worlds and ways" (Powell, "Listening"). Rhetorical alliance, which has been practiced by America's tribal nations for thousands of years (Powell, "Down" 40), negotiates a "mutual understanding across cultures and communities" while honoring the particularities of each speaker's positionality and context (King 220). Pedagogies of alternative rhetorics based in alliance building would envision the writing classroom as "a meeting place, but one not cast in the vocabulary of domination and subordination or colonizer and colonized, of only clashing and grappling" (216). In other words, such pedagogy would look toward reciprocity and relationality rather than an agonistic encounter between individuals and ("dominant") culture.

A pedagogy of rhetorical alliance would conceive of writers and their communities as potential collaborators invested in the development of their interconnected futures. The student who acquires a relational approach to alternative rhetoric would see themselves forging alliances across disparate communities in order to change the conditions of our shared worlds. Understanding the work of alternative rhetorics as alliance making locates the "meaning" of alternative rhetorics within a relational network, emphasizing context rather than any inherent quality of a text. Alliances are then never fixed conditions, but "community-based process[es] of making" (De Hierro et al.) that require ongoing reflexivity and renegotiation.

As communal practices, alliances demand more than making space for other voices. Alliances hold us responsible for our deeply entwined histories—responsible not in the sense of attributing blame, but in the sense of Krista Ratcliffe's "responsibility logic," through which we listen for the "historically situated discourses that are (un)consciously swirling around and through" these rhetorics, and "evaluate politically and ethically how these discourses function and how we want to act upon them" (Ratcliffe 208). Toward that end, scholarship on teaching American Indian rhetorics places a heavy emphasis on histories—on which narratives have been told by whom and to what ends. To teach American Indian texts without reducing them to token examples,[4] instructors must begin with an understanding of how America's colonial history positions Native communities differently than other minority groups in their struggle to maintain literal and rhetorical sovereignty (Lyons; Powell, "Rhetorics")—that is, the ability of indigenous peoples to exercise self- and community-determination independent from US governing bodies (Watanabe 39).

For example, Lisa King's "Rhetorical Sovereignty and Rhetorical Alliance in the Writing Classroom: Using American Indian Texts" offers questions to help students (and instructors) recognize rhetorical sovereignty and find opportunities for rhetorical alliance. Through detailed considerations of the rhetor's own affiliations as well as the text's multiple audiences, classes can focus discussions of Native texts within Native frameworks. The goal of these practices is to enable the responsible incorporation of Indigenous knowledges into our classrooms without tokenizing these texts or relegating them to area studies curricula. The robust archive of materials for teaching Native rhetorics should be explored on its own terms, so I will not duplicate that work here.[5] Instead, I argue that we must extend these conscientious approaches to pedagogies of alternative rhetorics, which are also dependent on their particular histories.

By practicing rhetorical alliance as teachers of rhetoric and composition, we must attend to the particularity of each text and its contexts. Rhetorical alliance requires that we take responsibility for the histories that we introduce to our classes—that we know more than just the texts on our syllabi, and that we learn about the values, exigencies, and objectives attached to those texts. In bridging alternative rhetorics with rhetorical alliance, I hope to enact that sort of responsibility—"[moving] away from the model of individuality and into the communal" (Riley-Mukavetz). While alternative rhetorics were not named as such until recent decades, and while much of this work traces its origins to Bizzell's "Hybrid Academic Dis courses," stories have long channeled experience and history into practices of survival, resistance, and worldmaking. In the following section, I offer a deeper exploration of the resonances among alternative rhetorics and rhetorical alliance by describing how a particular writing class found both allyship and discursive alternatives through their personal writing. Those discoveries began with investigating how students pressed one another for deeper "reflection" in one another's narratives. From this experience emerged a theory of reflection as a means of alliance making, which I have used to structure personal writing units in composition and creative writing classes for beginning and advanced writers.

REFLECTION AS RELATIONALITY

When we ask our students to reflect, we may in fact be asking them to perform particular subjectivities that they may or may not be prepared (or willing) to perform. (K. Alexander, "Story" 47)

In a 2015 study, Kara Poe Alexander found significant inconsistencies between what writing teachers described as reflection and what they marked as reflection in student papers. In fact, as a discipline, we have struggled to reach any functional consensus about the definition of reflection—despite its pervasive usage (K. Alexander, "Story"; Yancey). In one of the field's few extended explorations of reflection, Kathleen Blake Yancey speculates about why the field has remained relatively silent on "what works" as reflective student writing: "Even in the best of circumstances, revealing what we value in such a text makes us vulnerable in ways that discomfit" (82). Without having read this body of literature, and without any training in composition theory, my students arrived at a similar conclusion as Alexander: that more explicit discussions of "reflection" would help students sharpen their uses of personal narrative and perhaps even "provide deeper resonance" for writers making sense of their lives (K. Alexander, "Story" 63).

Below, I offer a story—or, constellated stories—of how we took a relational approach to personal writing; how an openness to alternative perspectives allowed students to strengthen connections among individual and communal narratives; and how offering my own definitions of reflection allowed students to challenge and renegotiate those expectations. The course description emphasized that we would adopt "both a personal and socially-minded approach to creative nonfiction [. . . to] consider how our stories engage the stories of others." Toward these goals, I gave students three key terms: 1) *personal narratives* (the author's own experiences); 2) *public narratives* (e.g., institutional patterns, communal practices, cultural assumptions); and 3) *relational setting* (the relational network of public narratives with which the personal narrative engages).[6] Keeping an eye on these three elements, we mapped the strategies of various "alternative" rhetoricians before delving into the students' own writing.

The reading selection surveyed a wide array of rhetorical strategies for relating the personal to the public. Some essays, such as David Sedaris's "A Plague of Tics," delivered a mostly linear narrative in vivid personal detail. Our discussion focused on how Sedaris's experience destabilized certain public narratives—narratives, for example, around mental illness and child behavior. Other essays, such as Eula Biss's "Sentimental Medicine," aligned closer to literary journalism, in which the author's own experience initiates explicit analysis of shared histories and cultures. We also turned to texts that collapsed genre distinctions such as Elisa Washuta's *My Body Is a Book of Rules* and Claudia Rankine's *Citizen* to explore how the layering of images and events might invite deeper appreciation for the multidimensionality of lived experience.

With every reading, we mapped the context by tracing how authors connected personal memories to larger cultural narratives—at times through explicit reflection, sometimes by juxtaposing their experiences with communal mythologies, and at other times by using language to draw attention to certain moments or images.[7] We tracked where and how these connections were made, with what sorts of transitions and imagery, and with how much specialized vocabulary or knowledge. While we covered a wide range of topics, I intentionally limited the number of readings so that we would have more time to delve into the related histories. For example, to engage Rankine, we needed a vocabulary for discussing racism as a system rather than a singular act. We needed to understand microaggressions and their place within racist structures and antiracist work. Even the book's cover—the severed cap of a dark hoodie, mounted to a wall—required awareness of the complex, entangled histories of hoodies, hoods, and racist thought.[8] When the students began crafting their essays, they carried this relational view into their own writing. We discussed each draft in a large group workshop as well as our online discussion board. Early on, I noticed that students used the term *reflection* as an ambiguous catchall, which stood for a wide variety of specific, rhetorical moves that connect individual stories with social exigencies. In search of more precise language, we tried to locate reflection in the relationships among individual experience and public narratives. Using our key terms, we were able to name and negotiate the efficacy of different rhetorical moves, identifying specific strategies that we saw as "reflective" within each particular relational setting. What resulted was a fluid exchange among texts and contexts. Each draft initiated a discussion that reflected *and* refracted authorial perspectives, audience expectations, and the mythologies of their wide-ranging communities. Inspired by Jacqueline Jones Royster and Gesa Kirsch's "critical imagination," we asked "what is there and not there," and speculated "about what could be there instead" (20). In the sections that follow, I discuss three very different student essays and the ways our discussions of "reflection" fostered more dialogic encounters between the "personal" and the cultural.[9]

Evan: Exposition

The evolution of Evan's writing presents perhaps the most straightforward example of how redefining reflection helped us navigate the connections among individual experience and communal expectations. Early in the semester, Evan spoke with me about a topic he wished to explore in writing. He had just recently come out as gay, which met a lot of resistance in his very conservative hometown. His essay, "The Man in the Mask," worked to disentangle the different identities to which he felt beholden. While the first draft did contain both personal narrative and larger public themes, the connection seemed a little forced. He offered one scene of personal experience, but otherwise made broader generalizations about LGBTQ experience. Evan's classmates discussed possible revisions using different interpretations of the word *reflection*. On our class forum, one student wrote, "I thought your mask metaphor was very well done, but I think you could add more reflection . . . to really show the significance of the metaphor both personally and publicly." A second student made a similar point, but with a very different understanding of reflection. She wrote, "I want more expansion on certain stories that can strengthen this 'mask' you had on. You gave one specific scene with your friend, but besides that it was a lot of reflection about general experiences with little specific grounding for the kind of pain you are describing." The first respondent seemed to think that the piece lacked reflection and the second suggested that the overemphasis on reflection needed "grounding" through more specific scenes. During workshop, I proposed that these two perspectives were actually two different approaches to the same concern.

The metaphorical mask, which stood for the narrator's performance of normative masculinity, provided a metaphorical commentary on gender policing.[10] As both of the above quotes note, however, the essay relied heavily on describing the mask itself rather than detailing experiences —personal or otherwise—that concretized the metaphor. The mask was introduced first through vivid description:

> I knew exactly what I was, and it *terrified* me. I felt that my only option was to begin work on my mask, so that by the time high school came around it would be expertly crafted. I would closely study the expressions, mannerisms and gestures of my straight male friends and thread each and every one into that mask; I would examine the world's view of what it meant to be a man and use it as a stencil to carve out holes for its eyes and mouth. Each morning I would fasten

it tightly to my face. I was going to wear that mask and I was going to wear it so well that I would soon find no need to take it off. After that, I could get to the point where it would no longer be just a mask, but a part of myself.

While the passage was powerful on its own, as the second student remarked, it had little connection to specific experiences. What one respondent referred to as "reflection" and another as "grounding" was the need for connections from the abstract world of metaphor to the world of lived experiences.

The class agreed unanimously that the most powerful moment in the essay was its single scene, which moved away from metaphorical description and into physical action. The narrator is playing video games with a friend when he discovers that he can select the female avatars as long as he laughs at their weaknesses and celebrates their defeats: "This way it wouldn't seem as though I actually enjoyed playing as the girl. As long as I exhibited the fact that I knew girls were weaker and therefore lesser, I was golden." Here, we see the narrator shaping his mask—carving a new face from the bloodless stone of heteronormativity. This powerful moment, though, did not necessarily connect with the broader (and perhaps overly general) claim that the essay makes about LGBT life—more specifically, that *all* LGBT youth must either shield themselves through performed normativity or "face crushing external factors."

Admittedly, the template that I gave students for charting their engagement with public narratives is simplistic and reductive, but it also served as a helpful heuristic for exploring this disjuncture. In our discussion, the class arrived at the statements shown in Figure 1. Students focused on how the specificity of the video game scene highlights the wide reach of misogynistic and masculinist values. The vivid detail illuminated, even for readers who felt removed from queer experiences, the pressure to perform gender norms. The scene, however, mostly delves into the narrator's temporary feeling of triumph—his small sense of victory that he could inhabit, for a moment, a feminine figure if he also trumpeted misogynistic values. The essay's latter claim—that LGBT youth *had* to accommodate gender norms or face dire consequences—then seemed broad and abstract. In terms of the essay's metaphor, the video game scene showed the construction of the narrator's mask but did not fully explore its burden. How did its weight accrue over time? What forces—internal or external—caused it to fracture?

After Evan's peers encouraged him to incorporate more detailed, personal scenes in his revisions, he and I continued to meet regularly throughout the drafting process. I worried that the class's enthusiasm would create a whole new set of pressures to disclose. In Evan's own words, though, writing became "a way to process the things that have happened." In our meetings, he described his narratives as a means of illuminating and sometimes pushing back against the cultural scripts that surrounded him—an experience that inspired him to pursue an English major.

Events	Personal Significance	Public Concerns
As a child, the narrator hides his preference for female video game characters by celebrating their deaths.	The narrator learns to perform gender norms.	Those who do not conform to normative expectations of gender and sexuality are often taught to mimic them from a young age.
?	?	"You see, all LGBT youth at some point have to make a choice: either embrace who you are and face crushing external factors or, drown yourself in order to make way for another self that is much more accommodating to the norm."

Figure 1. Evan's narrative.

Evan's final draft incorporated a new scene in which the narrator pledges a fraternity during his freshman year of college. In hazing rituals, the pledges are renamed faggots, among other homophobic slurs. Evan writes:

> For most boys, this name meant absolutely nothing. It was only a word—one they had picked up during games of recess football [. . . .] Each sting chipped away at my fashioned exterior, I was slowly being split open [. . . .] Most kids come to college and are fearful of its uncertainty; I was fearful of its certainty. I was certain that continuing down this path would leave me uncertain about who would come out on the other side—uncertain if anyone would come out at all.

Evan also uses the mask to transition into a more explicit (but less universalizing) discussion of struggles faced by LGBTQ and gender nonconforming individuals:

> All I do know is that I got lucky. I still have a lot of my life ahead of me, and I have a whole bunch of people who love me as me, not as the mask. Others don't get so lucky. Some continue to hide

behind their mask for so long that they permanently blend into a collage of other people. Some, who finally find the strength to take off their mask, aren't embraced by their loved ones. Some are left homeless. Some would rather die than face that hate.

After detailing his own struggles, Evan takes this moment to contextualize his experience within a larger social landscape—one in which LGBTQ youth constitute 40 percent of the homeless youth population and attempt suicide at a much higher rate than their straight counterparts.

To return to the chart we made, Evan's new scene helped shape both the narrative arc of his individual story, as well as the larger argument he was trying to make about LGBTQ experience (see Figure 2). The addition of this second scene also brought out yet another connection that galvanized students during our workshop discussion. In the video game scene, the narrator is being trained in social norms and self-censorship by adopting misogynistic stances. In the fraternity scene, that training continues through homophobic hazing rituals. Of his performed misogyny, Evan writes, "In no way am I condoning or justifying these negative attitudes toward 'femininity,' but rather pointing out their source." That source is the same public narrative that privileges normative masculinity and disciplines the narrator for his deviances. While individual experiences of misogyny and homophobia vary widely, many could be traced to the script that compels Evan to emulate the "macho, beer-loving party boys that everyone knew and loved." By situating his experiences within a relational network of competing narratives and expectations, Evan was able to derive relevant social commentary without making his story stand in for all LGBTQ youth.

Events	Personal Significance	Public Concerns
College-aged Evan endures homophobic slurs as part of his fraternity hazing process.	The performance of gender norms begins to take its toll on the narrator. ("Each sting chipped away at my fashioned exterior")	Other LGBTQ youth face even more crushing external pressures. Some are unable to thrive under such conditions. ("Others don't get so lucky")

Figure 2. Evan's revised narrative.

Jen: Motifs

Whereas Evan used a more straightforward combination of action and exposition to work through the sociocultural relevance of his narrative, Jen arrived at a more subtle but equally effective strategy. Through the use of motifs, Jen was able to strengthen the meditations on wealth disparity that appeared muted in her first draft. Like Evan, Jen made substantial revisions between her rough and final drafts and responded enthusiastically to the class discussion.

Jen's essay, "The Broken Coconut," began as a detailed account of her childhood traveling to and from India, where she visited extended family. The narrative opened by juxtaposing the warmth of her family and the bustle of the city streets with the impoverished image of India that she presented to her American peers:

> "Yeah, it's really dirty and gross. I hate India. There's dust and poor people everywhere, and everyone makes fun of my accent," I boasted to a group of wide-eyed first graders one morning. I wanted to seem as American as possible, as if admitting that some part of me actually enjoyed this foreign land made me different.

The essay goes on to reveal that Jen's extended family is actually quite wealthy. Amid scenes of beachside resorts and seventy-two-hour weddings, the narrator details a memorable encounter: She, her aunt, and her mother are being driven through the streets of India. A woman carrying a young child taps on the window. The narrator tries to offer them money, but her aunt intervenes, telling Jen, "We can't always give them money. The more we give the more they'll come flocking to us. The best is just to pretend they aren't there and they'll leave." The essay itself, however, also seemed uncertain what to make of this encounter. A few other scenes contained brief mentions of class difference, but the narrator's explicit discussions focused on the tension between her American identity and her familial bonds.

On the discussion forum, students praised Jen's use of detail and character development but also grappled with the narrative's brief encounters with economic inequality. One student wrote, "Your sources of conflict in the story are powerful, but a little disjointed. Your qualms with your family's relationship with the lower class, and your attempts to assimilate with two disparate cultures . . . I would like to see you connect them with a little bit of reflection." Overwhelmingly, the class agreed. Another student added, "I think these are both very interesting aspects of the story, and I think there could be a way to link them both without presenting them as two different ideas." The goal of "reflection," in this particular instance, was to connect the narrator's transnational identity with her thoughts on class differences. Jen resolved these concerns through the strategic use of imagery.

In the first draft, the titular "broken coconut" appeared only at the very end of the story. It was a compelling final image, but one without context or precedent. The narrator recalls seeing a broken coconut smashed on the side of the road. She writes:

> A nearby dog was sniffing it with seemingly mild interest. Everyone else stepped around it, pretending it didn't exist. The shell was green, not brown, like the kind I used to drink when I was little. I later learned that just meant it was a young coconut that had not matured yet. Too bad. It never had a chance.

The class remarked on the coconut's sudden appearance. On the forum, one student suggested that Jen "make the coconut a motif . . . That way it won't look as thrown on at the end." She added, "However, I loved the metaphor brewing with it." In Jen's revision, the coconut did in fact emerge as a motif— and one that connected the two divergent themes identified by her peers.

In Jen's final draft, the coconut moves between worlds and cultures much like the narrator herself. In the narrative's first glimpse of India, Jen and her family encounter a mother and child who are selling balloons. Jen's eyes lock with those of the child. She can't look away. The girl drinks from a small green coconut and juice dribbles down her chin. Jen's mother admonishes, "Don't look at them, you'll encourage it." Coconut juice reap pears, though, several scenes later when the narrator moves to college. Her floor mate explains this new health trend: "It's great. It's imported from Thailand you know, and it's pure coconut water. Kind of expensive, but so worth it." Figure 3 frames this scene through the course's three key terms: *events, personal significance,* and *public concerns.*

Events	Personal Significance	Public Concerns
In India, Jen's family tells her to ignore a mother and child who are selling balloons on the street. The child is drinking from a coconut.	After encountering the same artifact in drastically different contexts, the narrator is struck by the arbitrariness of cultural and economic capital.	The narrator observes how gross inequities are often invisible in everyday life. ("It was almost twisted, how this was simply a supplement for us. Something we took for granted.")
In the United States, Jen's college floor mate explains coconut water as a health fad.	("Just like the one the little girl was drinking at her mother's hip. Just like the kind I used to drink.")	

Figure 3. Jen's narrative.

While Jen does not make direct claims like Evan, her use of repetition and metaphor invites deeper examination of the cultural forces at play. This time, the essay's closing image layers atop these other scenes: "Everyone else stepped around it, pretending it didn't exist." The coconut becomes the proverbial elephant in the room—the ponderous weight of class inequity that many choose to ignore. Unlike Evan's "mask" metaphor, Jen's central image is less a direct symbol of her chosen topic. Through multiple iterations across multiple contexts, though, Jen uses that image to mull over the complexities of wealth distribution and the varied ways people become complicit in exploitative practices.

Michael: Framing

Perhaps the least direct approach to "reflection" came from Michael's essay, "Politics and English as a Second Language," which began as a word-for-word transcript of a phone call between Michael and his mother. To capture their bilingual exchange, he recorded all his mother's words in Mandarin, verbatim, and all of his own in English. Michael used the "comments" feature on Microsoft Word to offer translations of his mother's Chinese, but otherwise provided no further commentary. Their conversation focused on the 2016 presidential election and his mother's choice to support Donald Trump—a decision that Michael struggled to understand.

Both on the forum and in our workshop, the class wrestled with the intended "meaning" of this essay. Numerous students asked for "a little more reflection," particularly to strengthen the essay's meditation on politics. One classmate put it most bluntly: "I would suggest that you add reflection. Right now this is a lifeless script." Michael also had strong opinions, though, and was not easily swayed by his classmates' suggestions that he offer more direct interpretations of this conversation.

Michael explained his reasoning and his reservations to me in an email, offering them as a list:

- I wanted to write about my mom and why she supports Trump, but I didn't want to include any sort of condescension or judgment, which I think is the tone of a lot of articles about Trump supporters.
- I didn't want to be accused of twisting her words in any way.
- I also thought it was important that her words—both Mandarin and English—be preserved. That she should speak for herself, in her own trans-Pacific dialect.

He was concerned that the sort of "reflection" his classmates were seeking would impose too much of his own voice on the conversation. He had intentionally made the text difficult. He wanted the reader to struggle for meaning alongside the interlocutors. In some places, he chose not to translate the Mandarin at all, and in others, he offered hyperlinks to online resources that explained the historical and current events referenced in the dialogue.

I agreed with Michael that directly interpreting the conversation for his readers would diminish the significance of the essay, but I also wondered if the initial draft was so ambiguous because the author himself had not yet decided what to make of it. In our discussions of this project, he seemed uncharacteristically uncertain. I do not remember the exact words that I left on Michael's draft, but he repeated them back to me in an email:

> I've been thinking about the discussion we had in class, and whether I'm "not doing the hard work of making connections and arriving at a larger understanding yourself," to quote the comment you made on my draft. When I read that, I said (out loud) to myself, "She's onto me."11 Because that's exactly right.

In our subsequent conversations, Michael and I agreed that ambiguity had its place as a rhetorical strategy—especially given his topic. To help Michael wield that ambiguity more intentionally, however, we also talked through his motives and possible interpretations of the conversation. In trying to communicate his thoughts to me, he arrived at a solution.

Michael's first revision began by describing how he recorded this conversation. He explained that he spoke into a microphone while he recorded his mother's voice through a laptop program. When he emailed me that description, he asked:

> Does it make literal sense? As in, do you get that because of the way I recorded the phone call I ended up with two mp3 files—one of my mom and one of myself—and that each file only contains one voice, so that taken individually it sounds like a single voice addressing silence, but when the files are combined a dialogue is formed, and that when I layered the two files on top of each other I realized they were almost perfectly in sync.

When I read his message, I said (out loud) to myself, "That's it." That description captured the experience of reading his dialogue. It sounded neither like two divergent voices, nor like a consensus, but like two voices coming together.

In his final draft, Michael merged the initial revision with the language from his email to me:

> My mom's voting for Trump. I called her to ask why. The stereotypical Trump supporter, if the articles I've read are true, is male, white, undereducated and underemployed. My mom's female, Chinese, has a PhD and works as a community college professor.
>
> We talked for a while—about China and America, communism and democracy, collectivism and individualism—switching between Mandarin and English. I recorded her voice with Audacity on my laptop; I recorded my voice with a microphone. I ended up with two mp3 files, one of my mom and one of myself. Taken individually, each file sounds like a single voice addressing silence. When the two are combined, our voices fit into the other's silence, almost perfectly in-sync.

The first paragraph gives just enough context to connect the narrative more clearly with the political exigency. The second paragraph, particularly with its ending lines, uses descriptive language and metaphor to capture the complex mother-son relationship that unfolds through the rest of the narrative. Together, these two short paragraphs hint at the writer's intent even without dictating how the essay should be read. It situates the reader within the 2016 presidential campaign season, and then more specifically within a powerful familial bond. The author's respect and deep empathy for his mother then stands in stark contrast to—in his words—"the condescension and judgment" used to represent the stereotypical Trump supporter.

To refer back to the course's key terms, Michael's new introduction brought in the public narratives to which his essay responds (see Figure 4). In an environment of hyperpartisanship and snap judgments, the narrator reaches carefully into the personal history of one Trump supporter, and he does it with respect and care. Michael asks about his mother's experiences during the Chinese Cultural Revolution and her support of Maoist ideology. They connect this background to her stances on US policies regarding homosexuality, immigration, and religious freedom. At times, Michael pressures his mother's conservatism, but she often changes the topic or asks that they drop the issue. Although neither Michael nor his mother arrive at a dramatic change of heart, the conversation also does not feel like a standstill. After discussing the rationale behind Trump's proposed immigration restrictions, Michael's mother asks about this essay—specifically, she asks if he would anonymize her character: "Just say you interviewed someone who grew up in China." Michael responds, "it's very important that I say that it's my mom, 'cause this is, y'know, this is the person I care about most . . . if I can't understand the person I care about the most, like, how can I understand anyone?" She concedes, "For your sake, I'll agree."

Events	Personal Significance	Public Concerns
The narrator records a conversation with his mother.	The narrator fails to persuade his mother to reconsider certain ideologies, but also reaffirms their connection and their ability to respond empathetically.	The writer responds to a political climate in which oppositional parties are quick to caricature one another without listening.

Figure 4. Michael's narrative.

I include Michael's essay not just for its creativity, but also because it challenged my own expectations of what could count as reflective prose. When I wrote my syllabus and assignment guidelines, I thought of reflection as more direct engagement with other stories. For example, even Jen's essay offered more explicit critique through its descriptive language. During Michael's workshop, most of the class asked for transparent insight into the narrator's thoughts and reactions. Michael's revision creatively responded to their search for clarity—for connection—without surrendering more personal detail. His final draft situates the narrative within larger public conversations, juxtaposing this dialogue with a polarized political climate. It also withholds the narrator's own personal reactions. It pushes back against our assumptions that we can *know* any other individual's thoughts and feelings. Instead, the narrative focuses on the words of Michael's mother – and in doing so, asks the reader to do the same.

In fact, perhaps the most remarkable element of this class was the way that students listened and responded to one another. The many resonances that emerged among student essays made it clear that the classroom had become a site of connectivity—in King's words, a "meeting place" where disparate histories converged. For example, the class carried terms that emerged during Evan's workshop into discussions of other narratives. Across wide-ranging topics, they prompted one another to dig deeper into the roles of "toxic masculinity" and "the way girls are enculturated." One student took up concerns from both Evan's and Michael's essays and used her third assignment to delve into narratives of gender that influenced the 2016 presidential election. Another student, who described himself as straight, white, and upper-middle class, used this vocabulary to revise an essay about his early infatuation with hip-hop culture. Whereas the original draft focused entirely on his friend group and their music production, the next draft revisited those events to reconsider how the narrator's positionality allowed him to ignore the complex and intertwined histories of hip-hop, race, and gender.

THE CLASSROOM AS RELATIONAL SETTING

The above passages draw heavily from the class's online forum because those posts often shaped the in-class discussions. They allowed me to emphasize the students' voices and to minimize my own. We started by identifying trends among the forum responses and asking for respondents to elaborate on their thoughts. Throughout, we tried to avoid vague evaluative judgments such as "I think you should . . ." or "It's better if." Instead, we focused on the effects of different narrative strategies. For example, rather than simply agreeing or disagreeing with the debate about whether Michael should offer more direct explanations of his mother's words, I asked the class how such a change would affect the essay and the experience of reading it. In the few rare instances when I disagreed with the majority consensus of the class, I put my opinion up for debate—again through a specific consideration of how different options might (re)shape the narrative and the ways it engaged its relational setting.

The workshop discussions were often so energetic that I was reluctant to impose my opinions, especially if I disagreed. I chose to offer my thoughts on occasion, though, because—even though I hoped that these essays would find a life beyond my classroom (and at least several have)— I could not ignore the fact that I would ultimately be assigning grades to them. In Yancey's words, I would be "award[ing] the A's and valorize[ing] the truths" (77). The reality that I was (in some ways) still the primary audience and arbiter of these essays also motivated my search for more precise understandings of what we mean by *reflection*. I hoped to give students a candid and dialogic conversation about the "public narratives" of our classroom. Certain students, such as Michael, were then able to renegotiate our shared expectations. Reflection, across these varied instances, entailed more deliberate engagements with the narrative's relational setting—with relevant cultural forces and institutional patterns. The specific form of that engagement, though, was open to interpretation, and students were able to use creative approaches to assert more control over their narratives.

Of course, there are many limitations to quantifying the complex and at times enchanting work of narrative. The above summaries are reductive. They discount the more sophisticated connections that students made through descriptive language, through layers of metaphor and imagery, and through meter and style. In *ALT DIS*, Helen Fox writes, "As witchcraft, writing is high art" (59). She goes on to argue that even though we might disagree with "the game"—the abstract and sometimes exclusionary conventions that privilege certain forms of language in the academy—we are still responsible for teaching our students how to play. The assumption about alternative discourses, though, is that students will automatically know how to play—that their experiences translate easily into legible and effective critiques of our shared cultures. We write often about the need to teach such genres, but far less about how to teach them. If we understand what personal writing comes to "mean" *in relation to* shared narratives (like all rhetoric), we might develop more robust ways of discussing how individual stories engage our shared understandings.

To return to Gilyard's critique—that no matter how liberally we "tweak" the discourses of power, we also maintain them[12]—I recognize that when I teach alternative rhetorics, the rhetorical strategies that seem most effective to me are informed by twenty-four years of formal academic training in the United States. To be more specific, my readings are shaped by a queer resistance to normativity and a feminist analysis of the "techniques of power" (Ahmed 90). My worldview is also calibrated by postcolonial critiques of Eurocentrism, which I learned from my immigrant parents long before I encountered the critical vocabularies of Said, Spivak, or Bhabha. The counsel I give students will work better in some contexts than others, and though I can try to anticipate different scenarios and reactions, I will make mistakes. Rhetorical alliance also provides an answer here: "The critical question is not 'How do I avoid ever making a mistake?' but rather 'What do I need to do after I make a mistake?'" (De Hierro et al.).

An alliance-oriented pedagogy of personal writing necessarily embraces the recursive nature of writing and rhetoric—the fact that texts are both products *and* the process through which those products are revised. In "revealing what we value" (Yancey 82), we open ourselves to critique from students and colleagues, but we may also find allies who will help expand our perspectives and refine our actions. Only by rendering our beliefs legible—by fixing them temporarily, imperfectly, and vulnerably in some form—can we create the conditions for discussion, negotiation, and change. With this understanding, my students seemed genuinely *excited* by disagreement. Moving fluidly between writing as product and as process, students regarded conflict as generative. The clashing of perspectives became catalysts for growth.

However partial my summary of our short semester may be, I present it here in hopes to further disciplinary conversations about what we ask of students in personal writing assignments, how we might better communicate those expectations with our classes, and how we might open the university to "alternative" ways of seeing the world. I also hope that, by regarding our classrooms as a relational setting—as a site where different narratives meet, struggle, and possibly even align—we might also create more opportunities for students to share their experiences and to be heard. In teaching personal writing as relational rhetoric, we might amplify our students' voices and—to borrow Michael's words—allow those voices to fill our silences.

Acknowledgments

For their thoughtful feedback and support, I would like to thank Drs. Jonathan Alexander and Helen Fox as well as the anonymous reviewers of CCC. *I am also greatly indebted to the scholars of alternative rhetorics for their ongoing conversation(s) and to Native rhetors and theorists who have modeled richer understandings of communing-through-rhetoric. Thanks, also, to Debra Hawhee, Laura Brown, and Sarah Adams for reading all the things, and to my students for their trust and courage.*

Notes

1. Though Wallace uses the singular term *rhetoric*, I choose to describe this thread of scholarship as *alternative rhetorics* to acknowledge the wide range of rhetorical strategies that it encompasses.

2. Though Bizzell called it "hybrid academic discourse" at the time (and later revised her terminology to "alternative discourse"), I am using *alternative rhetorics* here for consistency.

3. Not all literacy narratives are alternative rhetorics, and not all alternative rhetorics are literacy narratives. However, especially in composition studies where we have so closely followed the interrelations among language and colonialism, the two genres have a lot of overlap. Examples include Villanueva's *Bootstraps* and Gilyard's *Lives on the Boundary* as well as two of Wallace's major examples—Douglass's *Narrative* and Anzaldúa's "How to Tame a Wild Tongue."

4. Alexander and Rhodes call this reduction the "flattening effect" of uncritical multiculturalism in their 2014 article.

5. See *Survivance, Sovereignty, and Story* (King et al.) for work by Lisa King, Sundy Watanabe, Qwo-Li Driskill, Gabriela R. Ríos, Rose Gubele, Kimberli Lee, Malea Powell, Andrea Riley-Mukavetz, Joyce Rain Anderson, Jessica Safran Hoover, and Angela Haas. Other resources include *Native Appropriations* and the open-access journal *Decolonialization: Indigeneity, Education, & Society*.

6. These terms were largely inspired by Margaret R. Somers's relational theory of narrative identity. In future iterations of this class, I intend to explore other sociological approaches to narrative—for example, Eduardo Bonilla-Silva's discussion of how "story lines" enable abstractly antiracist "frames" (54) while also reifying racist practices.

7. We mapped in a literal sense, creating visual diagrams inspired by Tim Bascom's "Picturing the Personal Essay."

8. The cover image is David Hammons's *In the Hood*.

9. All students have consented to my use of their essays and forum posts. For anonymity, they have all been given pseudonyms. This study has received IRB approval.

10. Following the conventions of many creative nonfiction workshops, we used the word *narrator* to distinguish the *I* speaking from the page from the writer sitting in our classroom.

11. In the two years between the teaching of this class and the publication of this article, I have transitioned from using *she/her* pronouns to *they/them* and have requested students follow this when referring to me.

12. Gray-Rosendale and Gruber also acknowledge that "no rhetoric is fully 'alternative' but always both rewrites the tradition and inevitably becomes part of it" (4).

Works Cited

Ahmed, Sara. *Living a Feminist Life*. Duke UP, 2017.

Alexander, Jonathan, and Jacqueline Rhodes. "Flattening Effects: Composition's Multicultural Imperative and the Problem of Narrative Coherence." *College Composition and Communication*, vol. 65, no. 3, 2014, pp. 430–54.

Alexander, Kara Poe. "From Story to Analysis: Reflection and Uptake in the Literacy Narrative Assignment." *Composition Studies*, vol. 43, no. 2, 2015, pp. 43–71.

—. "Successes, Victims, and Prodigies: 'Master' and 'Little' Cultural Narratives in the Literacy Narrative Genre." *College Composition and Communication*, vol. 62, no. 4, pp. 608–33.

Bartholomae, David, and Peter Elbow. "Interchanges: Responses to Bartholomae and Elbow." *College Composition and Communication*, vol. 46, no. 1, 1995, pp. 84–107.

Bascom, Tim. "Picturing the Personal Essay: A Visual Guide." *Creative Nonfiction*, no. 49, 2013, www.creativenonfiction.org/online-reading/picturing-personal-essay-visual-guide.

France, Alan W. "Dialectics of Self: Structure and Agency as the Subject of English." *College English*, vol. 63, no. 2, 2000, pp. 145–65.

Biss, Eula. "Sentimental Medicine: Why We Still Fear Vaccines." *Harper's Magazine*, Jan. 2013, harpers.org/archive/2013/01/sentimental-medicine/.

Bizzell, Patricia. "Hybrid Academic Discourses: What, Why, How." *Composition Studies*, vol. 27, no. 2, 1999, pp. 7–21.

—. "The Intellectual Work of 'Mixed' Forms of Academic Discourses." Schroeder et al., pp. 1–10.

Bonilla-Silva, Eduardo. *Racism without Racists: Color-Blind Racism and the Persistence of Racial Inequality in America*. 5th ed., Rowman & Littlefield, 2017.

Carpenter, William, and Bianca Falbo. "Literacy, Identity, and the 'Successful' Student Writer." *Identity Papers*, edited by Bronwyn T. Williams, Utah State UP, 2009, pp. 92–108.

De Hierro, Victor, et al. "We Are Here: Negotiating Difference and Alliance in Spaces of Cultural Rhetorics." *Enculturation*, no. 21.

Eldred, Janet Carey, and Peter Mortensen. "Reading Literacy Narratives." *College English*, vol. 54, no. 5, 1992, pp. 512–39.

Fox, Helen. "Being an Ally." Schroeder et al., pp. 57–67.

Gilyard, Keith. "Literacy, Identity, Imagination, Flight." *College Composition and Communication*, vol. 52, no. 2, 2000, pp. 260–72.

—. *Voices of the Self: A Study of Language Competence*. Wayne State UP, 1991.

Glenn, Cheryl, and Andrea A. Lunsford, editors. *Landmark Essays on Rhetoric and Feminism: 1973-2000*. Routledge, 2015.

Gray-Rosendale, Laura, and Sibylle Gruber. "Introduction." *Alternative Rhetorics: Challenges to the Rhetorical Tradition*, State U of New York P, 2001, pp. 1–16.

Gunter, Kimberly K. "Braiding and Rhetorical Power Players: Transforming Academic Writing through Rhetorical Dialectic." *Journal of Basic Writing*, vol. 30, no. 1, 2011, pp. 64–98.

Hammons, David. *In the Hood*. 1993, Tilton Gallery, New York.

Howe, LeAnne. "The Story of America: A Tribalography." *Clearing a Path: Theorizing the Past in Native American Studies*, edited by Nancy Shoemaker, Routledge, 2001, pp. 29–48.

King, Lisa. "Rhetorical Sovereignty and Rhetorical Alliance in the Writing Classroom: Using American Indian Texts." *Pedagogy*, vol. 12, no. 2, 2012, pp. 209–33.

King, Lisa, et al., editors. *Survivance, Sovereignty, and Story: Teaching American Indian Rhetorics*. Utah State UP, 2015.

Lu, Min-Zhan. "From Silence to Words: Writing as Struggle." *College English*, vol. 49, no. 4, 1987, pp. 437–48.

Lyons, Scott Richard. "Rhetorical Sovereignty: What Do American Indians Want from Writing?" *College Composition and Communication*, vol. 51, no. 3, 2000, pp. 447–68.

Miller, Richard. "Fault Lines in the Contact Zone." *College English*, vol. 56, 1994, pp. 389–408.

Murray, Robert D., Jr. "Power, Conflict, and Contact: Re-Constructing Authority in the Classroom." *Race, Rhetoric and Composition*, edited by Keith Gilyard, Boynton/Cook, 1999, pp. 87–103.

Native Appropriations | Representations Matter. http://nativeappropriations.com/. Accessed 29 Oct. 2017.

Powell, Malea. "Down by the River, or How Susan La Flesche Picotte Can Teach Us about Alliance as a Practice of Survivance." *College English*, vol. 67, no. 1, 2004, pp. 38–60.

—. "Listening to Ghosts: An Alternative (Non)Argument." Schroeder et al., pp. 11–22.

—. "Rhetorics of Survivance: How American Indians Use Writing." *College Composition and Communication*, vol. 53, no. 3, 2002, pp. 396–434.

Rankine, Claudia. *Citizen: An American Lyric*. Graywolf P, 2014.

Ratcliffe, Krista. "Rhetorical Listening: A Trope for Interpretive Invention and a 'Code of Cross-Cultural Conduct.'" *College Composition and Communication*, vol. 51, no. 2, 1999, pp. 195–224.

Riley-Mukavetz, Andrea. "On Working from or with Anger: Or How I Learned to Listen to My Relatives and Practice All Our Relations." *Enculturation*, vol. 21, 2016.

Royster, Jacqueline Jones. "Academic Discourse or Small Boats on a Big Sea." Schroeder et al., pp. 23–30.

Royster, Jacqueline Jones, and Gesa Kirsch. *Feminist Rhetorical Practices: New Horizons for Rhetoric, Composition, and Literacy Studies*. Southern Illinois UP, 2012.

Schroeder, Christopher L., et al., editors. *ALT DIS: Alternative Discourses and the Academy*. Boynton/Cook—Heinemann, 2002.

Sedaris, David. "A Plague of Tics." *Naked*. Phoenix, 2002.

Somers, Margaret R. "The Narrative Constitution of Identity: A Relational and Network Approach." *Theory and Society*, vol. 23, 1994, pp. 605–49.

Spivak, Gayatri Chakravorty. *An Aesthetic Education in the Era of Globalization*. Harvard UP, 2013.

Villanueva, Victor. *Bootstraps: From an American Academic of Color*. National Council of Teachers of English, 1993.

Wallace, David L. *Compelled to Write: Alternative Rhetoric in Theory and Practice*. Utah State UP, 2011.

Washuta, Elissa. *My Body Is a Book of Rules*. 1st ed., Red Hen P, 2014.

Watanabe, Sundy. "Socioacupuncture Pedagogy." *Survivance, Sovereignty, and Story: Teaching American Indian Rhetorics*, edited by Lisa King et al., Utah State UP, 2015, pp. 35–56.

Williams, Bronwyn T. "Heroes, Rebels, and Victims: Student Identities in Literacy Narratives." *Journal of Adolescent & Adult Literacy*, vol. 47, no. 4, 2003, pp. 342–45.

—. "Speak for Yourself? Power and Hybridity in the Cross-Cultural Classroom." *College Composition and Communication*, vol. 54, no. 4, 2003, pp. 586–609, doi:10.2307/3594186.

Yancey, Kathleen Blake. *Reflection in the Writing Classroom*. Utah State UP, 1998.

V. Jo Hsu is an assistant professor of English and the associate director of the Program in Rhetoric and Composition at the University of Arkansas. Their research and teaching focus on the interrelations among identity, narrative writing, and struggles for social justice. Their current project examines intergenerational narratives among queer Asian Americans and considers what these archives can teach us about our cultural and academic institutions, as well as how they might help us envision more inclusive pedagogical theories and practices. Jo has yet to find a third-person pronoun that feels entirely like home.

Supplemental Material

"Reflection as Relationality: Rhetorical Alliances and Teaching Alternative Rhetorics"

V. Jo Hsu

Part I: Reflection on the Origins of the Article

I started graduate school studying creative writing, and like many MFA students, I taught first-year composition. Most of the textbooks we used for FYC situated the "personal essay" as the first assignment, describing it as an "accessible" genre that students would find less challenging than the traditional research paper. I contrasted this understanding of the personal essay with the difficult, vulnerable work of creative nonfiction workshops – how terrifying it was to surrender our truths to peer criticism; how impossible it felt to even carve that truth into a shape that others would recognize. My research began with this incongruence. I wanted to know: What did first-year students lose when we delivered them a reductive version of an otherwise sophisticated and powerful genre? How can we better teach them to access the potential of personal essays for cultural analysis and critique?

Part II: Description of Research Methods, Findings, and/or Pedagogical Impact

I was fortunate in that this essay emerged organically from my work as a teacher. I did not originally envision a publication. I wanted to design a course that could explore how creative nonfiction can illuminate the interdependence of the "personal" and the "public." We would consider how individual experiences are conditioned by surrounding social and institutional formations and how an individual's life chances are affected by the ways they align – or fail to align – with different categories of social belonging (e.g. gender, race, sexual orientation, disability, class, etc.). To design the class, I combined what I had learned from creative writing craft classes with my background as a rhetorician, creating lesson plans that explored the rhetorical impact of "creative" devices—for example, balancing action vs. reflection; figurative language; scene vs. summary; and character and plot development.

Perhaps even more critical to the execution of the class, however, are the actual relationships we form within the classroom. Meaningful discoveries are high stakes; they require us to risk the stability of our worldview and to be willing to discuss them with our peers and teachers. More, they require us to respect our peers and teachers enough to allow them into those worldviews—

to augment or expand what we think we know. I've taught this class three times now, and it feels like a new (exhilarating, gratifying, difficult) experience every time. Because the students' own workshop contributions compose a significant part of the curriculum, the class is driven by the students. It moves in the directions that they take it. I adapt throughout the semester so we spend more time on topics that they find interesting; we detour into creative strategies and methods that they tend to use, and we modify our reading schedule to find writers who touch on resonant ideas or narrative forms.

For any of these explorations to work, teachers have to establish and model discursive practices conducive toward vulnerability and mutual care. I see this as one of the greatest responsibilities and gifts of my job—that I get to earn students' trust every semester, or at least try. No matter what class I'm teaching, I start with that foundation. While other courses might not be as personalized (in that students are not writing directly from the personal), I do keep an eye toward relationality—how do I highlight the ways we are *already* in relation with the material and one another? How do I nurture these relationships so that students are interested and invested in not only the content but in one another's engagement with the class? Like most teachers, I imagine, I have varying success with each class, but I too am learning with every step and misstep, and I hope to have the privilege of doing so for many years to come.

Part III: Discussion Questions

1. In their exploration of rhetorical alliance, Del Hierro et al. write, "The critical question is not 'How do I avoid ever making a mistake?' but rather 'What do I need to do after I make a mistake?'" Consider examples of public rhetoric following a "mistake"—be that a public figure's individual apology or a nation's reckoning with its own violent histories. In what ways are these responses conducive toward alliance? In what ways do they foreclose or inhibit relationality?

2. This essay focuses on an abstraction that writing teachers often discuss as if its meaning is self-evident: "reflection." What are other terms in writing instruction that could use clarification, complication, and/or deeper exploration? What does it mean to you? What do you find confusing or challenging about it?

3. We often notice the oversights of social and structural norms when our experiences come up against their limitations—for example, if you use a wheelchair, you are probably more attuned to how many entryways, walkways, and other spaces presume that everyone has

walking privilege. Recall a moment when your own experience exposed the exclusions of a shared norm. What histories have helped entrench this assumption, policy, or practice? What institutions and/or which people have the power to change these structures? What arguments would be persuasive to these different constituencies? What genres might suit those arguments? What are their strengths and weaknesses?

COMMUNITY LITERACY JOURNAL

Community Literacy Journal is on the Web at http://www.communityliteracy.org/

The *Community Literacy Journal* is an interdisciplinary journal that publishes both scholarly work that contributes to theories, methodologies, and research agendas and work by literacy workers, practitioners, and community literacy program staff. We are especially committed to presenting work done in collaboration between academics and community members, organizers, activists, teachers, and artists. We understand "community literacy" as including multiple domains for literacy work extending beyond mainstream educational and work institutions. It can be found in programs devoted to adult education, early childhood education, reading initiatives, or work with marginalized populations, but it can also be found in more informal, ad hoc projects, including creative writing, graffiti art, protest songwriting, and social media campaigns. For us, literacy is defined as the realm where attention is paid not just to content or to knowledge but to the symbolic means by which it is represented and used.

Decolonizing Community Writing with Community Listening[1]

Part of a special issue on community listening, Rachel Jackson's article is concerned with responsible connection in communities that have been historically denigrated. In "Decolonizing Community Writing with Community Listening," she draws our focus to story and narrative as critical literacy. Writing in dialogue with Kiowa elder Dorothy Whitehorse DeLaune, Jackson argues, "In order to decolonize community writing in this academic context, we must listen—as invited community members—to the story of Kiowa cultural literacy on Kiowa terms." We find this piece to be an especially important reminder to scholars who engage in research in (and as) marginalized communities to remain deeply mindful of our practices to avoid exploitation.

---

1. *Community Literacy Journal*, vol 13, no. 1. © 2018 Community Literacy Journal

Decolonizing Community Writing with Community Listening: Story, Transrhetorical Resistance, and Indigenous Cultural Literacy Activism

Rachel C. Jackson with Dorothy Whitehorse DeLaune

This article foregrounds stories told by Kiowa Elder Dorothy Whitehorse DeLaune in order to distinguish "community listening" from "rhetorical listening" and decolonize community writing. Dorothy's stories demonstrate "transrhetoricity" as rhetorical practices that move across time and space to activate relationships between peoples and places through collaborative meaning making. Story moves historic legacies into the present despite suppression enacted by settler colonialism, and story yields adaptive meanings and cultural renewal. When communities listen across difference, stories enact resistance by building a larger community of storytellers, defying divisive settler colonialist inscriptions, and reinscribing Indigenous peoples and their epistemologies across the landscapes they historically inhabit.

A Story about Story

Dorothy Whitehorse DeLaune, who proudly identifies as a full-blood Kiowa, spoke only the Kiowa language until the age of six. Born in 1933 to a father who was in his mid-60s and who taught her to speak her tribal language, she is one of the remaining fluent native speakers of Kiowa alive today. She serves as a vital source of cultural knowledge and a respected Elder in her community. Recently turned 85 years old, Dorothy's spryness, wit, and unstoppable commitment to her people keep her spirit strong. She lives her days recalling language, stories, and songs that shape the Kiowa cultural landscape, residing in memory, inhabiting a people and their history. Dorothy feels pressed to share what she knows, as she says, "before it's too late." She inherits her commitment to Kiowa cultural literacy from her Elders, particularly her father, "Charley" Whitehorse (Tsane Thiye Day in Kiowa). He kept Kiowa

Ohoma (War Dance) songs alive throughout federal prohibition. Despite the suppression of Native American ceremonies during the Ghost Dance movement of the early 20th century, he hosted gatherings to sing the songs in secret. Dorothy grew up listening to her father sing these songs with his hand drum every morning on their back porch. She carries these songs, and the many stories attached to them, in her heart. They are who she is.

I have worked with Dorothy for eight years, picking her up once a week from her home in Anadarko, Oklahoma, stopping by the "Step and Fetch" on the corner to get her 32-ounce Pepsi, and making our way to the cultural literacy class, formally called the Kiowa Clemente Course in the Humanities. We co-teach this class for the University of Science and Arts of Oklahoma. The community calls the class Kiowa College. My role in the course began as the Instructor of Record, but I have also always been a student, learning Kiowa language and culture alongside the class participants. Now I spend most classes transcribing and translating Kiowa on a projected screen as words, phrases, and names arise from Dorothy's memory and enter class discussion. Over more than a decade, the class also began to inform my research, as I gained experience at the intersection of Native rhetorics, cultural literacies, and community engagement. Each Thursday night, the class meets to practice the Kiowa language and learn Kiowa ways that include oral tradition, songs, military and women's societies, protocol, ceremony, history, and values.

On our drive, Dorothy tells me stories. She tells me about the last week's events in the community, the memories that have come to her on restless nights, and the Kiowa words, phrases, and songs she wants to record, transcribe, and translate. We keep an ongoing list. I have learned from Dorothy that in Kiowa Country everything has a story—usually more than one. Working with the Kiowa cultural literacy class for eleven years, I've spent most of that time listening. The Kiowa tell stories in episodes that function also as stories within stories, simultaneously drawing connections between them while also tying them to the contexts in which they are told. Story, or hayn tday gyah, structures Kiowa epistemology. Kiowa stories connect not only to each other but also to the storied landscape within which they reside. Stories unite people in relationships with the land and with each other.

Recently, after I told Dorothy about my idea for this article, she told me a story of the relative from whom her father, "Charley" Whitehorse (ca. 1873 – 1949), received his name. Whitehorse the warrior (1847-1892), her father's uncle, led war parties under the last Kiowa Chief, Lone Wolf (Khooyie Pah Gaw). That night, Dorothy told me a story about Whitehorse the warrior. In 1875, following the Kiowa's final military subjugation at Palo Duro Canyon, he was taken along with Lone Wolf to the Fort Marion prison in St. Augustine, Florida. This story is around 143 years old, spanning four generations. Dorothy tells me it has never been written down, until now. She learned it from listening to her father and older brothers tell it many times. I share it with readers now because Dorothy shared it with me in the context of our discussion of this article. This means she sees a relationship between the story of Whitehorse and the story of Kiowa cultural literacy and community listening that I am telling here.

That evening, as we waited at the stoplight on Central Avenue on the way to class, the winter sunset on the Southern Plains laid long shadows on the Anadarko streets. Dorothy and I consider each other relatives and interact like good friends. Like most everyone else in the Kiowa community, I call her Grandma. Her laugh makes me laugh, and we enjoy each other. We also work together and trust each other. It is with her, and with her permission, that I write this article. As we pull out of the Step and Fetch drive-through, our conversation resumes. I remind her I am working on this article draft, and she begins to tell a story. I hit record on the voice memo application on my phone. Dorothy continues with a story of Whitehorse at Ft. Marion:

> So, when they got down there, I guess in one incident they counted them out first because they wanted to make plaster casts of their faces. It's kind of funny. The Kiowas had seen what they done to the Cheyennes. If someone puts something on your face and fills it with powder, you'd be afraid too. They thought they were death masks, that they would be killed, that they were getting witched. (DeLaune #2)

Dorothy explains that the plaster molds used to make the masks must have looked like books to the Kiowa warriors. The Kiowa language, like Kiowa stories, works through description, comparison, and analogy. At any rate, the warriors had no words in Kiowa for a plaster cast face mold. The word for book, khoot, was the closest descriptive fit.

> When they went in there, to have these masks made, they had to figure out what to do. Lone Wolf told Whitehorse, "I'm gonna give this to you and you shoot it." Lone Wolf grabbed the mold and yelled, "Khoot baht taht tday! Shoot the book!" So, Whitehorse shot the book. And they got punished for that. They got the ball and chain and put in the prison dungeon. (DeLaune #2)

Khoot is also part of the Kiowa word for school, khoot aim, and for pencil, khoot ah daw, and for map, daum khoot gaw (Gonzales 123). This repetition of the word suggests the Kiowas saw a relationship between these objects that connects them all as western literacy practices.

Whitehorse the warrior and Dorothy's father Charley refused to be educated in English. Neither read or wrote in English and, more striking, neither read or wrote in Kiowa. Their relationship to literacy remained entirely dependent on the aurality of the Kiowa language, and listening was a primary function of that literacy. As Scott Lyons (Ojibwe/Mdewakanton Dakota) articulated so powerfully nearly twenty years ago, centuries of "cultural violence . . . located at the scene of writing . . . set into motion a persistent distrust of the written word in English" among Native American peoples (449). Writing was a weapon of the enemy. Books and anything associated with them, or even resembling them, were suspect. Even as Kiowas gained text-based literacy through missionaries, boarding schools, and seminaries, they retained the cultural practice of story and listening. Story and listening, like resistance—and, in this case, as resistance—is part of being Kiowa.

Dorothy and I continue toward class as the western Oklahoma sky illuminates our discussion and the sun sinks slowly behind us. I listen as she finishes the story by adding, "Whitehorse was my dad's mother's brother. Whitehorse didn't have any children, so when Grandma was expecting dad, he said to her, 'If you have a boy, I want to give my name to him.' That's why we're Whitehorse" (DeLaune #2). In inheriting Whitehorse's name, her father, and now Dorothy, inherit his cultural legacy.

Story Decolonizes Academic Discourse

At this point in the narrative I am led by western academic practice to impose a theoretical framework, a chronology, a colonial logic, on these stories. In writing an academic article, I am expected to present a clear argument, a well-honed thesis, and rigorous analysis with "credible" evidence as support. Western academic discourse privileges heuristics, taxonomies, categories, genres, and terminologies intended to impose rational order on otherwise organic ideas and spontaneous meanings. These practices provide clarity for western minds in so far as they "settle" these meanings, subordinating them to the logics that govern them. This is not an appropriate way to treat the stories I am telling here, particularly if decolonization is a goal. For the purposes of this article, settling meaning also interferes with the praxis of community listening, like laying a map on the storied landscape that erases those who live there. Written text has historically operated in much the same way in Indigenous contexts, determining and enacting limits while enforcing control and silencing Native peoples. Kiowa storytelling, as a culturally literate act that depends on community listeners for collaborative meaning making, invites us to listen without limitations. It asks us to imagine possibilities instead of parsing print. It urges us to attend to the potential meanings and possible actions the story opens: the relationships between the past and the present situation, between peoples and places, between "then and now" and "us and them." In this way, it asks us to understand why the story is being told, as it is being told.

In writing about Kiowa storytelling, I want to practice Kiowa storytelling, demonstrating how I understand it to work. As a decolonial move, I choose storying instead of articulating an argument, recalling theory, or constructing a literature review. Kiowa storytelling calls us as scholars to experience a kind of community listening, one that is specific to the Kiowa community and wholly different from established (largely western) community writing practices. Kiowa stories make meaning that is not captured by print or motivated by the goal of producing text or authorship. Rather Kiowa stories build relationships by extending cultural knowledge and values through an Indigenous cultural literacy practice aligned with historical resistance to western hegemony. Western literacy practices perpetuate western hegemony. In order to decolonize community writing in this academic context, we must listen— as invited by community members—to the story of Kiowa cultural literacy on Kiowa terms. I must tell the story without relying on the academic discourse that Writing Studies privileges, but rather on the integrity inherent in Kiowa epistemology and the literacy practices that extend from it. If we listen, the stories speak for themselves, as Indigenous peoples have always spoken for themselves.

While I am not Kiowa, I am enrolled Cherokee and a Native Studies scholar committed to the goals of decolonization. This means I believe the Americas are Indigenous lands that belong, despite the rhetoric, violence, and genocidal tactics of settler colonialism, to the Indigenous peoples who have historically inhabited them. Narratives of US history by contrast present settler colonialism and western expansion as discreet, naturalized, inevitable phenomena, "settled" once and for all through supposedly benign federal policies. In actuality, these were genocidal policies that included violence, militarism, containment, land theft, removal, relocation, and assimilation. The Academy, as a western institution on an Indigenous landscape, places both explicit and implicit limits on Indigenous voices, practices, and perspectives to avoid unsettling these narratives. Dakota scholar and activist Waziyatawin writes, "A growing number of [Indigenous scholars] believe that as Aboriginal intellectuals we can best be of service to our nations by recovering the traditions that have been assaulted to near-extinction" (Wilson 69). As a Cherokee woman and Indigenous scholar interested in community writing, I forward storytelling and community listening as a means of recovery and resistance that provide possibilities for decolonizing academia and community writing in multiple ways. I choose story because it creates resistant spaces for cultural regeneration and community building both within Native communities and beyond them.

The stories Dorothy shares allow us to understand how Kiowa story performs transrhetorical resistance by moving meaning across temporal, spatial, and cultural locations and thereby creating relationships across these sites in order to form the broader movements upon which decolonization depends. Kiowa storytellers do not ask us to analyze their stories or take them apart. They ask us instead to put them together by bringing what we know —not as scholars but as humans —into storied space in order to engage and participate in the story, to share in making the narrative rather than taking control of it. Stories enact intimate, interpersonal relationships built on trust that the stories will be told again, in the right ways, and in connection with other stories. Rather than appropriating these stories for colonial purposes, the task for scholars committed to decolonization "is to challenge the academy as an agent of colonialism and carve a place for [Indigenous] traditions as legitimate subjects of scholarly study, but on [Indigenous] terms" (Wilson 73). This means continually listening to our communities.

In this article, working primarily from stories Dorothy told me in a series of interviews, I tell a story (made up of stories connected to other stories) of community writing to demonstrate how Kiowa storytelling functions as decolonized cultural literacy that depends upon community listening. While I draw in part from the concepts of "cross-cultural conduct" and "rhetorical listening" (Royster qtd. in Ratcliffe *Rhetorical Listening* 1), I believe Dorothy's stories disrupt these concepts, decolonizing them for Indigenous landscapes. In Native spaces, I characterize "community listening" as transrhetorical and define it as a literate act that engages listeners as collaborators in meaning making across multiple sites. These listeners work together with storytellers to construct and sustain cultural knowledge by building storied connections across difference. Like other decolonial tactics, Kiowa storytelling enacts a collectivity that operates across traditional Indigenous cultures. Kiowa stories therefore provide a counternarrative amidst the dominant settler culture inscribed on the landscape and against hegemonic history, the English language, and subsequent cultural erasures. Rather than the singular, monolithic narratives voiced by objective authority in the western tradition, Kiowa stories live and grow, nourishing and expanding culture across sites of knowing and defying the fixed and finalized print of colonial control. Kiowa stories continue to be told because listeners become tellers, building connections across time and locations.

For Kiowas, listening is composing, not consuming. Kiowa story intervenes in the western rhetor/audience (speaker/listener) binary by calling listeners into collective identity and a shared responsibility for cultural knowledge.

Anthropologist Gus Palmer (Kiowa) explains that Kiowa stories "open and remain open so the listener is able to interact with the storyteller by adding comments, asides, stories, interpretations, or other responses or remarks that make the story grow" (109). "Growing" a story suggests that Palmer, like me, observes listeners adding meaning throughout the storytelling process, creating the narrative with the storyteller, and holding accountability for its telling. In this way, Kiowa storytelling resists settled narratives and cultivates instead the continual rewriting and renewal of Indigenous culture and history. Kiowa storytelling not only disrupts colonial discourse. It also performs culturally literate community action as a means of decolonization.

These stories also demonstrate how story operates transrhetorically. I define transrhetoricity in the context of Royster and Ratcliffe as rhetorical patterns that move across time and cultural locations, above fixed rhetorical situations, and beyond limited categories to activate dynamic intersections of race and place that honor difference. In Indigenous spaces, story provides a vehicle of transrhetorical resistance, effectively moving historically silenced legacies and cultural knowledges into the present context to yield adaptive meanings and cultural renewal to the extent that we listen to them together. Likewise, my project ultimately extends Kiowa resistance into the broader community-writing community and asks us to consider the ways we reinscribe settler colonialism in our work. It invites us to listen differently, *with* a community rather than *to* a community or *for* a community. Kiowa stories as a kind of community listening call us to consider the ways in which community writing occurs beyond the colonialist implications and limitations of printed text. In the historically marginalized realms of aurality, meaning remains dynamic and continual despite settler colonial force. If community-writing scholars and advocates seek social justice through their work with diverse communities at intersections of identity that include place, race and ethnicity, class, and gender, then community listening helps us to honor the dynamism operating at these intersections. Likewise, by acknowledging the transrhetorical resistance occurring across the sites where we engage communities dealing with the shared consequences of settler colonial history, together we can understand community writing more broadly as decolonial work. Community listening defies the divisions settler colonialism inscribes on communities while restoring Indigenous peoples and their epistemologies to the landscapes they historically inhabit. By acknowledging the Indigenous landscapes on which our communities reside and the rights of Indigenous peoples—and all peoples—to their own cultural literacies, we align the goals of community writing with the goals of decolonization.

Decolonizing Rhetoric and Transrhetorical Listening

After a decade of listening to Kiowa stories, I still struggle to articulate how these stories work and what they mean. Though I am a Native woman, I am not Kiowa. My sense as a community listener is that Kiowa stories make meaning beyond articulation. "Growing" Kiowa stories, as Palmer suggests, requires making new connections that depend on listeners' imaginations, their willingness to let go of their assumptions, and their desire for clear-cut conclusions. Doing so requires a different kind of listening, transrhetorical listening, that moves meaning across, above, and beyond two-dimensional, dualistic, and linear models. That transrhetorical movement facilitates a web of simultaneous possible meanings also makes it decolonial. Kimberly Wieser, Native Studies scholar of Choctaw and Cherokee descent, characterizes this aspect of Native American rhetorics as "indirect discourse" (xiii). In her recent publication, *Back to the Blanket: Recovered Rhetorics and Literacies in American Indian Studies*, she explains how story works for multiple purposes in Indigenous contexts. She also underscores how story depends upon the co-construction of narrative and the communal articulation of meaning:

> Indigenous American articulation of philosophy and science—who we are and how we see the world, what our position in it is in relation to the rest of creation, how other aspects of creation relate to each other—has often been accomplished by indirect discourse, by saying something without directly saying it. We are traditionally taught by story, and typically explain by story, not merely exposition. Stories, along with oratory, can rhetorically function as argument in Native cultures. Knowledge—cultural, familial, and individual—is often embedded in narrative and must be deduced. (xiii)

In settler colonial situations, the cultural imperative for survival combines with the cultural practice of listening to become community action. Wieser writes, "existence hinges spiritually and culturally on remaining 'storied peoples'" (9). In settler colonial contexts, the telling and the listening become a unified act of resistance and meaning making, a process that has occurred continually across time, whereby listeners become storytellers themselves, equally empowered in mapping out multiple meanings together.

One story told to me by Dorothy helps me to simultaneously explain and demonstrate this process of transrhetorical meaning making. She has shared this story many times with me over the years I have known her. I have also heard her tell it to others. Each time she uses the story to connect the past to the time and place in which she tells it. Her stories function this way here as well, so that readers must draw out the connections listeners had to make for themselves on each occasion. Dorothy does not state these connections directly. Her strongest memory of her father, which she tells here, comes to her as part of a larger story. As she talks, I listen and, in this case, I record, transcribe, and write her stories into the story I am telling now. Every morning, when she was a child, Dorothy remembered her father playing his hand drum and singing Sate Ahn Gyah's death song. I asked her once in an interview who inspired her cultural activism, and she answered by telling me this story:

> Daddy would get the hand drum and he'd sing that man's song every morning. And then he'd say a few side words and then we'd hear him praying. And it was always facing to the east. He says, it says, "Sate Ahn Gyah ee daw gyiye ain tdoe hadle." He saved us a song and I will sing... "Gyah daw tdaw. Gyah daw khoon tdaw." And then it says, "Sate Ahn Gyah ee daw gyai ain tdoe hadle." And it says, "I'll sing it and I'll sing it forever 'cause he saved it for me." And he sang that. And we were no descendant of that man. (DeLaune #1)

These are not the words of the death song itself, but rather words Charley Whitehorse inserts as he sings, adding to the song's story as he sings it. Sate Ahn Gyah (ca. 1800 – 1871), Sitting Bear, was a member of the Kiowa's most elite Warrior Society, the Koiye Tsane Gaw (Horse Soldiers). Dorothy explains:

> You stake yourself to the, you know when you're in combat, you stake yourself. And you couldn't let loose unless one of your friends came by and cut you loose. And they stood there until their death." (DeLaune #1)

In battle, the Koiye Tsane Gaw stake themselves to the ground and face the enemy, an act that embodies their spiritual commitment to fight to the death for the Kiowa land and people. I hear in this story resonances between Dorothy's cultural literacy activism, her father's singing, and Sate Ahn Gyah's fierce resistance in battle. Even after multiple tellings and multiple listenings, the meaning of these connections continues to move and change.

Because the process of listening in Kiowa storytelling requires collaboration between the teller and the listener, community listening in this Indigenous space (and others) differs in some ways from "rhetorical listening" as it has been taken up in writing studies. Responding in part to Jacqueline Jones Royster's call for the construction of "codes of cross-cultural conduct," Krista Ratcliffe argues for the practice of "rhetorical listening" as a trope for "interpretive invention" (*Rhetorical Listening* 1). In *Rhetorical Listening:*

Identification, Gender, and Whiteness, Ratcliffe maintains that sites of cross-cultural interaction and exchange provide the antidote for "the US culture's dearth of discursive possibilities either for articulating intersecting identification or promoting cross-cultural dialogues" (*Rhetorical Listening* 3). "Interpretive invention" and "cross-cultural dialogue" provide useful ways to think of meaning making in Indigenous contexts, yet they are still concepts grounded in the western rhetorical traditions. In particular, cross-cultural dialogue carries forward western binary logics that reassert mean-making as a process occurring between two parties. While it is tempting to understand listening to Indigenous storytelling through the lens of Aristotelean rhetoric and dialectic, to do so in Indigenous contexts foregrounds rhetorical theory as a western cultural logic rather than listening for Native epistemologies via Native cultural literacy practices.

"Community listening" decolonizes "rhetorical listening" to the extent that it reflects Indigenous community practices that transrhetorically resist the binaries inherent to western dialogics. To be fair, my focus here centers on community literacy practices, whereas Ratcliffe takes up public discourse, inclusive of literature, scholarship, and classroom conversations. Within communities, particularly Indigenous communities, the possibilities for co-constructing narratives and meaning are necessarily different. Ratcliffe's applications of rhetorical listening have also been effectively aimed at understanding whiteness, or rather how whiteness, which she characterizes as "unstated," "signifies as an assumed norm, which haunts discourses on any topic" ("In Search" 282). She suggests, "at its best, whiteness studies questions the dominant culture's tendency to define race in binary terms of black/white while only articulating blackness" (Ratcliffe "Eavesdropping" 88). Ratcliffe acknowledges here how whiteness enforces itself as the presumed norm against which white culture compares, measures, and articulates "other" perspectives. Indeed, this portion of her argument applies to what I am attempting to discern here, that is, how whiteness haunts community writing discourse and silences other cultural perspectives. This rhetorical silencing, which Ratcliffe positions rhetorical listening to interrupt, results from how "rhetorical theories were presented as ahistorical structures that could be lifted from, say fourth-century BCE Greece and dropped into" other contexts unchanged ("Eavesdropping" 87 – 88). The ahistorical movement which she points out mirrors the historic western imperialism that animates settler colonialist expansion. Settlers transplant colonial values wholesale, without regard for the Indigenous peoples or cultures already living in place on the landscape. Rather than relying on listening to Indigenous cultures and adapting to new contexts, settler colonialism and the discourses that accompany it depend on displacing and erasing those cultures.

I also hear in this passage the binary of black/white reiterating a problematic settler colonial frame that has historically defined and restricted racial categories and suppressed otherwise far more complex relationships enacted across difference. Such constructions reproduce the limits of dialogic western rhetoric that Indigenous community listening and transrhetorical meaning making resist. Native Americans (among others) are not represented in the black/white binary at all, which replicates the distinct racial policies of assimilation versus segregation authorized by the U.S. federal government to control Native American and African American populations. Settler colonialism is built upon, as Tuck and Yang put it, "an entangled triad of settler-native-slave" (Tuck & Yang 1), where the militias that formed to repel Native Americans from the land eventually also functioned as slave patrols (Dunbar-Ortiz 60). Tuck & Yang remind us of Franz Fanon's unyielding assertion in *The Wretched of the Earth* that decolonization "sets out to change the order of the world" and only becomes clear when we can "discern the movements which give it historical form and content" (Tuck & Yang 2). Indigenous cultural literacy practices such as storytelling and listening work transrhetorically to move and make meaning in traditional ways that defy historically reductive, false divisions to reveal a complex web of relationships both within and between communities. By focusing on the white/black binary as an object of study and critique, Ratcliffe also reinscribes it. Kiowa storytelling and listening resist the imposition of such colonial constructions, refiguring not only racial binaries that reinforce disconnection and isolation, but also potentially restructuring the way rhetoric works in the world and how we understand cultural literacies.

Co-constructing a narrative, particularly in and with community, differs entirely from the rhetor/audience binary where ideas are seemingly exchanged between two parties and the rhetor retains authority over the audience. When Dorothy tells me a story, she is not asserting an argument but rather drawing a connection to the meaning we are making together in the moment she tells it. The listening involved in these two processes necessarily differs as well, as community listeners do not function as a passive audience but rather as active participants. My job as a listener is to work alongside Dorothy to draw those connections. Wieser explains that for Native Americans, "argument does not proceed the way it does in the kind of academic discourse [where] the rhetor leads the hearer/reader to a specific conclusion." Rather, "meaning making is equally distributed" and the listeners "must make active choices […] particularly when argument is done by analogy, by putting pieces of discourse in association with the actual context" in which a story is being told (Wieser 11). Additionally, Kiowa storytellers rely on listeners to draw connections to their own sources of cultural knowledge, including their experiences, family histories, and other stories they have heard before. Story as a "rhetorical practice highlights communal meaning-making systems" (Wieser 12). As such, stories promote Indigenous literacy practices such as community listening while also sustaining Indigenous rhetorics and cultures.

Kiowa Cultural Literacy Practices and Resistance

Anadarko, Oklahoma, sits in the southwestern portion of the state, a small rural town that hit its economic peak in the earlier part of the 1900's and remained fairly strong through the mid-century. Like many rural towns based on agricultural economies and fluctuating oil prices, since then the town has struggled with steady decline and increasing poverty. Built on top of the historic lands of the Wichita and Caddo peoples, which then became the treatied lands of the Kiowa, Comanche, and Apache, the town and surrounding landscape tell the story of a complex settler-colonial history and a persistent, though obscured, Indigenous presence. Anadarko, for instance, while currently considered a part of the Kiowa, Comanche, and Apache reservation, takes its name from a smaller tribal group affiliated with the Caddo. Thus, the settler colonial map blurs distinctions between peoples, cultures, and histories. According to Eve Tuck and Marcia McKenzie in "Decolonizing Perspectives on Place," "in Indigenous worldviews, relationships to land are . . . familiar, and if sacred, sacred because they are familiar" (51). They point to "the tendency to romanticize Indigenous relationships to land inside the Western cultural tradition" as "a misunderstanding of the nexus of Indigenous identity and land" (Tuck and McKenzie 51). Land, story, and identity intertwine in Indigenous epistemologies, so that a particular location presents layered narratives and storied connections that comprise the present landscape.

Clearly, the Kiowas have lived *on* this land and *with* this land prior to recorded histories of the landscape. Their survival depended on *knowing* the land—the weather patterns and seasons, the waterways and windbreaks, the plants and animals, and the people. Kiowa stories, especially when told in the Kiowa language, retain this cultural knowing. In Indigenous contexts, the impacts of 500-plus years of post-Columbus colonization continue to erode Native cultures and languages. While it is difficult to argue against the central role languages play in cultural epistemologies and community identities, the settler colonial formula simply reverses this: to erase a people, erase their language. Adam Gaudry, a Métis scholar and Indigenous Studies professor at the University of Saskatchewan, argues for "insurgent research" methodologies aimed at decolonization. He puts it plainly:

> It is no secret that most Indigenous languages in North America are in danger of being lost forever, nor do we kid ourselves that the hegemony of the English language is anything but responsible for this. There is a well-developed body of Indigenous research that demonstrates the centrality of Indigenous languages in understanding an Indigenous worldview. (129)

For Native peoples living in settler-colonial contexts, then, community writing is more accurately understood as cultural literacy, because the work in these communities focuses not on reading and writing or producing texts. It focuses instead on sustaining cultural knowledges via tribal cultural literacy practices, despite historic suppressive forces, and revitalizing the Native stories and languages that house them. Any reading or writing of texts necessarily serves this goal.

Indigenous cultures are oral cultures, which also means they are aural cultures. Listening is as critical a literacy tool as speaking well. For Kiowa people, speaking well means telling stories well, particularly in community contexts. Dorothy teaches language while sharing stories, incorporating Kiowa words, phrases, names, and locations, and singing songs in Kiowa. Community listeners share their own stories in response, making them grow by compiling narratives and co-constructing Kiowa cultural knowledge to forward into the future. In these stories, I hear the historic persistence of the Kiowa people using Kiowa literacy practices to work against cultural erasure, and so I also see resistance in action. Community listening becomes a critical tool, particularly when today's Elders learned Kiowa aurally and used it orally, rather than textually. Elders rely on other community members to listen to their stories, to place them on the storied landscape, to thread them together and connect them to their own family histories, to make meaning of them, to share them with others. Kiowa culture depends on these stories, so the stakes for storytellers and storylisteners are high. These are their stories. These stories are who they are, who their children and grandchildren are. These stories make them Kiowa.

The story Dorothy tells of Sate Ahn Gyah's death, the story that explains the origin of the song her father sang every morning, and one I've heard her tell many times, comes to mind here. Sate Ahn Gyah participated in multiple war parties and raids in the years prior to the Red River War (1874 – 1875). General William Tecumseh Sherman arrested Sate Ahn Gyah, along with several others, for their participation in raiding a wagon party of would-be settlers. They were imprisoned at Ft. Sill, Indian Territory (now Oklahoma), and ordered to trial in Texas, making them the first Native American war leaders to stand trial in U.S. Court. In an act of defiance, Sate Ahn Gyah refused to be taken to trial. This is how Dorothy explained it to me, after telling me the story of her father singing Sate Ahn Gyah's death song.

> They caught those three together at Ft. Sill and they already had those other two, BigTree [Ah Daw Ate] and Sate Thiye Day [White Bear], in custody. And they were gonna put this old man in one of the other wagons. They were taking them to prison in Texas. The real Kiowas, that's the way I was told, you say when you have medicine, you say, "Daw daw." He had medicine and he told, he said, "I'm not going alive." Some of the Kiowas used to say he ingested that knife. (DeLaune #1)

Sate Ahn Gyah refused to get in the first wagon. They put him in irons and loaded him in a second wagon. Other versions of the story say he chewed his own wrists out of the iron cuffs and pulled a knife from his throat to attack the guards, killing two of them.

> Course they rode on off with Sate Thiye Day and Big Tree. Sate Ahn Gyah said he wasn't gonna go past where that creek was. And they said the soldiers were laughing at him. "That old man can't do nothing." And all of a sudden he appeared with a knife. He broke hisself out of the handcuffs and he got two of them before they filled him with bullet holes, and yet he lived long enough leaning against the tree, singing that song. (DeLaune #1)

This is the song Dorothy's father sang each morning while she listened as a little girl. This is the story Dorothy told to explain the cultural sources of her literacy activism, a story that in this telling recalls both Sate Ahn Gyah's and her father's resistance, all born from a deep commitment to the Kiowa people and their landscape.

KIOWA COMMUNITY LITERACY AS DECOLONIZED CULTURAL LITERACY

The Kiowa Clemente Course in the Humanities, across the nearly fifteen years since the class began, intersects distinct cultures, interests, and institutions. It began in conjunction with the Clemente Course in the Humanities Program of the National Endowment for the Humanities. Developed by Earl Shorris in conjunction with Bard College, the Clemente Course model rests on beliefs Shorris articulated in his 1997 book *Riches for the Poor: The Clemente Course in the Humanities*: namely, that exposure to the humanities instills "the poor and the unschooled" with the power to reflect and think critically rather than react to forces that oppress them (Vitello). According to the Clemente website, "[T]he aim of the course [model] is to bring the clarity and beauty of the humanities to people who have been deprived of these riches through economic, social, or political forces." Shorris piloted the first course in the Roberto Clemente Family Guidance Center in Manhattan's East Village in 1995. In its early iterations, the curriculum consisted of canonical readings from multiple western humanities disciplines such as logic, history, literature, art, and philosophy. Shorris passed away in May 2012 at the age of 75, with Clemente Courses being offered on five continents in locations as variant as the Yucatan and Darfur. Anadarko, Oklahoma, is one of these locations.

The Kiowa Clemente Course development began in 1998 under Dr. Howard Meredith (Cherokee), Professor of Indian Studies at the University of Science and Arts of Oklahoma in Chickasha. A small group of Kiowa students, led by Jay Goombi and including Jackie Yellowhair, along with Kiowa Elders Alecia Keahbone Gonzales, Bob Cannon, Richie Tartsah, and J.T. Goombi, developed the curriculum by adding Kiowa cultural content, community interests, and pedagogical practices to the Clemente Course model. Shorris includes a description of their process in the last chapter of *Riches for the Poor*, entitled "Other Countries, Other Cultures" (248-249). Jay Goombi (Kiowa), one of the students who participated in the course design and implementation, consulted with tribal Elders for input into the course format and content. Multiple conversations between USAO's Indian Studies students and these Elders resulted in a unique community-driven curriculum, one that incorporated transrhetorical inquiry from the start, that developed a comparative, interdisciplinary humanities model that revised, or rather decolonized, the original Clemente Course model for an Indigenous context.

From the beginning, the Kiowas who participated in the collaborative course design included both USAO students and Elders. Together, they rewrote the course objectives to meet their cultural needs, demonstrating one way that decolonization works at an Indigenous community literacy site. Instead of aligning with the problematic goal to disseminate the western canon and "help" the "unschooled," the Kiowa Clemente Course took a comparative humanities approach by studying western texts alongside Kiowa oral tradition, story, and song, putting them in conversation where meaning could be negotiated. Instead of turning to western texts for "clarity and beauty" as in the original Clemente Course curriculum models, the Kiowa Elders wanted to study them for other reasons. As Jay Goombi, now a writer and activist, explained to me early on in my own involvement with the course, the Elders saw the inclusion of western texts as a means to "understand white ways." They wanted to understand western culture, not to better adopt it, but to better subvert it where it conflicts with Kiowa values and practices, adapting it only where it is useful to do so. Likewise, the Elders wanted each class to include a beginning and closing prayer, a shared meal, and a Kiowa language lesson. Each of these original components of the class privileges Kiowa community needs and cultural practices over western educational goals, and the class still includes them. The course was originally entitled, "Yee p'ay gyah maw tame aim" which means in Kiowa "two ways of knowing."

My involvement with the class began in 2007 when the class still used the comparative humanities model developed in its original design. During my first few years of teaching, students and community participants began to express in class a desire to omit the western content entirely. At first, this was an awkward conversation to have as the instructor assigned to present the western perspective on the weekly topic. However, after listening to several semesters of comments, complaints, and suggestions, and acknowledging dwindling attendance, I worked with the Elders involved in the class to redesign it. Now, the course focuses completely on Kiowa language and culture, and our weekly attendance averages between 20 and 30 people, a testament to the community's approval. Not everyone enrolls for college credit. Many come just to listen, practice, and learn about their language, culture, and history, to hear the stories of who they are. Though students can only enroll for a total of six hours of credit over two semesters, many return year after year. Over time, they also take on roles and responsibilities, which include providing food for the class meal and sharing cultural resources from their own family histories and archives. In this way, the class dynamic reflects Kiowa community and cultural practices. In any given semester, we prioritize deep inquiry into the topics that emerge from student interest and discussion, and the group identifies course priorities collaboratively, thinking through together what they would like to learn next. They depend on Dorothy's knowledge to help them.

Our course texts range the full spectrum of modalities. They do include books produced by several white ethnographers, the earliest of which, Jane Richardson Hanks' *Kiowa Law and Status*, was published in 1935 and based on oral interviews with prominent Kiowa Elders of that era. Dorothy's father Charley Whitehorse was one of the Elders Hanks interviewed. Dorothy was two years old at the time. He recorded a total of sixty songs with Hanks and in class, we use Hanks' archival sound recordings as cultural resources. These recordings include a wide range of songs, from ceremonial songs belonging to specific Kiowa societies, to child-rearing songs, to Kiowa Christian hymns. We listen to them and transcribe them collectively into Kiowa, and then translate them with Dorothy's help into English. We also use other ethnographic and archival texts (written in English) and photographs, many of which have been brought to class by students from their own family collections. For instance, in class we read aloud from the papers of Morris Doyeto. He was the grandfather of one of our returning students, Martha Addison. His personal papers reside in her possession. Doyeto was educated outside of the Kiowa community and completed seminary in Chicago in the 1920's. Doyeto's explications in English of Kiowa religious and ceremonial history are not only rich in cultural information, but they also provide an opportunity to observe and discuss the influence of western education and text-based literacy on Kiowa stories and storytelling.

One of the key characteristics of traditional Kiowa storytelling that Dorothy models for the class regards their cyclical nature. That is, Kiowa stories are told in cycles according to the seasons. For instance, the stories of the primary deity in Kiowa culture, the Zie Day Tahlee or Split Boys, must only be told in the springtime after the first thunder. In our class, Dorothy shares these stories in preparation for our annual field trip, which she describes as a pilgrimage. The trip includes a visit to at least two of the ten Medicine Bundles sacred to the Kiowa people. In one of Doyeto's treatises, he writes down in English a long series of episodes related to the Zie Day Tahlee which we use in class as a primary text. The stories tell of the boys' origin, exploits, and heroism as they use their medicine to confront monsters and make the world safe for the Kiowa to inhabit. The class participants take turns reading Doyeto's version aloud, one episode at a time. The room grows still as these sacred stories fill the air between us, drawing us into relationship with the past. Everyone focuses together, and I can almost hear us listening. We are rapt. Throughout Doyeto's rendering of these stories, he characterizes the Zie Day Tahlee as "the Author of Religious Liberty and Freedom from Tyranny," a rhetorical move that the students never fail to notice—and question. Through our discussions of his possible motives for identifying the Zie Day Tahlee in this way, Doyeto's stories allow us to see both the dissonance between his cultural upbringing and his western theological training as well as how they intersect. We discuss his motivations and the impact of writing the stories down. This conversation, still centered on story, acknowledges the influence of western thinking on Kiowa culture while also disrupting it and decolonizing the course curriculum. Because the community prefers to focus on Kiowa content, the western humanities component has been permanently dropped from the syllabus and course calendar.

STORY AS TRANSRHETORICAL LISTENING AND CULTURAL CONTINUANCE

Dorothy's father, Charley Whitehorse, even though he received the name of a great warrior, never saw battle. Born in approximately 1873, he was a small child when the Kiowas lost their last military battle with the United States at Palo Duro, and Whitehorse was taken to prison in Florida. Still, Dorothy's father inherited along with his name a legacy of resistance, one that he continued through the turn of the century as the Kiowas faced allotment and the lottery that opened their remaining lands to white (and black) settlement in preparation for statehood. Federal assimilation policy included the prohibition of Indigenous ceremonial practices, which began most famously with the Battle of Wounded Knee. The violent and unprovoked U.S. aggression against the Lakota decimated a camp of primarily women, children, and Elders with the goal of suppressing the Ghost Dance Movement. Kiowa ceremonies included not only a yearly Sun Dance, but the songs and dances of the Kiowa military societies. When I ask Dorothy what resistance means to her, she tells me this story:

> Well, in 1919 my dad was the head of one of our three existing, now existing, Kiowa organizations. One was the Gourd Clan. One was the Black Leggings. And the other one was the Ohoma War Dance Society. We had ten, but the others had gone out of existence. I guess it was earlier than that. Early 1900's when they made us quit the Ghost Dance and everything. Well, uh, they told these organizations, if you don't quit, you're not getting any rations. But my dad kept on. They'd put up the teepee after dark, and pray all night, and then break it down before daylight. And then, uh, they never quit dancing. Danced in secret. All through my homeplace. (DeLaune #1)

Her story connects her father's resisting the suppression of Native ceremonies to her own work to sustain Kiowa culture. Never having learned how to read or write in Kiowa or English, Charley Whitehorse learned these songs by listening to his Elders sing. He saved them by singing them for and with his community, despite the risk of punishment.

The sixty songs he recorded for Hanks several years later in 1933 include Sun Dance (Kxaw Tdoe) songs, Tohn Kohn Gaht (Black Leggings) songs, Tdiye Pay Gaw (Gourd Clan) songs, in addition to Ohoma War Society songs. In one of Hanks' recordings of him singing, Dorothy's father inserts words into the song, as he did with the Sate Ahn Gyah's Death Song that he sang each morning on his back porch, adding his own story to the stories the songs tell of Kiowa history. He pauses between the lyrics and addresses the listener directly, appending phrases in Kiowa that suggest his own motivations for recording them. They translate roughly as: "I feel good when I sing these songs because my grandfather sang them to me"; "these songs are the only things we have left"; and "after I am gone you'll still hear me" (DeLaune #3). In these phrases, he calls the listener into the song and the song's story, to listen as he did, and to learn them as he did.

In another song, he inserts a prayer for Dorothy, who was only a small child on the floor next to him, listening as he sang. He says, "Tdoe dohn gyah thohm kaw day ah ahm mah hope," or "the one crawling on the floor, let that one be proud/persevere" (DeLaune #3). Dorothy, whose Kiowa name is Daw Tsai Gyah Ahn Thah Gyah (She Comes With Good Prayers), thrills when she hears him pray for her. She was named as an infant in a Peyote meeting. Her father passed when she was only sixteen years old. Despite Dorothy's strong memories of his singing, the Hanks recordings house many songs that would have otherwise been lost had Charley Whitehorse not kept them to share with others:

> The only Kiowa organization that never died out completely was the Ohoma. My dad led that. And to this day, if you came to the Ohoma ceremonials, we have a song. It's the resistance song. It's by no means radical, like let's kill 'em or anything. People will say, "Sing the resistance song." It says, "Don't quit dancing, 'cause you enjoy it. Even if we have to go to jail, we're gonna keep dancing." And those are the Kiowa words. "Dah ba tohn pahnt bah." It says, "Let's go on and go to jail, okay?" To me, that's where I get it. From my dad, I guess. He defied 'em. (DeLaune #1)

These are the stories she tells when I ask her to explain resistance. Sustaining her culture—as her father did, and as Whitehorse the warrior did before him—and telling these stories comprise the same resistant, cultural, and literate act.

The community listening enacted in Dorothy's storytelling connects her great uncle Whitehorse the warrior's story, Sate Ahn Gyah's story, her father's story, and her own story to the larger story of Kiowa resistance, and now, through this publication, to the broader community writing network. These stories decolonize our academic understandings of community writing by asking us to participate as community listeners co-engaged in making meaning from them. What possible meanings we hear in them depends upon how we listen transrhetorically to the stories and to each other in understanding them together. These stories ask us to consider how and where we extend them and to whom we tell them. Who we are depends upon listening as a community to storied landscape rather than the *settled* landscape. Where we reside and the connections we make between our own locations and others—and how we make those connections as scholars committed to decolonization—matter to our work. We are telling a story together that moves across spaces and beyond time, sustaining Indigenous knowledges, languages, and literacy practices that nourish the cultural continuance of Native peoples to whom this land belongs.

Stories survive not just through the telling, but through communities listening to them together, adding to them, building them into larger narratives that connect us in relationship with each other, and telling them again. Charley Whitehorse recorded Sate Ahn Gyah's Death Song, the one Dorothy heard him sing every morning as a child, with Hanks in 1933, knowing he would be heard again in the future beyond his own death. Sate Ahn Gyah, the Kiowa war leader who staked himself to the ground in battle and who chose death as resistance to leaving the Kiowa landscape as a prisoner of the United States, leaned up against an old Cottonwood tree as he died from gunshot wounds. As he died, the story—as Dorothy shares it—says he sang:

> "Haw ah gome," I walk around. "Ahdle haw ah oiye boiye gome thaw day." I won't be here forever. "Oiye p'iye day kee oiye boiye kxaw." Only the sun will be here forever. "Oiye dohn gaw kee ay oiye boiye kxaw." Only the land will be here forever. (DeLaune #1)

Though the sun and the land may outlast them, as long as the story of Kiowa resistance continues to be told so that others can listen, the Kiowa people will continue as well.

Works Cited

The Clemente Course in the Humanities. National Endowment for the Humanities, 2015, clementecourse.org. Accessed 22 Nov. 2015.

DeLaune, Dorothy Whitehorse. Personal Interview #1. 1 May 2014.

DeLaune, Dorothy Whitehorse. Personal Interview #2. 4 January 2018.

DeLaune, Dorothy Whitehorse. Personal Interview #3. 21 January 2018.

Doyeto, Morris. Private Family Collection.

Dunbar-Ortiz, Roxanne. *Loaded: A Disarming History of the Second Amendment*, City Lights Books, 2018.

Gaudry, Adam J. P. "Insurgent Research." *Wicazo Sa Review*, vol. 26, no. 1, 2011, pp. 113-136.

Gonzales, Alecia Keahbone. *Thaum Khoiye Toden Gyah: Beginning Kiowa Language*, University of Science and Arts of Oklahoma, 2001.

Goombi, Jay. Personal Interview. 5 June 2014.

Hanks, Jane Richardson. *Kiowa Law & Status*, U of Washington P, 1940.

Hanks, Jane Richardson. Jane Richardson Hanks Papers. Edward E. Ayer Manuscript Collection, Newberry Library, Chicago, IL.

Lyons, Scott Richard. "Rhetorical Sovereignty: What Do American Indians Want from Writing?" *College Composition and Communication*, vol. 51, no. 3, 2000, pp. 447-468.

Palmer, Gus, Jr. *Telling Stories the Kiowa Way*, U of Arizona P, 2003.

Ratcliffe, Krista. "Eavesdropping as Rhetorical Tactic: History, Whiteness, and Rhetoric." *Journal of Advanced Composition*, vol. 20, no. 1, 2000, pp. 87-119.

Ratcliffe, Krista. "In Search of the Unstated: The Enthymeme and/of Whiteness." *Journal of Advanced Composition*, vol. 27, no. 1, 2007, pp. 275-290.

Ratcliffe, Krista. *Rhetorical Listening: Identification, Gender, and Whiteness*, Southern Illinois UP, 2006.

Shorris, Earl. *Riches for the Poor: The Clemente Course in the Humanities*, W.W. Norton & Company, 2000.

Tuck, Eve, and K. Wayne Yang. "Decolonization is Not a Metaphor." *Decolonization: Indigeneity, Education & Society*, vol. 1, no. 1, 2012, pp. 1-40.

Tuck, Eve, and Marcia McKenzie. *Place in Research: Theory, Methodologies, and Methods*, Routledge, 2015.

Vitello, Paul. "Remembering Earl Shorris." *Clemente Course in the Humanities*, 2 June 2012, clementecourse.og/about-us/remembering-earl-shorris. Accessed 18 February 2014.

Wieser, Kimberly G. *Back to the Blanket: Recovered Rhetorics and Literacies in American Indian Studies*, U of Oklahoma P, 2017.

Wilson, Angela Cavender. "Reclaiming Our Humanity: Decolonization and the Recovery of Indigenous Knowledge." *Indigenizing the Academy: Transforming Scholarship and Empowering Communities*, edited by Devon Abbott Mihesuah & Angela Cavender Wilson, U of Nebraska P, 2004, pp. 69-87.

Rachel C. Jackson (Cherokee Nation of Oklahoma) completed her PhD in the Composition/Rhetoric/Literacy Program at the University of Oklahoma in 2016. She currently holds a Diversity Post-Doctoral Fellow position in the Rhetoric and Writing Studies Program at Oklahoma State University. Her research examines local activist rhetorical strategies in the context of historical suppression, particularly as activist rhetorics operate transrhetorically across cultural locations to build collective action. Her community-engaged projects focus on sustaining Native American languages and cultural literacies and forwarding Indigenous voices and perspectives. She works with tribal leaders and community members across Oklahoma to develop and implement classes, workshops, and projects. Her work has appeared in *College Composition and Communication, College English*, and *Rhetoric Review*. She is a Ford Foundation Fellow, a Fellow with the Newberry Consortium on American Indian Studies, and a recipient of the 2017 Berlin Award and 2017 Ohmann Award from the National Council of Teachers of English.

Dorothy Whitehorse DeLaune is a widely acknowledged and highly honored elder in the Kiowa community. She works as a cultural advisor, storyteller, and language teacher with many programs and offices in the Anadarko area. She is Co-Instructor for the Kiowa Clemente Course in the Humanities (University of Science and Arts of Oklahoma) and serves as project staff for Kiowatalk.org. She is an active member of the Kiowa War Mothers Society and the TOHN KOHN GAHT (Kiowa Black Leggings) Society.

Supplemental Material

"Decolonizing Community Writing with Community Listening: Story, Transrhetorical Resistance, and Indigenous Cultural Literacy Activism"

Rachel C. Jackson with Dorothy Whitehorse DeLaune

Part I: Reflection on the Origins of the Article

The origin of this article begins with our longstanding and ongoing relationship, based in our collaboration as co-facilitators of the Kiowa Clemente Course in the Humanities, the Indigenous humanities course detailed in the essay. As friends, we share many personality traits as well as life commitments. We are both open, easy, and curious with people, and we understand ourselves as connected to long histories and vital communities of our respective peoples. In our time alone together, over the phone or during long car rides through the Oklahoma countryside, we talk like sisters with each other, sharing stories and struggles, and laughing like no one in the world can hear us. This article originates, as it begins here, with our conversations on our journey together building a community-based cultural literacy project and adapting it to the assets, interests, and needs of the Kiowa community. According to the course design, Kiowa cultural knowledge centers the course in terms of pedagogy and content. Dorothy holds an honored role as an elder, a knowledge keeper, a storyteller, a first-language Kiowa speaker, and a grandmother to many members of the community. She teaches as she speaks, her words spirited with Kiowa culture and life, her observations and ideas animated by Kiowa values and sensitivities, and her speech marked by cultural practices and proclivities appearing in subtle patterns and rhythms as she talks. One of these patterns is this: if you ask her a question, she tells a story. Over our nearly ten years of collaboration and conversation, the same stories continue to bear repeating, each time in a new context and (thus) in a new way. The stories accumulate meaning with each telling, remaining alive and without end, deepening connections for listeners as well as inscribing themselves in the community's cultural memories. As an Indigenous cultural and rhetorical practice, storytelling works in a wholly different way than Western academic discourse. The challenge of sustaining Indigenous cultural knowledge within an academic context (whether from within the university itself or through an academic article) requires presenting that knowledge in and against the language and discursive practices of an historically oppressive settler-colonial institution. Our working relationship teaches us both new ways of meeting or, rather, managing this challenge while privileging Indigenous practices such as reciprocity and collectivity. "Decolonizing Community Writing with Community Listening" emerges as much from this challenge as it does from our conversations, because in many ways this challenge occurs, like the article itself, at the center of our relationship.

Part II: Description of Research Methods, Findings, and/or Pedagogical Impact

The research process Rachel undertook as a doctoral candidate required institutional review board approval and formal research protocols. Field interviews, as a qualitative research method (used in ethnographic methodologies) and informed consent, proved a flexible form for engaging cultural literacy workers in an open discussion about activism and resistance. All field interviews were transcribed and coded for emergent rhetorical patterns, practices, and themes. Rachel first formally interviewed Dorothy for this dissertation research. That interview, conducted on May 14th, 2014, is incorporated and cited in the article along with subsequent interviews we conducted after committing to writing this piece together. In many ways, the connections we draw in the article between Dorothy's own cultural commitments and those of her father, emerge newly for both of us as a result of sitting with these stories to discern what meaning they lend to our understanding of community literacy activism, resistance and transrhetoricity, and the role stories play in sustaining Indigenous knowledges. The article, we hope, demonstrates the type of transrhetorical listening for which it argues, as we attempt to make apparent in the text our process of making meaning together while occupying and bridging different cultural/institutional spaces. We have found transrhetorical listening an effective tool for sustaining a community-based Indigenous cultural literacy project such as the Kiowa Clemente Course. As the article establishes, our storywork informs our teaching, enabling us to strengthen connections between course objectives and stories told and to invent new ways of engaging students/listeners in the process of meaning making during and between classes. This includes taking the time to ask what connections arise for students/listeners between the stories Dorothy tells and the stories they have been told by other elders and integrating the broader matrix of meanings that emerge into class discussion as well as course planning. Engaging such a matrix highlights to us as well as course participants the collective agency necessary for sustaining Indigenous cultural knowledges in colonial contexts, while also building a broader community archive of Kiowa stories.

Part III: Discussion Questions

1. In order to facilitate audience engagement with the article that replicates listener engagement with Kiowa stories, the authors attempt to resist drawing concrete conclusions and fixed interpretations as story episodes appear in the article and instead draw connections. In your experience as a reader, to what extent does their resistance of this Western writing convention succeed and how? Was it frustrating or liberating to encounter Dorothy's stories in this way?

2. How does the author's relationship, detailed early in the article, shape the construction of community literacy and community listening for which the stories advocate? In what ways does it complicate and/or illuminate the role of the community-engaged scholar?

3. The article makes a subtle claim that in sharing Kiowa stories with readers it also conscripts them in the process of sustaining Indigenous cultural knowledge, a position that comes with the responsibility to collaborate as a meaning maker. How does your encounter with these stories shape your understanding of Indigenous cultural literacy activism as well as your role in it?

COMPOSITION STUDIES

Composition Studies is on the web at https://comp-studiesjournal.com/

In publication since March 1972, *Composition Studies* holds the distinction of being the oldest independent journal in writing studies. Consistent with its beginnings as a forum for discussing teaching strategies, Composition Studies continues to publish scholarship about teaching writing but has expanded to include a wide range of historical, theoretical, and exploratory studies related to writing, pedagogy, administration, literacy, and emerging areas of interest. The journal's interest in growing with the field is perhaps best illustrated by a statement in the mission welcoming work that doesn't fit neatly elsewhere.

Decolonial Potential in a Multilingual FYC[1]

"Decolonial Potential in a Multilingual FYC" by Cruz Medina is a pedagogically focused article that argues for the cultural legitimacy of a bilingual fyc course. This is an idea whose time has come, and Medina explores it through a grounded study that is both informed by current theories and anchored in practical details relevant to teachers around the US.

---

1. *Composition Studies*, vol. 47, no. 1 © 2019 by Laura Micciche.

Decolonial Potential in a Multilingual FYC

Cruz Medina

Scholars in rhetoric and composition have questioned to what extent the field can be decolonial because of the gatekeeping role that writing plays in the university. This article examines the decolonial potential of implementing multilingual practices in first-year composition (fyc), enacting what Walter Mignolo calls "epistemic disobedience" by complicating the primacy of English as the language of knowledge-building. I describe a Spanish-English "bilingual" fyc course offered at a private university with a Jesuit Catholic heritage. The course is characterized by a translanguaging approach in which Spanish is presented as a valid language for academic writing. The students' writing highlights the enduring influence of colonialism in the form of monolingual ideology within the linguistically diverse geographical context of Silicon Valley, where the potential of decolonial practices are tempered by the economic power of the tech industry and its hiring practices, which have resulted in a low number of employed women and minorities in comparison to both national employment levels and diversity within the region.

Multilingual students experience monolingual ideology in their education, which undermines their abilities to communicate, make meaning, and be effective writers. A multilingual student, Selena[1], describes in her literacy narrative the feeling of vulnerability she experienced in elementary school when she moved from Mexico City, Mexico, to Toronto, Canada:

> I would rather be in a tank full of hungry sharks than once again be vulnerable to a language barrier that had barely been trespassed months before. I was determined to master the English language as to avoid another encounter where nobody could understand me and I couldn't understand them. . . . After having lived my entire seven-year-old life in Mexico City, my father received a job offer in Toronto, Canada. This resulted in my small four-member family to move two countries north into an unknown culture, weather, people, and more importantly language (at least by me).

Selena communicates the vulnerability of starting a new school as a young student who is unable to speak English and is an emerging multilingual learner in an academic institution that imposes assimilation. This article examines the literacy narratives of multilingual speakers in a fyc course themed as "bilingual," the first course in a two-course sequence, which was taught in Spanish. After examining these literacy narratives, I recognized students had used translingual theories we discussed in class to conceptualize their multilingual struggles not as obstacles they had to overcome but as advantages they could use to create new meanings and discover new knowledge. The negative experiences that students related to assimilation, isolation, and insecurity reveal the need for decolonial practices that redress the damage of assimilation and monolingual ideology.

Before moving on, I want to clarify how I'm using key terms in this article. By multilingual, I refer to someone who speaks or writes in more than one language, with linguistic abilities ranging from emerging skills to more complex rhetorical awareness of linguistic practices in a language other than what was spoken at home. The term bilingual describes the specific Spanish fyc course that I co-taught with my colleague Juan Velasco, which was followed by a second course in English. The term bilingual falls under the larger umbrella of multilingual; however, the application of bilingual is limited because it reduces multilingualism to two languages, whereas many of the student writers in this piece speak or write in more than two languages. The term translingual refers to the dispositions, theories, and frameworks that propose inclusive approaches to the use of multiple languages, or translanguaging, for communication, in spite of monolingual efforts to invalidate non-Standard Academic English (SAE). By translanguaging, I refer to "both the complex language practices of multilingual individuals and communities, as well as the pedagogical approaches that draw on those complex practices to build those desired in formal school settings" (Garcia, Johnson, and Seltzer 2). The writing examined in this piece is by multilingual students in a bilingual fyc taught with a translingual approach that was incorporated through readings, discussions, and writing assignments.

Within rhetoric and composition, African American, American Indian, and Latinx scholars have questioned the extent to which the field can, across university contexts, operate within higher education and against colonial paradigms undergirded by racism, sexism, classism, and other systems of oppression that impact whose voices or English(es) are valued (Gilyard; Powell; Villanueva, "On the Rhetoric"). Indigenous scholar Angela Haas explains that decolonial theory informs practices, methodologies, and pedagogies that examine

(1) how we have individually and collectively been affected by and complicit in the legacy of colonialism; (2) how these effects and complicities of historical and contemporary colonialism influence research and educational institutions, theories, methodologies, methods, and scholarship; and (3) how the effects and complicities of colonialism play out in our everyday embodied practices. ("Decolonial Digital" 191)

Indigenous scholars such as Ellen Cushman focus on the coexistence of language and digital spaces in her call for decolonizing digital archives for the purpose of sharing the Cherokee language ("Wampum"), and Qwo-Li Driskill advocates for decolonial skillshares and exposure to indigenous language to counter colonial perceptions of indigenous knowledge and communities ("Decolonial Skillshares"). The issues of language and intellectual production that are central to the rhetorical sovereignty of Indigenous scholars in writing studies provide generative support for considering how translingual practices in fyc have the potential to disrupt colonial practices. By incorporating languages other than SAE into classrooms, students create knowledge and become familiar with translingual practices that frame their linguistic differences as resources and embodied practices and that disrupt colonial monolingual narratives.

To that end, I assigned a literacy narrative in the required fyc class that I taught in English, which students took after completing the first course in Spanish with my colleague Juan Velasco. When I examined the student narratives, I recognized students had used the translingual theories we discussed in class to reconceptualize their multilingual struggles not as obstacles they had to overcome but as advantages they could use to create new narratives about their linguistic differences. This analysis does not posit that literacy narrative assignments on translingualism will be effective for teaching all English language learners across all institutional contexts; instead, this student writing reveals how reconceptualizing multilingual practices through the introduction of translingualism in a fyc course highlights the potential for redressing perceptions of language, people, and communities based on the colonial influence of monolingual ideology. Additionally, both multilingual writing and writing in different forms of English provide a heuristic for recognizing how composing always requires a rhetorical awareness of translating a writer's message and how competing ideologies affect audience reception, which highlights ideological factors.

THE BILINGUAL FYC COURSE

From 2013-2017, my institution offered four sections of an fyc two-course sequence that enacted a translanguaging approach. Serving approximately 80 students over four years, each class of approximately twenty students began the fyc course titled Critical Thinking and Writing 1 Bilingual in Spanish (CTW1) with my colleague Juan Velasco, which focused on analytical skills, before continuing the sequence with me in CTW2 Bilingual in English, which focused on argumentation, information literacy, and research. In this sequence, Spanish was presented as a valid linguistic mode of academic writing, and identities and experiences of multilingual students were validated through critical examination of monolingual ideology in course readings and discussion. The course theme of "bilingual" would have been better titled "multilingual" because multiple enrolled students grew up with languages other than English and Spanish.[2]

The bilingual fyc course was developed by English faculty[3] based on the understanding that multilingual students possessed linguistic resources that informed their rhetorical awareness and discursive skills, in part answering Ellen Cushman's language-based decolonial question, "How can teachers and scholars move beyond the presumption that English is the only language of knowledge making and learning?" ("Translingual" 234). Students opted into the bilingual course based on questionnaires they completed during orientation[4]. The students' levels of Spanish proficiency ranged from native speakers, those who have spoken Spanish as a first language, to native English speakers, who felt their Spanish speaking skills were still emerging, even though they passed Advanced Placement (AP) Spanish classes and tests in high school. Some AP students were the children of educators who spoke some Spanish with a care-giver growing up, while others learned English as a second language during their elementary education[5]. The students who learned Spanish in school tended to come from privileged backgrounds while the first-generation students spoke of immigrant parents, commuting to school and holding jobs[6]. With a student body of approximately 5,500 undergraduates, the twenty or so students who took part in the bilingual fyc courses each year were hardly a significant representation of the entire university; however, the percentage of Latinx students in each course exceeds 50% even though Latinx students make up only 15% of the overall student population.

In the first quarter of bilingual fyc (CTW1), my colleague Juan Velasco[7] conducted the course in Spanish, providing space for students to discuss the spectrum of their languaging abilities, including positive and negative experiences associated with their multilingual identities. Velasco introduced Gloria Anzaldúa's *Borderlands/La Frontera* as a central text to provide a model for thinking about writing as an expression of multiple linguistic identities and translanguaging with English, Spanish and Nahuatl. Steven Alvarez suggests that translingual literacy studies could undergird a decolonial definition of literacy that "contribute[s] to a necessary shift in literacy studies by treating heterogeneity in contact zones as the norm rather than the exception" (19). He continues, the "rhetorical dimension of translingual literacies allows it to consider communicative competence as not restricted to predefined meanings within individual languages" (19). The diverse population of students in the bilingual fyc, which included white, Latinx, African American, Asian American, and Middle Eastern American students, understood linguistic heterogeneity because it was a part of their lived experiences as multilinguals. By addressing the negative impact of monolingual ideology on the linguistic abilities of multilinguals, the translingual readings, discussion, and analysis contribute to the decolonial potential of this framework, which decentralizes a singular, authoritative version of language.

During the second fyc course in the two-course sequence (CTW2), which focused on argumentation and research, I assigned readings that theorized multilingual experiences within monolingual university writing classrooms, articulating important arguments about diversity within a single language. The students read Paul Kei Matsuda's "Myth of Linguistic Homogeneity," which problematizes teaching SAE as a primary goal of writing instruction and describes how the myth of linguistic homogeneity privileges monolingual English speakers. Students agreed with Matsuda's claim that "the dominant discourse of U.S. college composition not only has accepted English Only as an ideal but it already assumes the state of English-only, in which students are native English speakers by default" (637). Additionally, many agreed with Matsuda's explanation that "resident second-language writers" and "native speakers of unprivileged varieties of English" are harmed when educators assume English homogeneity (648). The class next read Bruce Horner et al.'s "Language Difference in Writing: Toward a Translingual Approach" and discussed how translingualism speaks to the myth of a singular English and frames linguistic difference as a resource. Students appreciated learning that a translingual approach "acknowledges that deviation from dominant expectations need not be errors; that conformity need not be automatically advisable; and that writers' purposes and readers' conventional expectations are neither fixed nor unified" (Horner et al. 304). These articles not only helped establish a shared vocabulary for discussing how audiences base responses to linguistic differences on monolingual ideology but also proposed a framework for advocating using languages other than English in the writing classroom.

Following the Matsuda and Horner et al. pieces, I assigned a literacy narrative assignment that asked students to discuss their experiences with reading and writing while reflecting specifically on language and identity. These narratives generated inquiry about language and multilingualism that often resulted in preliminary research topics. For the literacy narrative assignment, the purpose was to "write a literacy narrative that draws on your experiences with reading and writing, identifying how these experiences have contributed to how you see yourself negotiating the different ways that people think about language" (see appendix). Students were asked to treat their experiences with language, whether positive or negative, as generative sites of analysis that should be supported or complicated by quotations from the course readings. In the assignment, I emphasized "negotiating" the different ways that audiences think about language because a translingual approach benefits from the understanding "that English is always a language in translation" (Pennycook 34) and "recognize[es] all language use as acts of translation" (Horner, NeCamp and Donahue 287), thereby framing linguistic "difference as the norm of all utterances" (Lu and Horner, "Introduction" 208). Literacy narratives allowed students to focus on their diverse uses of language, creating a space where they could describe tangible instances of how audiences' respond to language difference and what those responses reveal about their ideology. These moments of translation and negotiation provide generative experiences for writing literacy narratives because students are keenly aware of the moments when they have been made to feel inferior for their language use. Through writing, multilingual students express how they experience frustration, rejection, and feelings of not belonging that motivate the work of translingual scholars, providing more critical perspectives on monolingual ideology's colonizing effect.

Isolation

One of the reasons that introducing translingual theory into writing classes supports decolonial practices has to do with its ability to create more inclusive spaces for knowledge creation, counteracting the isolation that marks multilingual speakers as "others." Below I return to the quote by Selena in which she describes her feeling of vulnerability after having moved from Mexico City to Toronto, Canada, without knowing English:

> I would rather be in a tank full of hungry sharks than once again be vulnerable to a language barrier that had barely been trespassed months before. I was determined to master the English language as to avoid another encounter where nobody could understand me and

> I couldn't understand them...After having lived my entire seven-year-old life in Mexico City, my father received a job offer in Toronto, Canada. This resulted in my small four-member family to move two countries north into an unknown culture, weather, people, and more importantly language (at least by me).

Because she would prefer to be in "a tank full of hungry sharks," her experience as an English language learner arriving in an unfamiliar linguistic space is characterized as worse than living in constant fear due to her inability to communicate. Selena's response underscores the fear associated with the experience of forced assimilation to dominant linguistic practices through the linguistic containment she faced in school. Assimilation remains a topic of concern in literacy studies, because as Gregorio Hernandez-Zamora explains in *Decolonizing Literacy: Mexican Lives in the Era of Global Capitalism*, literacy learning is "not just a psycholinguistic process, but centrally... a cultural, political and ideological experience of *adopting and assimilating to the language, culture and ideologies of the dominant other*" (32). Fortunately, Selena describes her teacher in Canada as dedicating extra time to help her and another student who spoke only French, as well as "other classmates who not only tolerated us but also made a warm welcoming environment." The multilingual context of Canada no doubt informed the teacher's approach to language; however, Selena's experience speaks to the necessity of professional development opportunities to prepare educators to work with multilingual student populations (Canagarajah, "Translingual Writing"; Ferris and Hedgcock; Matsuda).

Selena's experience with the English language became further complicated when her family moved from Toronto to Corpus Christi, Texas, where she describes being exposed to Spanglish as a form of translanguaging that challenged her experiences with languages as being distinctly separate. She felt uncomfortable with the translingual practices of multilinguals in Corpus Christi because Selena's educational experiences in both Mexico and Canada had reinforced monolingual beliefs about the homogeneity of languages. Moving again from Texas to a small town in Montana, Selena references Matsuda's "Myth of Linguistic Homogeneity" to address the lack of diversity she faced when her English teachers focused primarily on grammar in her writing, a salient feature of her writing as a non-native English writer. Selena's teacher imagined that she had had the same experiences as the other students, so her teacher paid less attention to the content of her writing:

> [W]henever I was returned a red ink drenched homework assignment, I never connected that failure to the fact that English was indeed my second language but simply to the fact that I hadn't worked

hard enough or hadn't invested enough time into it. I had fallen victim to the idea that "'writing well' is the ability to produce English that is unmarked in the eyes of teachers who are custodians of privileged varieties of English." (Matsuda 640)

Although Selena makes no claims about discrimination because English was her second language, her experience demonstrates how the overemphasis of certain grammar rules enacts a form of linguistic discrimination that reinforces the exclusionary and punitive aspects of monolingual ideology. Even though Selena's writing teachers may have intended to contribute to Selena's transferable writing skills for future classes, the overemphasis of grammar and syntax correction served to demoralize Selena. "Drenching" an assignment with red ink overwhelms students and detracts from higher-level writing goals; it serves only to reinforce the gatekeeping role of colonial institutions that mark non-white multilingual students as inferior.

Selena's negative experience with writing, based on a teacher's overemphasis on a specific variety of English, highlights the need for translingual practices. These practices refer to the pedagogical "disposition of openness and inquiry the people take toward language and language differences" and the advocacy "to be more humble about what constitutes a mistake (and about what constitutes correctness) in writing" (Horner et al. 310-11). Enacting translingual practices reframes linguistic difference as a skill in the semiotic toolkit, following Suresh Canagarajah's assertion that "[t]he term translingual conceives of language relationships in more dynamic terms" (*Literacy as Translingual Practice* 8). Translingualism and translanguaging offer a dynamic paradigm for students to understand their multilingual identities and linguistic differences within monolingual universities where students like Selena have often been inculcated to think of multilingual abilities as a deficit.

In his literacy narrative, Julian describes the difficulty of growing up with parents who were emerging multilinguals, speaking primarily a non-privileged dialect of Spanish. After immigrating from Zacatecas, Mexico, to Aspen, Colorado, Julian describes the confusion that results from moving between two languages dominated by monolingual ideology:

> Before starting school, my parents had taught me their imperfect versions of Spanish; dialects coming from a rural area of Zacatecas, México. Both of them had received very little education and thus had little experience with the more academic forms of Spanish. I was raised very monolingual, to the extent that I wasn't even aware of all the other languages that existed in our surrounding community and around the world. Thus when I was taught to read and write in

English at school in Colorado, my mind was blown away and I felt very confused and frustrated.

Julian's experience highlights the clash of colonial influence. Spanish and English monolingual ideology negatively impacted his move between Mexico and the U.S. Julian's frustration follows what Anzaldúa argues in "How to Tame a Wild Tongue" about academic rules oppressing English and Spanish speakers: "Even our own people, other Spanish speakers *nos quieren poner candados en la boca* [they want to put padlocks in our mouths]. They would hold us back with their bag of *reglas de academia* [academic rules]" (76; my translations). The student's experience of moving between locations dominated by monolingual ideology highlights how the enforcement of "*reglas de academia*," in both English and Spanish, exert the worldview's power through standardization.

Anzaldúa's *Borderlands/La Frontera* articulates many of the frustrations multilinguals experience because of the standardization that monolingual ideology imposes, which is part of the reason why my colleague Velasco taught the first quarter in Spanish using *Borderlands/La Frontera* as the primary text in the course. Anzaldúa's translanguaging with English, Spanish, and Nahuatl provides students with arguments and experiences they can relate to about language and identity. For students like Julian, writing in a language other than English offers decolonial potential since their English abilities have been called into question due to their multilingual identity. The high percentage of Latinx students in the class provided an exigence for the incorporation of the Spanish language, which Anzaldúa describes as embodying a "tolerance for contradictions, a tolerance for ambiguity," with the mestiza who learns "to be an Indian in Mexican culture" (101). Native scholar Driskill also introduces Anzaldúa's *Borderlands/La Frontera* into courses where the indigenous Cherokee language is incorporated because the book supports the claim that "[l]anguage revitalization and continuance is one of the central struggles of Native people in the United States and Canada" (Driskill 65). Language provides a generative heuristic for helping students to arrive at a nuanced understanding of the deeply rooted and intermingled cultures and people who live on colonized indigenous lands in the U.S.

Maria, a first-year Latina in my class who was actually a junior because of dual-enrollment credits, describes having felt, or having been made to feel, as though her first language of Spanish was inferior for creating knowledge. In her literacy narrative, she interprets her experience through the myth of linguistic homogeneity and translingualism**,** revealing how monolingual ideology is internalized and used to subjugate speakers of non-dominant varieties of English. She advocates for translingualism:

> Throughout my education, I always viewed English as a superior language to my native Spanish language due to the constant separation of students into classrooms of different English levels. . . . Enacting a translingual approach to learning institutions is essential to break the borders that are built between several languages and their variations.

Maria's advocacy for a translingual approach follows Cushman's view, expressed in "Translingual and Decolonial Approaches to Meaning Making," that translingualism offers potential for decolonial practice because of its premise that knowledge can be made in languages other than English. Maria's literacy narrative also underscores Juan Guerra's reasons for using of translingual theory in writing classrooms. Guerra argues that translingualism "introduces more of our students in the first-year and advanced writing courses to the competing ideologies that inform their current writing" ("Cultivating" 232). Using multiple languages in the writing classroom, Maria appreciates how a writing course creates a space where multilingual students can reclaim agency over their linguistic practices while addressing competing ideologies in those practices. For multilingual speakers like Maria, monolingual ideology manifests in a colonial rhetoric of assimilation urging students to should hide their abilities and identities as people who are able to speak more than standard U.S. English. When instructors teach languages other than English as contributing to knowledge in academic institutions, they create a space where decolonial practices serve to reveal how colonialism has benefited from erasing alternative epistemologies, cultures, and communities in order to justify expansion and "discovery" of occupied territories.

What makes Maria's experience further indicative of how colonial ideology discriminates against multilingual students is that she entered the university with junior-level status as a result of dual-enrollment courses, and yet she was still indoctrinated to believe her linguistic heritage made her academically inferior. Maria's heightened awareness about the impact of monolingual ideology demonstrates why students should be taught "communicative practices as not neutral or innocent but informed by and informing economic, geopolitical, social-historical, cultural relations of asymmetrical power" (Lu and Horner 208). Despite Maria's academic success, she was still left feeling that her linguistic heritage was framed as inferior by the pervasive monolingual ideology. Maria's experience is atypical for the many Latinx students who internalize myths of monolingual superiority because hers remains a relative success story. Many times, Latinx students with Spanish as their first language or heritage language are less academically successful because they are segregated in public and charter schools through implicit and explicit linguistic and socioeconomic containment (Blume; "Choice Without Equity").

INSECURITY

The feeling of insecurity that Maria describes demonstrates the impact of monolingual ideology, although the continued use of the term "broken English" by the multilingual students in their literacy narratives shows how these beliefs are internalized and then manifested, often to describe the linguistic differences of family members. One student, Kerry, defines the Korean English she spoke when she was young as a kind of "broken English." She writes, "As a child, I was raised by my grandparents who spoke broken English yet primarily spoke Korean. Thus, I spent most of my youth speaking to them in what I called 'Ko-nglish,' a mixture of grammatically incorrect Korean and English." Kerry's description of her family's English echoes Matsuda's point about the implied connection between grammar and intelligence and his critique of educators "who judge the writer's credibility or even intelligence on the basis of grammaticality" (640). That Kerry was made to feel shame or embarrassment about her family members' way of communicating with the world demonstrates why decolonial and anti-racist scholars continue to critique the colonial imperative of assimilation (Baca, *Mestiz@*; Martinez; Villanueva, *Bootstraps*). When arguing for integration rather than assimilation, these scholars seek to recognize and increase the epistemological work recognized, as well as "the breadth of meanings available within a language," such as variations across Chicanx English, African American English, and Hawaiian English (Pennycook 43). In addition, the continued use of concepts such as "broken English" undermines the dynamic nature of language and of how language changes across genres, in different contexts, for different audiences.

However, Kerry also comments on how Anzaldúa's *Borderlands/La Frontera* re-conceptualizes effective writing by emphasizing the content of what is being communicated, rather than focusing primarily on grammar. Kerry writes,

> Our [fyc in Spanish] professor showed us a variety of writing pieces with mixes of Spanish and English or grammatically incorrect Spanish, emphasizing that the message and content were more important than just the grammatical contents. He similarly encouraged us to not focus as much on the grammar in our Spanish, but more about our content as well as expressing our writing in creative manners. This was a complete change from all the previous standard language

classes that I had taken . . . languages could intermingle, mix, and vary in an artistic manner, rather than be something that needed to be corrected.

Kerry's appreciation of the "artistic" intermingling of languages and the attention to writing content demonstrates how translingual practices can create decolonial disruptions, positively impacting how students perceive their own language use. By drawing attention to how and what Anzaldúa writes, the course reveals "decolonial potential, [where] translingual approaches need to avoid simply changing the content of what is studied and taught and work toward dwelling in the borders to revise the paradigmatic tenets of thought structuring everyday practices" (Cushman, "Translingual" 236). When Kerry writes about Anzaldúa's writing and the fyc's approach to language, she alludes to how the course impacts the tenets of thought regarding her everyday practices with language and writing. As Cushman notes, the decolonial potential of translingual practices is rooted in unsettling what students have been taught about the possibilities of writing. The "creative manners" that Kerry mentions also speak to a broadened definition of writing that includes multiple modes and semiotic resources for knowledge-making available to students.

While discussing the potential for constructing knowledge in the Cherokee language, Ellen Cushman calls for decolonizing digital spaces, a result of which might be multimodal composing. Both translingual and multimodal digital writing draw on a wide range of composing resources in non-alphabetic, multimodal, digital, and multiple linguistic modes of communication (Baca, *Mestiz@*; Banks; Canagarajah, *Translingual*; Cushman, "Wampum"; Haas; Palmeri; Selfe; Shipka). Cushman supports a translingual approach though remains critical of its application in much the same way she calls on composers to remain critical of the media they use. Cushman explains that "a translingual approach to meaning making evokes a decolonial lens with its focus on the ideologies implicit in any tool chosen for meaning making (be it mode, media, or genre), as these are always laden with cultural, historical, and instrumental import for the people who use them" ("Translingual" 236). I would add that the responses digital texts generate can reveal an audience's ideology and conceptualization of writing. Like the additional affordances that digital, visual, and non-alphabetic modes offer students for communicating, translingualism offers another approach for understanding how linguistic diversity is regarded as a resource for intended audiences.

Similar to Kerry's experience with "broken English" and "Ko-nglish," a student named Jennifer highlights how translingual practices can teach multilingual students to view their linguistic differences as something to leverage rather than hide. In the following, Jennifer presents her Filipino mother's English as having a negative impact on Jennifer's idiomatic phrasing and pronunciation. Jennifer relays the feeling related to the use of "broken English" when she describes her mother's variations as grammatical errors:

> Many of the grammatical and pronunciation errors that my Filipino family regularly make when speaking or writing in English have been passed down onto my own use of language. Although English is my first language, I have still managed to adopt the same nuances as my mom as a result of primarily learning how to speak and write from her. Sometimes I catch myself mistakenly saying to "open" and "close" the light instead of "turn the light on and off," pronouncing the word "alumni" as "a-loom-ni", and interchangeably using the pronouns she and he.

Contextualized language practices such as the use of "open" instead of "turn on" are misidentified as grammatical errors within the dominant monolingual ideology. In reality, the language use by Jennifer's mother represents "the normal transactions of daily communicative practice of ordinary people" (Lu and Horner 212). These "normal transactions" of "ordinary people" like Jennifer and her mother demonstrate how overemphasizing privileged forms of English in the classroom can serve to uphold colonial standards that stigmatize linguistic variances, especially within the families of multilingual students.

Jennifer's response to her mother's English is an internalization of monolingual ideology, which manifests in the English Only movement, rebranded as "English Official." Through a decolonial lens, English Official demonstrates an enduring colonial project that privileges nativism and excludes non-white multilinguals from institutional power due to linguistic difference that mark multilinguals as "other." Here in California, monolingual ideology was concretized in the passage of Proposition 63 in 1982, making English the "official" language (Dyste). Opponents of English Official/English Only policy, Bruce Horner and John Trimbur explain that English Official policy "continues to exert a powerful influence on our teaching, our writing programs, and our impact on U.S. culture" (595). Students like Jennifer fear replicating the linguistic patterns of their parents because of the systematic remediation and poor assessment of multilingual students' writing, supported by state policy authorizing discriminatory practices at the programmatic and classroom levels. Tensions over which language can be used for knowledge production continue to be an issue at the state level, where legislation such as West Virginia's English official House Bill 3019 passed as recently as 2016 ("U.S. English"). These policies exert colonial power by delegitimizing the linguistic practices of anyone other than monolingual English speakers. With the majority of states having English as the official language, colonial paradigms operate through the establishment of a standard, against which the subjugated population always falls short (Bhaba).

DECOLONIAL IMPLICATIONS FOR MULTILINGUAL PRACTICES IN COMPOSITION STUDIES

The literacy narratives by students like Jennifer highlight the enduring influence that colonialism maintains through monolingual ideology, even in a geographical context as diverse as the Bay Area in northern California. The tech industry in Silicon Valley contributes to the colonial influence that flattens differences in the name of innovation and economic growth. The writing by the students in the bilingual fyc course brings to light how isolation and insecurity continue to impact multilingual speakers in composition classrooms. Even as my colleague Juan encouraged students to use both Spanish and English in their writing assignments to demonstrate how their multilingualism provided an additional semiotic resource, Juan noted how the students often self-censored their use of English when writing predominantly in Spanish. By adhering to monolingual practices in this multilingual writing class, students allude to how the prestige of SAE supersedes students' multilingual abilities. When students accommodate to the dominant language, they follow the logic of Western modernity that "is still at work assimilating and consuming" (Ruiz and Sánchez xvi). Students' desires to perform an educated version of English no doubt contributes to the discomfort that students described when speaking Spanish in a writing course. This is particularly poignant in Silicon Valley because diversity is often celebrated publicly as aligned with innovation (Massaro and Najera). The institutional context and its adherence to monolingualism support the belief that universities should be viewed as sites for job preparation exclusively, where learning rules translates into future employment.

My institution's geographical context of Silicon Valley also provides a useful metonymy for the juggernaut tech industry[8] to consider in the analysis of student literacy narratives because of the economic ethos of the area; that is, arguments for colonialism often use economic development as evidence of a positive net benefit. In "The Case for Colonialism," Bruce Gilley claims there is "evidence for significant social, economic, and political gain under colonialism: expanded education, improved public health, the abolition of slavery, widened employment opportunities, improved administration, the creation of basic infrastructure…access to capital, the generation of historical and cultural knowledge, and national identity formation" (4).[9] Gilley's claims that colonialism helped generate cultural knowledge contradicts accounts by native populations, such as the Nahua in what is now Mexico, where colonial forces destroyed literacy artifacts following contact with indigenous populations (León-Portilla). Similarly, Gilley's claims about abolishing slavery ring false given the forced conversion, labor and enslavement of native populations; colonial forces, ultimately, are those that benefit from inequitable economies and employment possibilities.

Within writing studies, decolonial theory continues to gain attention because it reveals and resists enduring colonial legacies that subjugate those marked by linguistic or racial difference. In *Decolonizing Rhetoric and Composition Studies*, Raúl Sánchez points to Walter Mignolo's influence on decolonial theory in writing studies: "Mignolo's decoloniality is of interest to scholars in our field who wish to continue expanding the concept of writing, especially as we continue to consider the rich varieties of Latin American and Latinx written experience past, present, and future" (87). Mignolo's influence in writing studies can be traced back to his work on breaking from colonial knowledge that standardizes and enforces beliefs about language ("Delinking"), his advocacy for epistemic disobedience ("Epistemic"), and his arguments for recognizing parallel sites of knowledge making (*Darker*). Mignolo's work is important for writing theory, methodology, and pedagogy seeking to break from colonial narratives about what is authorized as writing for knowledge-making and what knowledge is valued. Decolonial theory enriches the analysis of multilingual student writing because colonial ideology imposes itself through the control of indigenous knowledge and knowledge by people of color. In previous work, I drew on decolonial theory in the examination of texts by predominantly Latinx students in Tucson responding to culturally relevant assignments in the context of anti-ethnic studies legislation that targeted a program scaffolded around indigenous and Latinx ways of knowing. In the context of Arizona HB 2281, which sought to outlaw a program that increased graduation rates and state test scores for a predominantly Latinx student population, I argued for the application of "decolonial theory, writing, and practices [such] as those which work against hegemonic institutions and policies that support colonial assumptions of white supremacy" (Medina 61) because district administrators sought to discredit the work of the ethnic studies program. Through the analysis of student writing in these contexts, we can observe the decolonial potential through the benefits students describe from having experienced a de-centering of colonial knowledge and monolingual practices in the classroom. A decolonial framework provides a critical method for analyzing student texts because experiences with language cannot be separated from the social and cultural ecologies of student knowledge.

Decolonizing "Good Writing"

For decolonial practices to be effective, they need to be iterative and reconstituted by taking local institutional contexts into account. Indigenous scholars such as Driskill incorporate decolonial practices through Native American language usage in the classroom relating to the demographics of a particular geographic location ("Decolonial Skillshares"). By standardizing the use of language other than English, Driskill argues that "Indigenous languages not only carry cultural memory, because language is so central to rhetoric, they also change the way we think about rhetoric and how rhetoric works" (67). Unfortunately, my students' literacy narratives suggest that writing instruction and assessment continue to overly emphasize grammar and syntax. Decolonial scholars might argue that over-enforcing syntax and grammar is rooted in colonial belief systems dating to at least 1492, when "one writing system was so brutally and quickly imposed upon others" (Baca, "Rethinking" 232).

Multilingual students have been discouraged from using their linguistic resources because of how their language practices have been policed by assessment practices based on colonial standards that emphasize mimicry (cf. Bhabha) through assimilation. In both the students' literacy narratives and class discussions, their perceptions of themselves as writers reveal the negative impact grammar rules have had on them and their writing. In writing studies, the discussion of grammar can be traced back to the 1966 Dartmouth Seminar, where scholars in composition and writing studies fought for the recognition of writing as entailing more than grammar and syntax. However, recent critiques of Vershawn Young's use of African American English (AAE) in the 2019 College Composition and Communication Conference call for papers demonstrate the need for more inclusive understandings of linguistic diversity within the U.S. Responding to Young's language use, such as his assertion that "We gon show up, show out, practice, and theorize performance-rhetoric and performance-composition," contributors on the Writing Program Administration listserv (WPA-L) echoed colonial appeals to standards, arguing that Young's writing should reflect the English taught in first-year classes (Young). These national conversations about the centrality of SAE reflect what students described in their literacy narratives regarding the enforcement of monolingual ideology. Nationally and locally, the reduction of writing to little more than grammar stands in for monolingual ideology because of how English and writing become narrowly defined as homogeneous. Canagarajah points out that these responses demonstrate how "[m]onolingual ideologies have relied on form, grammar, and system for meaning-making, motivating teachers and scholars to either ignore strategies and practices or give them secondary importance" (*Literacy as Translingual Practice* 4). Students' focus on writing for content, not simply for correctness, supports advocacy for translingual practices. These practices can help make writing more relevant and can "push composition from its parochial status as a U.S.-centric, English monolingual enterprise to a discipline directly confronting, investigating, and experimenting with, rather than simply correcting, language practices on the ground" (Horner, NeCamp and Donahue 291). Presenting translingualism in the classroom increases student awareness of the evolving nature of language and disrupts monolingual arguments that negatively impact how multilingual students view the validity of their writing.

Translingual theories and practices contribute to decolonial practice when curricular materials and assignments call attention to monolingual ideology and provoke students' critical reflection on the discriminatory institutional practices that affect how multilingual speakers negotiate language use. This work—beyond making writing about more than error correction—counters deficit-model terminology embedded in phrases like "broken English" and proactively responds to naming the enduring legacies of colonialism and having *la facultad* to see beneath the surface of these structures (Anzaldúa 60). At this moment when xenophobia functions as a strategy in mainstream political campaigns[10], language remains a tangible curricular avenue through which to discuss the unequal distribution of power and the importance of critical communication for civil discourse. Instead of continually fortifying walls that separate and authorize language use, educators have the opportunity to engage students in critical discussion about language difference and multiple literacies and to continue the work of decolonizing the borders of what writing is and how it can be composed. The literacy narratives discussed here reveal the decolonial potential of providing students with an alternative paradigm through which to understand language differences. Translingual practices provide a pedagogical intervention for reframing discussion of linguistic difference within the classroom and for redressing how colonial legacies affect multilingual students' perceptions of themselves as writers.

Acknowledgments

Thanks to Juan Velasco and Sharon Merritt for making the bilingual writing class possible. Thanks to Bob Mayberry for the support with revisions, to Laura Micciche for editorial guidance, and to reviewers for generous feedback.

Notes

1. Student names have been changed.

2. This diversity of language is similarly reflected in U.S. Census data cited in a 2014 *Silicon Valley Index* report that the percentage of Spanish speakers is smaller in Silicon Valley compared to California and the rest of the U.S., with Chinese, Vietnamese, other Indo-European, and Tagalog spoken at higher rates by those who are five years and older (*Silicon Valley Index* 13).

3. Juan Velasco and Sharon Merritt worked together to develop the course in 2011. Velasco and I piloted it in its second year when I began at Santa Clara University in 2013.

4. The mechanism for identifying students for this class has been an issue since the inception of the bilingual fyc. Students are often uncertain about why they were placed in the course.

5. At this small liberal arts private institution, a student commuting can be indicative of a working class background, especially in the context of the visibly privileged student population.

6. Anecdotally, the division in cultural and economic capital between students who could have benefited from bilingual education and those students whose parents exposed them to immersion education highlights how outlawing bilingual education disproportionately negatively impacts students of color from lower socioeconomic backgrounds.

7. Juan Velasco earned a PhD in his home country of Spain and an additional PhD in Chicano Studies from UCLA.

8. When most students were asked why they chose to attend this institution, proximity to the Silicon Valley tech industry ranked highest.

9. Since the publication of this article, the journal has withdrawn this essay after it "received serious and credible threats of personal violence," according to the Taylor & Francis webpage.

10. The xenophobia evidenced in Donald Trump's remarks about Mexico as a country sending drug dealers and rapists to the U.S. is echoed by lesser-known political candidates such as Mike Pape (see Pape's campaign ad on YouTube).

Appendix

First Year Writing |
Session Year | **Literacy Narrative**

> A literacy narrative tells the story of a particular incident or a series of vignettes that contributed to the awareness of becoming literate. It is a meaningful narrative constructed with scenes, events, dialogue and detail that communicate experiences.

During this unit, we're engaging with writers whose writing addresses issues related to language, a writer's identity, and myths of a singular English. Some of these issues are described by Gloria Anzaldúa as literacy moments, and we will think of literacy "as a set of socially organized practices which make use of a symbol system and a technology for producing and disseminating it" and "apply this knowledge for a specific purpose in specific contexts of use" (Scribner and Cole 236). Because the theme of this class is education and identity, this writing assignment will ask you to reflect on aspects of literacy as they relate to your identity and your use of knowledge about language in specific situations.

Assignment: Write a literacy narrative that draws on your experiences with reading and writing, identifying how these experiences have contributed to how you see yourself negotiating the different ways that people think about language. For example, you might consider specific instances when you made conscious decisions about language that either achieved a desired outcome or perhaps when your choice of language led to an unexpected response from someone who thought differently about language than you. You will incorporate quotes from the course readings that support, refute or complicate your point and experience with language and literacy.

Required Texts: Paul Kei Matsuda, "Myth of Monolingualism" and Bruce Horner et al., "Toward a Translingual Approach"

Audience: For this assignment, you will be writing for an academic discourse community in a non-fictional style of writing that uses Standard Academic English as well as non-English to demonstrate your claim about language.

Should Include:

- A central claim/thesis about yourself as a reader/writer and how it reveals an aspect of your educated identity
- Clear scenes with description and explanation of significance of this scene
- Evidence in the form of quotes from Matsuda or Horner et al.
- Analytical explanation about how and why this experience impacted your identity as a reader, writer and educated person
- Paragraphs organized by content rather than focused on length

Remember that you are working to:

- Demonstrate how experiences from your life contributed to how you are critically aware of language
- Demonstrate critical thinking, which includes the whole process of selecting complex enough claims, appropriate evidence (and the appropriate amount of analysis)
- Demonstrate insights about experiences through analytical explanations
- Demonstrate the strategic use of details to communicate the tone and emotion of the experience

Format: MLA format, 12 pt font, Times New Roman, double spaced, 1-inch margins, page numbers (see MLA example on OWL Purdue on d2l), 3-4 pages, works cited page

Grading Rubric Criteria

Analysis: How effectively are experiences explained and their impact on literacy/education communicated?

Clarity: Did the scenes/experiences provide details, description or dialogue that communicated the feeling of the experience?

Organization: Did the sequence of events or the choice of included events contribute to an effective communication of experiences with education?

Academic Convention and Style: Did the style match the content of the scenes and analysis? Did the quotes effectively contribute to analysis of the experiences?

Process: Did you engage in the drafting activities with your group? Work across drafts to make the best summary possible?

Works Cited

Alvarez, Steven. "Literacy." *Decolonizing Rhetoric and Composition Studies: New Latinx Keywords for Theory and Pedagogy*, edited by Iris Ruiz and Raúl Sánchez, Palgrave MacMillan, 2016, pp. 17-30.

Anzaldúa, Gloria. *Borderlands/ La Frontera*. Aunt Lute, 1987.

Baca, Damian. *Mestiz@ Scripts, Digital Migrations, and the Territories of Writing*. Palgrave MacMillan, 2008.

---. "Rethinking Composition, Five Hundred Years Later." *JAC*, vol. 29, no. 1/2, 2009, pp. 229-42.

Banks, Adam J. *Digital Griots: African American Rhetoric in a Multimedia Age*. SIUP, 2011.

Bhabha, Homi. "Of Mimicry and Man: The Ambivalence of Colonial Discourse." *October*, vol. 28, 1984, pp. 125-33.

Blume, Howard. "Charter Schools' Growth Promoting Segregation, Studies Say." *Los Angeles Times*, 4 Feb. 2010, articles.latimes.com/2010/feb/04/local/la-me-charters5-2010feb05.

Canagarajah, Suresh, editor. *Literacy as Translingual Practice: Between Communities and Classrooms*. Routledge, 2013.

—. *Translingual Practice: Global Englishes and Cosmopolitan Relations*. Routledge, 2012.

—. "Translingual Writing and Teacher Development in Composition." *College English*, vol. 78, no. 3, 2016, pp. 265-73.

"Choice Without Equity: Charter School Segregation and the Need for Civil Rights Standards." *The Civil Rights Project: Proyecto Derechos Civiles*, 6 March 2012, www.civilrightsproject.ucla.edu/research/k-12-education/integration-and-diversity/choice-without-equity-2009-report.

"*College English* Call for Submissions: 'And Gladly Teach.'" NCTE, www2.ncte.org/resources/journals/college-english/write-for-us/#AGT.

Cushman, Ellen. "Translingual and Decolonial Approaches to Meaning Making." *College English*, vol. 78, no. 3, 2016, pp. 234-42.

—. "Wampum, Sequoyan, and Story: Decolonizing the Digital Archive." *College English* vol. 76, no. 2, 2013, pp. 115-35.

Driskill, Qwo-Li. "Decolonial Skillshares: Indigenous Rhetorics as Radical Practice." *Survivance, Sovereignty, and Story: Teaching American Indian Rhetorics*, edited by Lisa King, Rose Gubele, and Joyce Rain Anderson, Utah State UP, 2015, pp. 57-78.

Dyste, Connie. "Proposition 63: The California English Language Amendment." *Applied Linguistics*, vol. 10, no. 3, 1989, pp. 313-30.

Ferris, Dana R., and John Hedgcock. *Teaching ESL Composition: Purpose, Process, and Practice*. Routledge, 2004.

García, Ofelia, Susana Ibarra Johnson, and Kate Seltzer. *The Translanguaging Classroom: Leveraging Student Bilingualism for Learning.* Caslon, 2017.

Gilley, Bruce. "The Case for Colonialism." *Third World Quarterly*, 2017, pp. 1-17.

Gilyard, Keith. "The Rhetoric of Translingualism." *College English*, vol. 78, no. 3, 2016, pp. 284-89.

Guerra, Juan C. "Cultivating a Rhetorical Sensibility in the Translingual Writing Classroom." *College English*, vol. 78, no. 3, 2016, pp. 228-33.

Haas, Angela. "Toward a Decolonial Digital and Visual American Indian Rhetorics Pedagogy." *Survivance, Sovereignty, and Story: Teaching American Indian Rhetorics*, edited by Lisa King, Rose Gubele, and Joyce Rain Anderson, 2015, pp. 188-208.

Hernandez-Zamora, Gregorio. *Decolonizing Literacy: Mexican Lives in the Era of Global Capitalism*, 2010.

Horner, Bruce, Min-Zhan Lu, Jacqueline Jones Royster, and John Trimbur. "Language Difference in Writing: Toward a Translingual Approach." *College English*, vol. 73, no. 3, 2011, pp. 303-21.

Horner, Bruce, Samantha NeCamp, and Christiane Donahue. "Toward a Multilingual Composition Scholarship: From English Only to a Translingual Norm." *CCC*, vol. 63, no. 2, 2011, pp. 269-300.

Horner, Bruce, and John Trimbur. "English Only and U.S. College Composition." *CCC*, vol. 53, no. 4, 2002, pp. 594-630.

León-Portilla, Miguel. *The Broken Spears: The Aztec Account of the Conquest of Mexico.* Trans. Lysander Kemp, Beacon, 1992.

Lu, Min-Zahn, and Bruce Horner. "Introduction: Translingual Work." *College English* vol. 78, no. 3, 2016, pp. 207-18.

Martinez, Aja Y. "'The American Way': Resisting the Empire of Force and Color-Blind Racism." *College English*, vol. 71, no. 6, 2009, pp. 584-95.

Martinez, Aja Y, Cruz Medina, and Gloria Howerton. "Comment and Response: A Response to Kim Hensley Owens's '*In Lak'ech*, the Chicano Clap, and Fear: A Partial Rhetorical Autopsy of Tucson's Now-Illegal Ethnic Studies Classes.'" *College English*, vol. 80, no. 6, 2018, pp. 539-45.

Massaro, Rachel, and Alesandro Najera. *Silicon Valley Index.* Joint Venture: Silicon Valley Institute for Regional Studies, 2014.

Matsuda, Paul Kei. "The Myth of Linguistic Homogeneity in US College Composition." *College English*, vol. 68 vol. 6, 2006, pp. 637-51.

Medina, Cruz. "Nuestros Refranes: Culturally Relevant Writing in Tucson High Schools." *Reflections: A Journal of Public Rhetoric, Civic Writing, and Service Learning*, vol. 12, no. 3, 2013, pp. 52-79.

Mignolo, Walter. *The Darker Side of the Renaissance: Literacy, Territoriality, and Colonization.* U of Michigan P, 1995.

—. "Delinking." *Cultural Studies*, vol. 21, no. 2, 2007, pp. 449-514.

—. "Epistemic Disobedience, Independent Thought and Decolonial Freedom." *Theory, Culture and Society*, vol. 26, no. 7-8, 2009, pp. 159-81.

Palmeri, Jason. *Remixing Composition: A History of Multimodal Writing Pedagogy.* SIUP, 2012.

Pennycook, Alastair. "English as a Language always in Translation." *European Journal of English Studies*, vol. 12, no. 1, 2008, pp. 33-47.
Powell, Malea. "2012 CCCC Chair's Address: Stories Take Place: A Performance in One Act." *CCC*, vol. 64, no. 2, 2012, pp. 383-406.
Ruiz, Iris, and Raúl Sánchez. "Introduction." *Decolonizing Rhetoric and Composition Studies: New Latinx Keywords for Theory and Pedagogy*, edited by Iris Ruiz and Raúl Sánchez, Palgrave MacMillan, 2016, pp. xiii-xx.
Selfe, Cynthia L. "The Movement of Air, the Breath of Meaning: Aurality and Multimodal Composing." *CCC*, vol. 60, no. 4, 2009, pp. 616-63.
Shipka, Jody. "Transmodality in/and Processes of Making: Changing Dispositions and Practice." *College English*, vol. 78, no. 3, 2016, pp. 250-57.
"U.S. English Efforts Lead West Virginia to Become 32nd State to Recognize English as Official Language." U.S. English, Inc., 5 March 2016, www.usenglish.org/u-s-english-efforts-lead-west-virginia-to-become-32nd-state-to-recognize-english-as-official-language/.
Villanueva Jr, Victor. *Bootstraps: From an American Academic of Color*, NCTE, 1993.
—. "On the Rhetoric and Precedents of Racism." *CCC*, vol. 50, no. 4, 1999, pp. 645-61.
Young, Vershawn. "Call for Program Proposals: Performance-Rhetoric, Performance-Composition." NCTE CCCC, cccc.ncte.org/cccc/conv/call-2019.

Cruz Medina is Assistant Professor of Rhetoric and Composition at Santa Clara University. Medina wrote *Reclaiming Poch@ Pop: Examining Rhetoric of Cultural Deficiency* (Palgrave 2015) and co-edited *Racial Shorthand: Coded Discrimination Contested in Social Media* (CCDP 2018). His writing has appeared in *CCC, College English, Composition Studies* and other venues.

Supplemental Material

"Decolonial Potential in a Multilingual FYC"
Cruz Medina

Part I: Reflection on the Origins of the Article

The idea for this piece began in 2013 when I learned that my colleague at Santa Clara University, Juan Velasco, was teaching a bilingual first-year writing class. I was interested in the course because of my experience teaching at the University of Arizona in Tucson where I saw first-hand the impact of culturally relevant courses in the Tucson Unified School District. Despite the increases in state test scores and graduation rates (Cabrera et al.), the Ethnic Studies program in Tucson came under attack from the State Superintendents of Education, Tom Horne and John Huppenthal. Beliefs that the program was attacked because the success of Latinx students in Arizona unsettled beliefs about white supremacy seemed somewhat validated when it was discovered that anonymous comments posted online about wiping out Jews and Africans were written by Huppenthal (Roberts 2014). While the concern about the outreach of white supremacy prior to the 2016 election was out of the mainstream, white supremacists have since then marched with tiki torches, attacked and killed counter protesters in Charlottesville, and lynched joggers in Georgia (for a detailed explanation of lynching, see Ersula Ore's book *Lynching*).

Part II: Description of Research Methods, Findings, and/or Pedagogical Impact

This article underwent several iterations through the process of submission. It was flat out desk-rejected by the editor of one National Council of Teachers of English journal. The editor believed the journal had enough submissions or forthcoming articles on the topic of translingualism (I had seen only one such article). When the incoming editor of a different NCTE journal announced that the journal would be accepting articles for a new section on pedagogy emphasizing empirical methods, I emailed the editor with a query, despite my discomfort at having to argue for decolonial methods as empirically valid. Still, I explained the topic, hoping perhaps for some indication whether to submit. A short response from the editor said they could not be sure without seeing the entire manuscript. Ignoring this noncommittal response, I revised the manuscript following knowledge conventions of empirical scholarship, doing my best to transform the voices of the student writers into what could be more objectively called a data set. This "empirical" version received a revise and resubmit, which I completed based on the reviewer's feedback. When the revised article was rejected, I submitted this "empirical" version to *Composition Studies* somewhat self-deceived that this "objective"-sounding version benefitted from the most revision.

I am extremely appreciative of Laura Miccichi's editorial guidance with this piece, helping me to re-center student voices and validate the decolonial perspective that had been undermined in the pursuit of so-called empiricism. Laura gave me an encouraging revise and resubmit that recommended restructuring the article back to an organization that resembled the structure of the pre-"empirical" version. When my revisions still clung to the pseudo-social science format, Laura connected me with Bob Mayberry, a former *Composition Studies* editor, who offered generous and supportive feedback that helped me restore my faith in my writing. Unfortunately, my experience had been with editors who undermine the research of scholars of color through their adherence to exclusionary editorial philosophies or worse. Since the publication of "Decolonial Potential in a Multilingual FYC," I have conducted surveys and interviews with primarily Latinx scholars of color on their experiences with publishing. Exclusionary editorial practices are among the experiences of the scholars whose voices fill the pages in the manuscript that will appear in the forthcoming *Rhetoric Review* article (Medina and Luna 2020).

Pedagogically, when I teach genres of writing that include personal writing such as literacy narratives, autoethnography, or digital testimonio (Medina 2018), I let students know that including languages other than English is encouraged and worth consideration. These inclusions of languages other than English can be important when students feel like what someone told them can't necessarily be translated exactly to English or what the person said in another language was impactful, especially when encouraging or discouraging education. The work of decolonial scholarship arguing for writing in languages other than English parallels, and in many ways follows, scholarship advocating for Students' Rights to Their Own Language since 1974. Unfortunately, the statement by Geneva Smitherman and Victor Villanueva remains something of a dream deferred when it comes to the kinds of outcomes that are standardized in institutional rubrics; in many ways, the lack of action following policy statements underscore indigenous scholars and writers' skepticism of policies that follow traditions of broken treatise by the U.S. and other settler forces (Deloria, Jr. 1969). This is not meant to be an "I told you so" to any one journal but more context providing exigency for decolonial work that problematizes an overreliance on "empirical" methods that have been used, and continue to be used, to silence and marginalize and how scholars of color and writers researching multilingualism struggle for inclusion.

Part III: Discussion Questions

1. Other than multilingual writing, what kinds of decolonial practices can be incorporated into the classroom and supported at the institutional level?

2. In what ways can we encourage students to write in languages other than Standard Academic English?

3. What ways can we create goals, rubrics, and outcomes that honor multilingualism and values it beyond style or voice?

Works Cited

Cabrera, Nolan L., Jeffrey F. Milem, Ozan Jaquette, and Ronald W. Marx. "Missing the (Student Achievement) Forest for All the (Political) Trees: Empiricism and the Mexican American Studies Controversy in Tucson." *American Educational Research Journal*, vol.51, no. 6, 2014, pp.1084-118.

Deloria Jr., Vine. *Custer Died for Your Sins: An Indian Manifesto*. University of Oklahoma P, 1969.

Medina, Cruz. "Digital Testimonio: Latin@ Multimodal Storytelling." *Racial Shorthand: Coded Discrimination in Social Media*, edited by Cruz Medina and Octavio Pimentel. Computers and Composition Digital P/Utah State UP, 2018, http://ccdigitalpress.org/shorthand.

Medina, Cruz and Perla Luna. "'Publishing Is Mystical': The Latinx Caucus Bibliography, Top-Tier Journals, and Minority Scholarship." *Rhetoric Review*, vol. 39, no.3, 2020, pp. 303–16, DOI: 10.1080/07350198.2020.1764764.

Ore, Ersula J. *Lynching: Violence, Rhetoric, and American Identity*. UP of Mississippi, 2019.

Roberts, Laurie. "Roberts: John Huppenthal unmasked" AZCentral.com. USA Today network. June 19, 2014 | Updated 10:27 a.m. MT June 24, 2014, https://www.azcentral.com/story/laurie-roberts/2014/06/19/john-huppenthal/10901575/

THE JOURNAL OF MULTIMODAL RHETORICS

The Journal of Multimodal Rhetorics is on the web at http://journalofmultimodalrhetorics.*com/*

The Journal of Multimodal Rhetorics, or JOMR, is a completely online, open-access journal featuring essays and other items that examine multimodality in all of its cultural, material, temporal, and pedagogical manifestations. We highlight traditional multimodal practices and praxes that sustain our cultures and everyday lives to draw attention to the political dimensions of under/privileged modes, with the ultimate goal of making current scholarship more accessible and welcoming of wide audiences.

Powerful Marginality: Feminist Scholarship through Comics[1]

"Powerful Marginality: Feminist Scholarship through Comics" by Rachel Rys is from a special issue on comics rhetorics (guest edited by Dale Jacobs). Rys's essay considers comics' capacity to represent experiences and people rarely imagined as audiences. That is, she argues that by depicting those not typically conceived of as one's "imaginary audience," comics do not allow audiences to overlook issues and themes foregrounded by feminist scholars. This essay is a wonderful example of how authors can make vital arguments and theories, often dense and alienating, more welcoming for a wide array of audiences. Together, these essays express our journal's goal of making the latest scholarship accessible to all.

---

1. *The Journal of Multimodal Rhetorics*, vol. 3, no. 1 © 2019 by JOMR.

Powerful Marginality: Feminist Scholarship through Comics

Rachel Rys

This article examines how the comics medium can be used to address epistemological, rhetorical, and representational concerns raised by feminist scholars. Drawing together feminist studies and comics studies theories, I examine how the storytelling tools of the comics medium can create reflexive and situated narratives that make visible the relationship between the reader, the writer, and the text. Building on a growing body of scholarship presented in comics form, I develop my argument through both comics and prose. Through this graphic argument, I explore potential points of connection between feminist epistemology and comics narrative, examining how the comics medium can help feminist researchers to create meaning in ways that center positionality, subjectivity, and multiple truths.

Introduction

Over the past decade, comics scholars have developed sophisticated frameworks and vocabularies for deconstructing and analyzing feminist comics. By examining feminist comics across a range of genres and eras, these scholars argue that the verbal and visual complexity of the comics medium makes it particularly well suited for telling stories that deal with issues of embodiment, autobiography, and memory. Building on these arguments, I further contend that the comics medium is also well suited for presenting academic feminist research because the medium itself contains powerful storytelling tools that are aligned with feminist approaches to knowledge. In this article, I argue that the comics medium can be useful for feminist scholars who wish to present their research in reflexive and experimental ways. However, rather than just telling you about it—

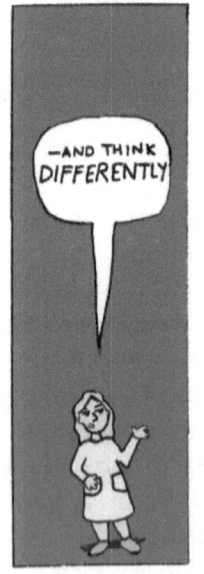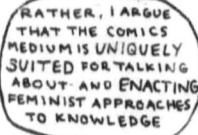

Powerful Marginality 87

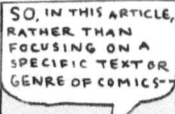

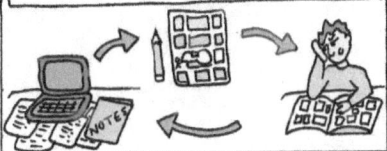

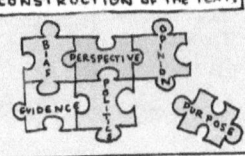

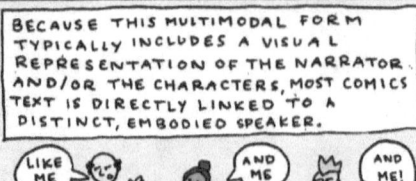

Powerful Marginality

Powerful Marginality 91

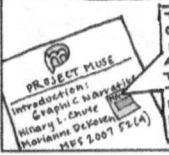

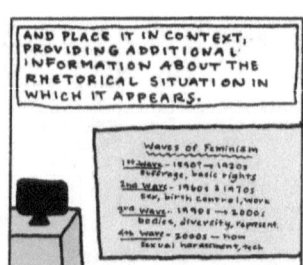

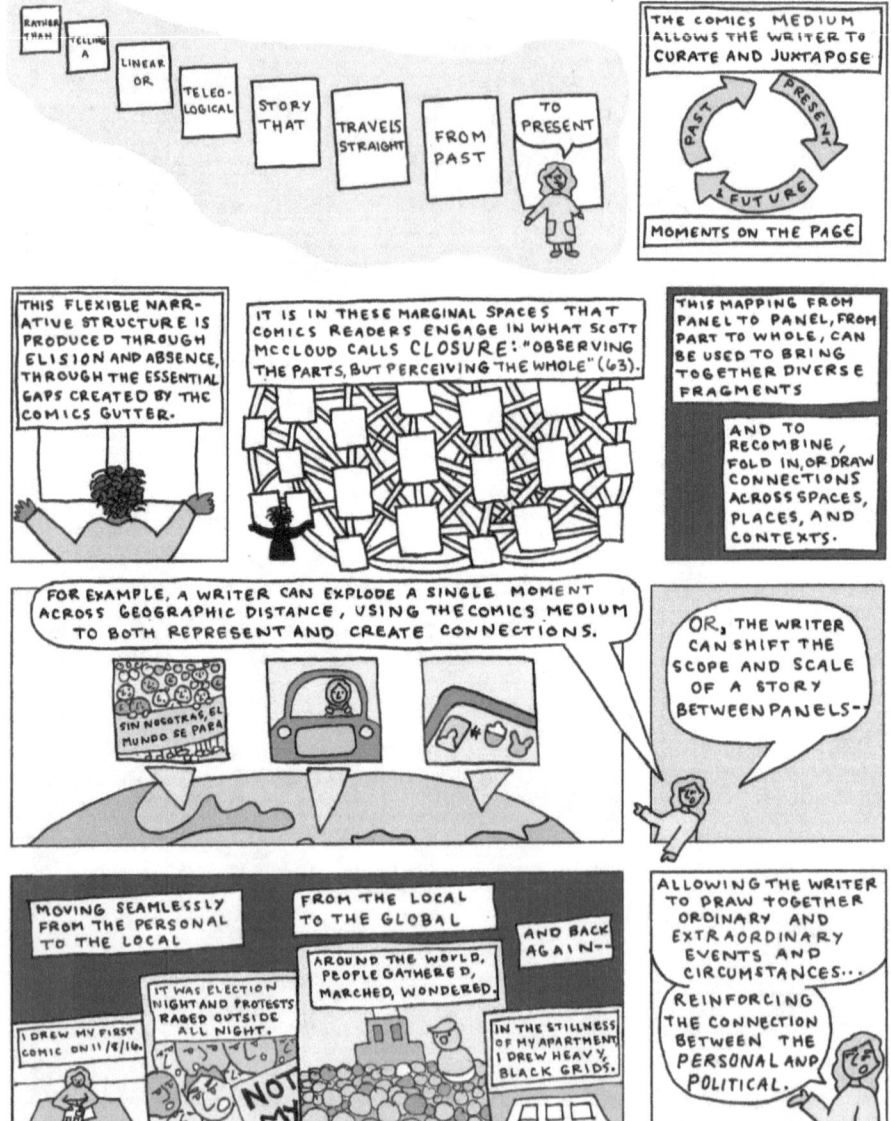

Notes

As I hope this exploratory comic has conveyed, my goal here is to gesture to some of the productive possibilities of the comics medium for feminist researchers who wish to create and share knowledge through emergent and experimental forms. Translating research across medium allows us to explore new rhetorical and representational tools—and to reflect on both the strengths and limits of our current approaches. As this is my first foray into experimental writing *and* my first attempt at making comics, these twelve comics pages have opened additional lines of both questioning and possibility.

The reference to "lines of flight" in my conclusion draws once more from Deleuze and Guattari, who argue that ruptured rhizomes can sprout anew along old lines or create "new lines of flight… directions in motion" (p. 35). This relationship between rhizomes and comics has been explored in multiple works and ways, including as a theoretical framework for analyzing comic book culture (Jeffery, 2016), as a visual metaphor (Sousanis, 2015), and as a flexible storytelling (non-) structure for the digital project *Rhizcomics* (Helms, 2017). Importantly, metaphors of connection and rupture, of roots and motion, offer powerful metaphors for critically examining identity and identity formation (Rodríguez, 2003, p. 22). Because reflexivity plays such a significant role in feminist studies scholarship, it comes as no surprise that many of the storytelling tools I analyze in this piece have been primarily discussed within the context of autobiographical and life writing comics. In fact, the first sections of my argument refer to a specific subset of narrative tools that are often used in first-person, single-authored comics—those that include an embodied version of the author-narrator on the page.

For feminist scholars, this close attention to the embodiment, practices, and habits of everyday life is essential. As Tolmie (2013) argues, comics are "precisely about matters of essential cultural urgency at the everyday level…" (p. xvi). Hillary Chute (2010) further argues that the ability to visualize the "ongoing procedure of self and subjectivity constructs 'ordinary' experiences as relevant and political" (p. 140). This visuality facilitates a political reading of everyday events, such as the panel below that brings together scenes from the International Women's Day strike in Spain, the repeal of the driving ban for women in Saudi Arabia, and the covert participation of Chinese women in the #MeToo movement (when the hashtag #MeToo was censored by the government, women continued to connect and share by substituting the characters or emojis for Rice 🍚 ("Mi") and Bunny 🐰 ("Tu")).

The comics medium offers a tactics of memory that pictures and recombines traces of everyday life. These same narrative tools are also available to feminist scholars—leaving an open opportunity for scholars to share not only their research *products*, but also their *process*: the situated interaction, decision-making, and thought processes that underlie scholarly work.

References

This project is indebted to the important work done by feminist comics scholars to identify specific narrative tools and to initiate conversations about the connections between identity, power, and form. While the comics medium offers incredible argumentative density, I have found it to be spatially and logistically challenging to incorporate the breadth of references expected of scholarly work into the comics form. Undoubtedly, the practices and politics of citation for scholarship written in the comics medium will require additional examination and experimentation—another line of flight perhaps?

Barker, M. & Scheele, J. (2016). *Queer: A graphic history*. London, UK: Icon Books.
   Bechdel, A. (2006). *Fun home*. Boston, MA: First Mariner Books.
Bui, T. (2017). *The best we could do*. New York, NY: Abrams ComicsArts.
Chute, H. (2010). *Graphic women: Life narrative and contemporary comics*. New York, NY: Columbia University Press.
Chute, H. & DeKoven, M. (2006). Introduction: Graphic narratives. *Modern Fiction Studies, 52(4)*, 767-782.

DeConnick, K. S., & Landro, V. D. (2015). *Bitch planet, vol. 1: Extraordinary machine*. Berkeley, CA: Image Comics.

Deleuze, G. & Guattari, F. (1987). *A thousand plateaus: Capitalism and schizophrenia*. Minneapolis, MN: University of Minnesota Press.

El Refaie, E. (2012). *Autobiographical comics: Life writing in pictures*. Jackson, MS: University Press of Mississippi.

Grosz, E. (1993). A thousand tiny sexes: Feminism and rhizomatics. *Topoi, 12*, 167–179. Hemmings, C. (2007). What is a feminist theorist responsible for? Response to Rachel Torr. *eminist Theory, 8*(1), 69–76.

England, K.V.L. (1994). Getting personal: Reflexivity, positionality, and feminist research. *The Professional Geographer, 46*(1), 80-89.

Helms, J. (2017). "Rhizcomics: Rhetoric, technology, and new media composition. Retrieved from http://www.digitalrhetoriccollaborative.org/rhizcomics/difference.html

Livholts, M. (2012). *Emergent writing methodologies in feminist studies*. New York, NY: Routledge. Losh, E., Alexander, J., Cannon, K., & Cannon, Z. (2013). *Understanding rhetoric: A graphic guide to writing*. Boston, MA: Bedford/St. Martin's.

McCloud, S. (1994). *Understanding comics: The invisible art*. New York, NY: William Morrow Paperbacks.

Newlevant, H., Taylor, H., & Fox, Ø. (2017). *Comics for choice*. USA: Open Source Publishing.

O'Leary, S., & Reilly, J. (Eds.). (2014). *The big feminist but: Comics about women, men and the ifs, ands & buts of feminism* (Second Edition). USA: Alternative Comics.

Petersen, E. B. (2016). Turned on, turned off: On timely and untimely feminist knowledge production. *NORA - Nordic Journal of Feminist and Gender Research, 24*(1), 5–17.

Robbins, T. (Ed.). (2016). *The complete wimmen's comix*. Seattle, WA: Fantagraphics. Rodríguez, J. M. (2003). *Queer Latinidad*. New York, NY: New York University Press. Ryan, M. (2004). *Narrative across media: The languages of storytelling*. Lincoln, NE: University of Nebraska Press.

Satrapi, M. (2003). *Persepolis*. USA: Panthenon Books.

Scott, J. (2016). *The posthuman body in superhero comics: Human, superhuman, transhuman, post/human*. New York, NY: Palgrave Macmillan.

Sousanis, N. (2015). *Unflattening*. Cambridge, MA: Harvard University Press.

Spivak, G. C. (1999). *A critique of postcolonial reason: Toward a history of the vanishing present*. Cambridge, MA: Harvard University Press.

Tolmie, J. (2013). Introduction: If a body meet a body. In J. Tolmie (Ed.), *Drawing from life: Memory and subjectivity in comic art* (pp. vii–xxiii). Jackson, MS: University of Mississippi Press.

Versaci, R. (2007). *This book contains graphic language: Comics as literature*. New York, NY: Continuum.

Wilkinson. S. (1988). The role of reflexivity in feminist psychology. *Women's Studies International Forum, 11*(5), 493-502.

Zinn, H., Buhle, P., & Konopacki, M. (2008). *A people's history of American empire project: A graphic adaptation.* New York, NY: Metropolitan Books.

Rachel Rys received her PhD in Feminist Studies from the University of California, Santa Barbara, specializing in Productive and Reproductive Labors. She also received a doctoral emphasis in Writing Studies and a Certificate in College and University Teaching.

Supplemental Material

"Powerful Marginality: Feminist Scholarship through Comics"

Rachel Rys

Part I: Reflection on the Origins of the Article

The earliest traces of this piece emerged in response to a frustrating classroom discussion and impromptu exercise. While teaching a senior capstone course on feminist theory, I found that my brilliant students often struggled to grasp and apply the nuances of some of our most theoretical readings. For example, many students narrowly interpreted the theory of *intersectionality*[1]—an expansive framework developed by Kimberlé Crenshaw which argues that oppressive structures are inextricably linked—as an argument about personal identities, rather than societal structures. Attempting to pivot from an unproductive discussion, I asked my students to spend a few minutes sketching out their understanding of the term "intersectionality." The drawings they created—which ranged from labeled Venn diagrams to chaotic traffic intersections to self-portraits pierced with labelled arrows—provided a concrete starting point for discussing the strengths and limits of each interpretation relative to the original text. Beyond making visible my students' specific struggles with this theory, this drawing exercise made me realize just how prevalent visual metaphors are in our academic social theories—and how profoundly these visual interpretations can facilitate or constrain our ability to apply abstract ideas. Building on my students' sketches, I began to develop a series of teaching resources that used visual representations to help students assess, clarify, and deepen their understanding of theory. These resources underscored the potential that visual and multimodal forms held for teaching academic theory in new and nuanced ways.

These realizations about the pedagogical potential of multimodality collided with my growing theoretical interest in the discussions and (non) traditions of alternative and emergent writing practices within the field of feminist studies.[2] Inspired by this history, I sought to develop a project that used visual and multimodal tools to interrogate and unsettle accepted conventions of academic writing in both focus and form. These dual commitments to pedagogy and form ultimately led me to the comics medium: As I drew, arranged, and annotated my visual teaching resources, I began to

---

1. For early discussions of intersectionality, see Crenshaw (1989, 1991).

2. For an introduction to alternative (or "emergent") feminist writing practices, see Livholts (2012).

recognize the early traces of a comic. More importantly, I began to recognize how the relationship between text and image, and between one panel and the next, facilitated a dynamic and layered narrative.

Although my early path to *comics-based research*[3] was primarily motivated by pedagogical and pragmatic interests, I quickly realized that the comics form was also *theoretically* aligned with feminist approaches to knowledge. My research focus thus turned to the comics medium itself, exploring the histories, conventions, and formal properties that make the comics medium not only a possible alternative form for feminist scholarship, but an alternative form that is particularly well-suited for this work. I chose to present my arguments through a *metacomic*—a self-referential comic that uses the comics form to talk about the comics form—in order to both discuss and demonstrate these storytelling tools in practice.

Part II: Description of Research Methods, Findings, and/or Pedagogical Impact

This piece was my very first experience writing in the comics form. Before I started this project, I first spent countless hours observing and analyzing how other comics creators had used the comics form to tell stories that engaged either explicitly or thematically with theories of marginalization, power, and social justice. I began by analyzing intentionally instructional comics, such as the short webcomics on the website *Everyday Feminism,* which use comics to explain concepts such as white privilege and asexuality. These comics use clear and repeated patterns to instruct and persuade, including an embodied narrator who speaks directly to the reader and who scaffolds their lessons by combining familiar physical teaching tools (like books and blackboards) with narrative teaching tools (like flashbacks and imagined or abstract sequences). Additionally, I also read and analyzed many feminist autobiographical and narrative comics, from *The Complete Wimmen's Comix*, a collection of women-authored underground comix published between the 1970s and 1990s (Robbins 2016), to *Comics for Choice*, a contemporary collection of short comics that explore personal and political stories about abortion (Newlevant, Taylor, and Fox 2017). These largely autobiographical comics use the cross-discursive and nonlinear structure of comics to call attention to the subjective and contested nature of time and memory. The arguments I ultimately present in this piece—that the comics medium encourages reflexive and situated writing, facilitates the circulation of contested narratives, and manipu-

---

3. Kuttner, Sousanis, and Weaver-Hightower (2018) define comics-based research as "a broad set of practices that use the comics form to collect, analyze, and/or disseminate scholarly research" (397).

lates time and space to create new connections—grew directly from these early observations.

While my piece argues for the many epistemological and pedagogical benefits of comics-based research, this form of scholarship also presents undeniable challenges—including the time-intensive process of planning, scripting, thumbnailing, sketching, erasing, inking, scanning, lettering, and coloring. Beyond the individual challenges of learning and executing scholarship in this form, comics-based research also presents material and procedural challenges to standard academic practices, including citation practices, peer review, and publication processes.[4] This form of research also brings up important questions about the longterm accessibility of multimodal scholarship; the expansion of comics-based research will require urgent and creative collaboration between scholars, editors, and publishers to ensure that comics-based research is accessible to assistive technology devices and translation services. Critical discussions about process and access are central to expanding and deepening comics-based research methodologies.

Despite the challenges that come with this work, the enormous potential of comics storytelling makes refining and reforming the processes of comics-based research worthwhile. As I hope this piece demonstrates, comics offer a theoretically, pedagogically, and rhetorically complex medium for creating and sharing feminist academic work. For feminist scholars, comics-based research offers an opportunity to not only question uninterrogated conventions of academic writing, but also to create new works that center questions of authorship, contested narrative, and temporality from the form up.

Part III: Discussion Questions

1. Did you respond to this piece of scholarship differently because it was written in the comics medium? How did your reading, notetaking, and discussion practices change when reading scholarship written in comics form?

2. What new audiences might comics-based scholarship create? What audiences might it discourage?

3. How did having an embodied narrator shape the argument of this piece? How would the piece be different if the narrator did not appear?

4. How could you apply the comics storytelling tools discussed in this piece to a different research topic?

---

4. For a discussion of some of the writing and editing challenges of comics scholarship, see Salter, Whitson, and Helms (2018).

Works Cited

Crenshaw, Kimberlé. 1989. "Demarginalizing the Intersection of Race and Sex: A Black Feminist Critique of Antidiscrimination Doctrine, Feminist Theory and Antiracist Politics." *The University of Chicago Legal Forum*: 39–67.

—. 1991. "Mapping the Margins: Intersectionality, Identity Politics, and Violence against Women of Color." *Stanford Law Review* 43 (6): 1241–99.

Kuttner, Paul J., Nick Sousanis, and Marcus B. Weaver-Hightower. 2018. "Drawing Comics the Scholarly Way: Creating Comics-Based Research in the Academy." In *Handbook of Arts-Based Research*, edited by Patricia Leavy, 396-422. New York: Guilford Press.

Livholts, Mona. 2012. *Emergent Writing Methodologies in Feminist Studies*. New York: Routledge.

Newlevant, Hazel, Whit Taylor, and Ø.K. Fox, eds. 2017. *Comics for Choice*. USA: Open Source Publishing.

Robbins, Trina, ed. 2016. *The Complete Wimmen's Comix*. Seattle, WA: Fantagraphics.

Salter, Anastasia, Roger Whitson, and Jason Helms. 2018. "Making 'Comics as Scholarship': A Reflection on the Process Behind *Digital Humanities Quarterly* (9) 4." *Kairos* 23 (1). http://kairos.technorhetoric.net/23.1/inventio/salter-et-al/.

LITERACY IN COMPOSITION STUDIES

Literacy in Composition Studies is on the web at http://licsjournal.org

Literacy in Composition Studies is a refereed open access online journal sponsoring scholarly activity at the nexus of Literacy and Composition Studies. With literacy and composition as our keywords we denote practices that are deeply context-bound and always ideological and recognize the institutional, disciplinary, and historical contexts surrounding the range of writing courses offered at the college level. Literacy is often a metaphor for the ability to navigate systems, cultures, and situations. At its heart, literacy is linked to interpretation—to reading the social environment and engaging and remaking that environment through communication. Orienting a Composition Studies journal around literacy prompts us to analyze the connections and disconnections among writing, reading and interpretation, inviting us to examine the ways in which literacy constitutes writer, context, and act.

Making Citizens Behind Bars (And the Stories We Tell About It): Queering Approaches to Prison Literacy Programs[1]

Alexandra Cavallero's "Making Citizens Behind Bars (And the Stories We Tell About It): Queering Approaches to Prison Literacy Programs," extends recent research on literacy education and citizenship by considering how images of the "good citizen" circulate in the context of prison education. Cavallaro contends that "While programs frequently invoke the language of citizenship in describing their goals, they do so without considering the particular challenges incarcerated people face in actually achieving this vision of citizenship--or indeed, if such a vision is ever possible (or desirable) for someone who has been incarcerated." Cavallaro's article draws from research in New Literacy Studies, queer studies, and critical prison studies to provide a framework that educators can use to both question and revise such constructions of citizenship in prison education. We nominated the article because it pushes forward longstanding conversations about literacy education and citizenship in new ways.

---

1. *Literacy in Composition Studies*, vol. 7, no. 1 © 2019 by Alexandra Cavallero. Creative Commons Attribution-NonCommercial-NoDerivs 4.0 Unported license.

Making Citizens Behind Bars (and the Stories We Tell About It): Queering Approaches to Prison Literacy Programs

Alexandra Cavallaro

Scholarship in literacy and composition studies has demonstrated the many connections between literacy education and citizenship production (e.g. Guerra, Wan). Despite often being neglected in conversations about literacy education and citizenship training, prison education programs and incarcerated students have a unique relationship to citizenship and can make an important contribution to that scholarship. By putting literacy studies in conversation with queer studies and critical prison studies, I argue that we as literacy educators and teachers can train ourselves to notice and push back against the harmful ideologies underlying the discourse around prison literacy education programs and citizenship education. This attention to language is essential because it has a material effect on the incarcerated students we teach, as well as the futures we imagine for our classes, programs, and the wider landscape of prison education.

Introduction

In June 2016, the US Department of Education reinstated access to Pell Grants for incarcerated students through their Second Chance Pell Grant Pilot Program, granting funding to 67 colleges and universities across the country. The goal of the initiative is to allow incarcerated individuals to receive Pell Grant funding and pursue postsecondary education in order to develop the skills necessary to "live lives of purpose and contribute to society upon their release" ("12,000 Incarcerated Students"). This pilot program reversed a 1994 Congressional change to the Higher Education Act (HEA) that rendered incarcerated students ineligible for Pell Grant funding, causing many prison education programs to shut their doors. While the future of the program currently remains uncertain, the availability of these grants increased access to education for students who had previously been barred because of their incarcerated status. In a press release announcing the program, the Department of Education frames its work as giving "deserving incarcerated individuals" access to higher education in an effort to "reduce recidivism, promote opportunity, and give justice-involved individuals a meaningful second chance" ("12,000 Incarcerated Students"). Similar language can be found in prison education programs across the country, whether they are Second Chance Pell Grant recipients or not. In mission statements, promotional materials, and media coverage, education and its attendant benefits (reduced recidivism, savings to taxpayers, increased employability) are consistently linked with the creation of "productive and engaged citizens" ("12,000 Incarcerated Students").

The problem with this image of the citizen reformed by education is that the students in these programs have all been rendered *non-citizens* as a result of their incarceration. During their sentences, they are denied many forms of civic participation and there are additional barriers to voting in twelve states even when their sentences are complete (NCSL). Even in states with no voting restrictions, their marginalized status will continue to follow them, and they will face sanctioned discrimination in the form of decreased access to employment, housing, and post-secondary educational opportunities and will be barred from many government assistance programs. Regaining anything that looks like the popular ideals of citizenship—voting, access to jobs and education, government assistance—will be difficult, if not impossible.

Given these contradictions and conflicts, why talk about citizenship and prison education together at all? Across the United States, prison education programs invoke the power of literacy education in the project of (re) making good citizens in the stories they tell about their work. In the programs' promotional materials, the figure of the citizen becomes a site of struggle, and this figure—the "bad citizen" in need of redemption and the potential for "good citizenship" in the future—is often central to the values that guide these programs. Literacy education becomes a focal point for the individual reform of deviant citizens, but this focus on the individual trains incarcerated people for a kind of citizenship that will not actually be available to them when (or if) they are released. Citizenship is frequently invoked as an ideal, but its complexity is elided. Examining these complexities opens up larger questions about the relationship between literacy and citizenship and the stories we tell connecting the two.

Recent scholarship in literacy and composition studies has demonstrated how the mythos of citizenship gets deployed to tell stories of who is included and who is not (e.g., Guerra; Wan). Such stories, argues Amy Wan, deserve our attention because "[h]ow a nation defines, constructs, and produces citizens communicates not only the ideals of that nation, but also its anxieties, particularly in moments of political, cultural, and economic uncertainty" (1). The development of mass incarceration in the US is a product of similar uncertainties. Because of persistent anxieties about race, legal scholar Michelle Alexander has demonstrated how new, institutionally sanctioned forms of discrimination replace the old—from slavery to Jim Crow to mass incarceration, where 1 in 15 black men and 1 in 36 Hispanic men can expect to be incarcerated in their lifetime, as opposed to 1 in 106 white men ("Mass Incarceration Problems"). Since educational programs are such a prominent feature of the carceral landscape,[1] and incarcerated people have a unique relationship to citizenship, I argue that we must include prison literacy programs in scholarly conversations about the relationship between education and citizenship. In many educational contexts, there is frequently an easy conflation of literacy education and the production of good citizens, a conflation that I argue is both especially tempting and especially damning in the context of prison education. While programs frequently invoke the language of citizenship in describing their goals, they do so without considering the particular challenges incarcerated people face in actually achieving this vision of citizenship—or indeed, if such a vision is ever possible (or desirable) for someone who has been incarcerated.

Incarcerated students make an important contribution to conversations about literacy education and the promise of citizenship both in spite of and because of their limited access to citizenship's privileges. In this article, I propose a framework to aid in interrogating the role that the production of citizens plays in the educational landscape of mass incarceration, and how teachers and scholars of literacy can intervene in these conversations. Drawing on three scholarly traditions concerned with prisons—New Literacy Studies (NLS), queer studies, and critical prison studies—I demonstrate how teachers and scholars of writing and literacy can intervene in the project of citizenship production by challenging and critiquing the logics of individualism that underwrite prison literacy programs. When we undo these logics, we can resist the individual narratives of redemption and transformation (e.g. Jacobi; Meiners and Sanabria) and envision possibilities that trouble the relationship between literacy education and the production of good citizens in prison.

In order to do this, we must take responsibility for the ideologies that show themselves in the materials that represent the work of prison education programs, including mission statements, promotional materials, and articles in local newspapers. While previous research has offered principles to guide our literacy work inside prison classrooms (e.g. Jacobi and Becker), I build on that work by turning an analytical lens toward the ideologies embedded in the ways we frame the literacy programs themselves, arguing for sustained (and queer) attention to the rhetorics of individual citizenship. A queer lens allows us to challenge the most common ideas about citizenship, calling our attention to the ways it often fails as an ideal, particularly for marginalized people. While we always need to be sensitive to the multiple audiences prison education programs are responsible to, we must also recognize that program materials don't just guide our work—they represent our work to a wider public and can reproduce harmful narratives about incarcerated people. This attention to language is essential because it has a material effect on the incarcerated students we teach, as well as the futures we imagine for our classes, programs, and the wider landscape of prison education.

In this article, I begin by outlining the intersections among literacy studies, queer studies, and critical prison studies, illustrating the ways their intersections might be productively mobilized in critiquing the role of citizenship in prison education. I then follow with a study of the "Higher Education in Jails and Prisons Programming List," demonstrating the prevalence of and problems with individualist, "bootstraps" ideologies in the construction of citizenship in these programs. I conclude with a framework, influenced by queer prison abolitionists and queer citizenship theorists, to guide the work of revising an d taking responsibility for the work of our public materials.

Education And The Carceral Landscape: An Interdisciplinary Framework For Queering Citizenship In Prison Education Programs

When I first stepped behind the walls of a prison three years ago as a writing instructor for the Education Justice Project, I quickly learned that prisons are built on and sustained by distinctly counter-productive logics. All across the country, while states routinely divert resources away from K–12 schools and public universities in times of budget crises, they do not hesitate to incarcerate their residents at nearly 4.5 x the cost (depending on the state) (Meiners 18). In Illinois, for example, where I earned my PhD and started my work as a prison educator, Erica Meiners describes the two different paths that such budget choices create with the phrase "going downstate," a metaphor that carries radically different meanings for different people: for wealthier Chicago residents, this means leaving the suburbs and traveling south to the prestigious (and expensive) University of Illinois (15). For poorer Chicago residents, their schools underfunded and crumbling, their neighborhoods ravaged by gentrification, this means traveling south to be incarcerated in the state's prisons, including the Danville Correctional Center, where I was a tutor and instructor for two years. Despite the conventional wisdom that tells us that these institutions are for those who deserve them (prisons for the worst of the worst, universities for the best of the best), these budget choices show that schools and prisons are linked by patterns of uneven resource allocation, illustrating that "these institutions do not merely reflect existing structures of power but reproduce and even exacerbate them" (Meiners 18).

Though I use Illinois to illustrate the ways that seemingly disconnected state institutions are analogous, such patterns repeat themselves across the country, and funding is but one of many points of intersection between public schools/universities and prisons. In California, for example, where I now work as an assistant professor, public colleges and universities are provided with furniture that, according to Angela Davis, is largely produced by incarcerated people (36). In fact, the number of connections between schools (and other institutions) and prisons is so overwhelming that scholars and activists have started using the phrase "prison-industrial complex" (PIC), a term that suggests that "criminalization and imprisonment filter through every aspect of how we live and understand ourselves and the world," including the design of educational institutions (Spade 3). Seeing prisons not as discrete buildings but as part of a web of institutions and practices demonstrates how prisons invisibly—and yet powerfully—permeate our lives in frequently unacknowledged ways. Acknowledging these intricate, often unspoken connections between prisons and schools/ universities, scholars in literacy studies, queer studies, and critical prison studies have separately interrogated the operations of the PIC. In literacy studies, scholars have examined the complicated role of writing in the prison environment, examining tactical methods of resistance (Plemons), considering the particularly fraught role of literacy sponsors (Jacobi), and researching the role of hope and possibility in the prison writing classroom (Berry, "Doing Time"). In queer studies, scholars and activists have resisted the incarceration and legal regulation of queer bodies (Stanley and Smith) and critiqued the use of legal frameworks as a means of protection (Spade). Finally, the field of critical prison studies offers frameworks for radically deconstructing the normalized operations of the criminal justice system (e.g. Davis), not merely offering solutions to reform it. Collectively, these three fields acknowledge that the PIC is both a product of and producer of normativity, that it dramatically impacts society's most marginalized, and that it uses literacy education as a component of its project of reform and punishment. The prison is as central to the work of literacy scholars (a field with a long history of commitment to questioning issues of power and privilege in language use) as it is to the political commitments of queer scholars and activists (whose projects critique injustices produced by normativity).

The intersections of the common concerns of these three fields can provide us with a framework to interrogate the normative ideologies embedded in prison literacy programs and offer a set of values to push this work forward. Queer theory and literacy studies' shared concerns with the operation of *normativity* and critiques of the *discourses of individuality* offer new insight on literacy education and citizenship when considered in the context of prisons. Following the work of Cathy J. Cohen and others who focus on queer theory's intersectional possibilities, I apply queer theory's critiques to a wider field of normativity, one that considers particular relationships to the power of state-sanctioned norms. Literacy, in particular, operates in this way, making it a good entry point into the operations of normativity in the PIC. Eric Pritchard's term "literacy normativity" captures these operations, describing literacy normativity as "the use of literacy to create and impose normative standards and beliefs onto people whom are labeled alien or other through textscapes" (28). In many prison programs, a lack of education and literacy are often cited as significant factors that led to incarceration in the first place. This actual or perceived "deficit" becomes a way to simultaneously label incarcerated people as non-normative citizens and provide an avenue of redemption for an offending body to reintegrate into society as a "good citizen." This mode of redemption, however, relies solely on a process of *individual* work. Whether or not you are "redeemed" into an acceptable citizen depends on the opportunities you take advantage of while incarcerated, via an educational project that promises to reform individual "criminals" into economically productive citizens.

The particular challenge with extending conversations to the construction of citizenship in prisons is that incarcerated people, according to Caleb Smith, are the product of paradoxes produced by carceral institutions, becoming divided figures as "a citizen-in-training but also an exile from civil society" (qtd. in Schorb 177). In order to address these paradoxes, I work to maintain an active tension between what Amy Brandzel calls "a politics of presence" and a "politics of radical critique." In her work on the queer politics of citizenship, Brandzel writes that a politics of presence requires "compassion toward the normative desires and aspirations for less vulnerability, more social belonging, and access to more life chances" (x), while a politics of critique requires "radical and downright cranky disdain for normativity" (xi). The tension between these two approaches forms the heart of my framework—it requires that literacy teacher-scholars who work in prisons remain cranky about normativity and normative aspirations (in this case, the ideology of individualism that guides prison education programs and the elusive promise of redemptive citizenship) while acknowledging the ways that the promise of such inclusion may seem like a compelling way to end the violence and suffering that this exclusion causes.

Maintaining such critical tensions extends the project of critique that is already familiar to scholars of literacy and composition: on the one hand, we have critiqued literacy's violence, and have expressed our disdain for the ways literacy renders people acceptable or unacceptable (e.g., through the politics of "standard English"). On the other hand, we recognize the potential power of literacy to effect change and the ways that denying access to literacy perpetuates the disenfranchisement of marginalized people. When it comes to an investigation of prison literacy programs and their role in the production of citizens, we must also maintain this critical tension between the individual and the systemic by working "to expose the intersectionality of normative belief systems and structures of thought, and offer suggestions as to how we might work against the reentrenchment of these processes" (Brandzel x). Examining this complex relationship to literacy in prison education programs, Patrick Berry has argued that "[w]hile we must find ways to maintain a critical stance toward overly optimistic accounts of literacy," we also "do ourselves a disservice if we do not recognize the multifaceted, sometimes contradictory ways in which writing accrues value in our lives" ("Doing Time" 138). Keeping these tensions at the forefront of our work, he argues, would help us develop pedagogies that are "mindful of the multiple objectives of literacy and writing instruction—objectives that go well beyond a focus on acquiring skills or gainful employment to the use of writing as a pathway toward understanding oneself in the world" (138). Throughout this project, I work to keep these multiple tensions between crankiness and presence, between violence and possibility, alive in my discussion of prison education work. In this way, I hope to move the conversation away from the more reductive, individualist constructions of the incarcerated citizen in a way that has material consequences for individual programs and the wider landscape of prison literacy education.

LITERACY FRAMEWORKS AND CASE STUDY METHODS

In order to more concretely and systematically study the ways that prison education programs across the country frame their work, I analyze programs from the "Higher Education in Jails and Prisons Programming List" (HEJPPL). Compiled by Victoria Bryan and Rebecca Ginsburg, this list contains information on 149 prison education programs across the United States. [2] From this list, I selected 54 programs across 25 states (including Washington DC and two national programs) for analysis. My primary criterion for selecting programs was the presence of a website, mission statement, or write-up so that I would have a stable set of texts to analyze. I also focused on liberal arts and humanities programs with literacy education[3] in some form or another, omitting programs that had only a vocational focus. I also omitted programs that were just for incarcerated youth since my interests are in higher education. Throughout my analysis, I leave the specific programs unnamed because my purpose is not to critique individual programs but rather to illustrate the larger ideological patterns that these programs follow. An analysis of these ideologies allows us to see the ways they are tied to larger social and political issues and how individual attempts at literacy education are never just about the individual but about constructing a (problematic) vision of citizenship. In instances where I reference specific examples from programs, I assign the programs pseudonyms in order to maintain this focus. In what follows, I show the prevalence of these ideologies and analyze their impact on our understanding of the connections between education, citizenship, and incarceration.

Reducing Recidivism And Making Good Citizens: Promoting An Individual "Choice" Discourse Through Literacy Education

In advertising and promoting their work, prison education programs offer an image of the kind of "good citizen" they will create through educational opportunities—one who makes up for their prior "mistakes" by being economically productive and not a burden to good, law-abiding taxpayers, an image that depends on a sense of individual responsibility and pulling oneself up by one's bootstraps. This vision is frequently supported by an emphasis on reducing recidivism, saving taxpayer money, providing a second chance, and improving future employment prospects, without considering the particular challenges incarcerated people face in actually achieving this imagined idea of citizenship. These attributes are featured prominently in the 54 programs I surveyed: 42 of the programs (over 77%) referenced at least one of these features, and 30 of the programs (over 55%) referenced two or more.

One of the most persuasive justifications for the presence of educational programs in prison is cost savings. Programs frequently emphasize that education can save money in order to argue that prison education will give taxpayers a good return on their investment, citing savings ranging from $36 to $97 million per year. Mid-Atlantic Prison Program, for example, informs us on their website that since the state spends over $60,000 a year to incarcerate just one person, the costs savings to each taxpayer attributable to this particular prison education program in "reduced re-incarceration rates could likely pay for the entire program" and should "be considered a mechanism to reduce the scope of prison [and] save the taxpayer money." Southern Prison Program cites different statistics, but nevertheless frames the importance of college education in terms of how much it can save the state's taxpayers: it costs $25,000 per year to incarcerate one person in this state, but "if college experiences could cut the recidivism rate in half, we could save the taxpayers millions of dollars." Second Mid-Atlantic Prison Program is even more direct in their budgetary comparisons, articulating the importance of a college education by directly comparing the cost of that education and the cost of incarceration: the daily rate of incarceration in their state is $115 per day, but the cost of attending a local state college is almost half that amount.

Along these same lines, programs foreground education and literacy in the service of job preparation and as producing marketable, directly transferrable skills. Many programs use general language to describe this job preparation: they describe the potential for "meaningful employment," "increased employment opportunities," "employment success," or "improved job prospects" upon release. Somewhat tellingly, these programs do not provide comprehensive information (beyond mentions of employment in a handful of "testimonials" or "success stories") on what kinds of jobs the former students were *actually* able to attain upon release. These vaguely articulated goals don't address the fact that while some employers are offered incentives to hire people with criminal records, employers are also legally allowed to discriminate against formerly incarcerated people, a stigma that no amount of education and no level of advanced literacy will remedy. And, even though they are in the minority, at least five programs require that incarcerated students pay for their courses (some at a reduced rate). Midwestern Prison Program requires "financial support to cover tuition and fees each semester," while Second Southern Prison Program pays for the courses while the student is incarcerated, but students must repay the state for the loaned amount *as a condition of their parole*. Given that incarcerated people are typically society's poorest—and that incarceration tends to exacerbate conditions of poverty because of its impacts beyond the individual and into communities—it is difficult to imagine how many incarcerated people would pay for the courses while incarcerated (or come up with the money once released).

Many programs extend their discussions of taxpayer savings by emphasizing education's role in reducing recidivism, with 61% of programs citing statistics that students who complete such programs return to prison far less than the approximately 68% national average. Though most programs avoid citing specific percentages (preferring, instead, to simply state that education programs contribute to reduced rates of recidivism), West Coast Prison Program boasts that the "recidivism rate among [their] graduates is just 6%."

East Coast Prison Program reports that "virtually none" of their students return to prison, boasting a recidivism rate of less than 3%. For educators who care about keeping students out of the criminal justice system, breaking cycles of incarceration and having fewer people return to prison is a positive result of these programs. However, like the other goals, the discussions of the ways in which educational programs reduce recidivism do not account for the complexity of systemic inequality. In many of these programs, recidivism is evoked uncritically; as Thom Gehring notes, recidivism often functions as "an unsophisticated, dichotomous, terminal variable," and the burden rests with the individual's own efforts to keep from returning to prison without acknowledging the many barriers in that process (Gehring 198). These programs position themselves as giving incarcerated people the resources they need not to recidivate so they are able to enjoy their freedom and rehabilitation once they are released, ignoring the many factors that make educational attainment limited in what it can accomplish in this regard (notably absent from these discussions are those who will never be released from prison). Education does not erase all the post-release challenges and barriers, such as when formerly incarcerated people are banned from government-sponsored food and housing support programs. Taken together, these discourses reduce literacy education to its instrumental value as line items on a budget sheet, simultaneously reducing the complexity of literacy education and overstating what that education can accomplish.

Narrating Redemption through Literacy Education

While many programs invoke just pieces of the individualistic ideologies in their project of producing good citizens, some programs bring a number of these characteristics together in the narratives they feature. Prison educators have critiqued the use of this type of narrative (e.g. Berry, "Doing Time"; Jacobi and Johnston), a literacy practice that Erica Meiners and Roberto Sanabria describe as constituting a "redemption genre" that follows a remarkably similar pattern: "I was born, committed evil, served time, saw the errors of my ways (found God), and I am now on the true path" (635). These are the narratives that tend to "capture public imagination—stories of admission, forgiveness, regret, familial hope and redemption" (Curry and Jacobi 11), and they are part of a larger project that requires incarcerated people "know" themselves (a la Foucault) "through highly regulatory and confining discursive practices" (Meiners and Sanabria 636) that are always— inescapably, unavoidably—mediated by the institution of the prison.

However, while we must acknowledge that "[s]uch narratives of transformation are, of course, distinctive and representative of these authors' powerful experiences," they also frequently "echo a romantic cultural script about the power of reading and writing that, while appealing to the public and especially to literacy educators, can overshadow what Morris Young (2004, 28) calls 'minor narratives' that fail to align with dominant tellings" (Berry, *Writing Lives* 105) and break out of the conventions of this genre. We cannot overlook or take lightly the materially important functions these narratives serve—many students see themselves in these renderings and they are rhetorically persuasive for the purpose of accessing material benefits, including obtaining necessary employment or speaking before parole boards. No other kind of narrative except one of individual responsibility and reform is going to get you released from prison or get you a job to support yourself. However, the almost complete lack of "minor narratives" that move away from individual redemption mask the larger factors—trauma or systemic structures of inequality—that contribute to incarceration exponentially more frequently than individual choices.

Of course, studying the complexity and range of the narratives used to support prison education programs is impossible when incarcerated people are largely absent from discussions of this work. While we cannot know the rationales behind each program's choice to use or exclude the voices of incarcerated people, there are numerous potential reasons for this absence: justice-involved people always face a real risk that their words will be later used against them in legal proceedings, and many prison administrations tightly control the writing that goes in and out of the prison, so that even programs that publish collections of incarcerated students' work (e.g. Speak-Out! (Curry and Jacobi)) must edit the published work to omit anything that might depict the prison in a bad light. However, over 56% of programs had absolutely no presence of incarcerated people in their materials. An additional 30% (17 programs) had some carefully contextualized quotes—in videos, in "testimonial" sections, or in reflections at award ceremonies. Only 8 programs (a mere 14%) have substantive narratives from currently (or, more commonly, formerly) incarcerated people, and only a few of them break from the script that Meiners and Sanabria identify. This absence speaks to the tight control institutions maintain over the ways the programs get narrated.

When they *are* included, many programs make redemption narratives a prominent feature of the way they frame their work. For example, a newsletter for Third Southern Prison Program contains an article very subtly titled "Redemption" that details the story of one formerly incarcerated student's journey through prison and to a life beyond through the redeeming power of education.

Though very little information is provided on this student's early life, he was incarcerated three times before he was 19 for gang-related activity. When he started his third prison sentence, he didn't take advantage of the prison's educational opportunities right away. Eventually, he "saw the error of his ways" (how he made this change is not explained) and decided that he didn't want to be involved in gangs anymore; instead, he "wanted to be an educated man." This marked a turning point in the narration of his life, or what Meiners and Sanabria would call finding "the true path." Though he was not eligible for a bachelor's program because he was up for parole in four years, he devoted himself to his studies, earning more than double the necessary credits for an Associate of Arts degree. While enrolled in this program, he and other incarcerated students saw a shift in their perspective on the world: "they began to see their involvement [with gangs] differently. They began having condescending attitudes to the thought patterns of their friends and the reasons for doing the kind of things they did." The three additional issues of the newsletter for Third Southern Prison Program are full of similar redemption narratives.

Third Mid-Atlantic Prison Program features "student success stories" where visitors to their webpage can "meet" some of the former students who have transformed their lives "through the power of higher education." The stories begin similarly: the students got involved with crime (drugs, gangs) and continued to get in trouble once they were incarcerated. One student is described as believing he had no value, no hope, and nothing to pass on to his own children. Another student describes how anger and fear led him in the wrong direction, eventually leading to his incarceration. A third student describes himself as "a street thug" with "no respect for [himself] or humanity." After these bleak beginnings, each of these students goes on to talk about the positive impact that higher education had on their outlooks and how instrumental it was in "turning their lives around." When the voices of incarcerated people are actually present in prison education program materials, they are frequently used to illustrate the desired outcome of prison education across the country—good citizens who have seen the error of their ways and have reformed themselves through hard work.

The repetition of these particular kinds of narratives—and the requirement that they are produced as part of the prison experience—illustrates Meiners and Sanabria's claim that "the PIC advances a quiet insistence that those incarcerated 'know' themselves in specific institutionalized ways" (643). This is one of many places where the push and pull between a politics of presence and a politics of critique is acutely felt; students are required to produce redemption narratives for parole boards and prison officials, and so we must acknowledge the current necessity of learning to narrate your life this particular way as a survival strategy; after all, "If an author knows that the audience does not have the ability to bear witness to her life in ways that will be productive for the author, the author can be engaging in tactics of survival" (Meiners and Sanabria 645). Narratives that follow these scripts are useful and desirable: useful for the prisons, in order to show that they are successfully rehabilitating offending citizens; for programs to show that they are helping prisons achieve their goals and pose no threat to their operations; and for incarcerated people themselves, as a tactic for survival and as a way to access material resources. However, a politics of critique asks us to begin to challenge the inclusion of these narratives in the work we do in our prison education programs. If we include and highlight narratives that provide "opportunities for writing and connecting outside of the self," we "might encourage prison writers to link their individual experience to more systemic understandings and critiques of current practice" (Hinshaw and Jacobi 77). The narratives in these examples simultaneously reinforce and ignore systemic problems; in the examples above, the crimes associated with gang activity or drug use/selling are positioned as a series of bad individual choices, and the decision to turn away from those activities is positioned as another individual choice that gives the incarcerated person a "second chance" (presumably to make up for the first chance they didn't take advantage of) to remake themselves through education. Absent from these narratives is any acknowledgement of the systemic inequalities that create conditions for gangs or underground economies. We need to make room for stories that show who the individual is in the world, stories that focus on *connectivity*—the way the individual person is connected to others in a web of social relationships. Literacy, in these kinds of narratives, becomes positioned as much more than a tool in a process of individual, bootstraps reform. Instead, literacy education is a dynamic process that doesn't just impact the individual but also their web of connections in their communities.

Constructing the Good Citizen through Higher Education

Collectively, these rhetorical characteristics have a common focus on reforming *individual* people into model citizens, focusing on the individual responsibility to build a "productive" life (defined as making economic contributions and not being a taxpayer burden) during their incarceration and beyond by participating in education programs. The collective vision of these education programs is implicitly supported by arguments "for what a person needs (or needs *to be*) in order to be prepared for a future and to act as a citizen" (Wan 22). Several programs explicitly evoke the language of citizenship, typically connecting transferable educational "skills" to transforming incarcerated people into good citizens. In Second East Coast Prison Program, for example, interviews with administrators linked good individual choices with creating productive citizens. Participating in this educational program, they argue, "is a concrete example of the positive choices these gentlemen have made to accomplish significant changes in their lives" because "we know that returning *citizens* to a global society armed with vocational and education credentials is truly the equalizer for positive productive citizenship, and greatly reduces the rate of recidivism" (emphasis mine). Collectively, they argue that the effect of education will improve the larger social order: "the more educated the citizenry, the better the social order."

However, as with the educational contexts in Amy Wan's study, the many challenges that formerly incarcerated people face "highlights the inequality among people's citizenship and the inadequacy of literacy as a sole solution" (26). Their newly acquired skills cannot overcome employment discrimination and their exclusion from the very social supports that would support a post-release life. No matter how educated, the scarlet letter of incarceration follows them as they attempt to navigate their supposed re-attainment of their citizenship status, a scarlet letter that burns ever brighter with the ways that electronic records make it more difficult to escape the stigma of incarceration. Furthermore, this framework ignores those incarcerated students with little or no hope for release.

This focus on the individual should be both familiar and unsurprising—individualism, or pulling yourself up by your bootstraps, is frequently evoked in discussions of literacy education. The problem with this, according to Victor Villanueva, is "if everything is reduced to individual will, work, and responsibility, there's no need to consider group exclusion" ("Blind" 6). What we fail to acknowledge is that for some "the bootstraps break before the boots are on, that too many have no boots" (Villanueva, *Bootstraps* xiv). If we only look at individuals to figure out why literacy education does not accomplish its inclusive democratic goals, we come to simple judgments about motivation and responsibility to make use of available resources. There's no need to contend with the larger structural forces of inequality. This focus on individual work, responsibility, and bootstraps is another manifestation of Harvey Graff's "literacy myth," the idea that literacy is linked to upward mobility, a myth that ignores the complex material, social, and economic factors that act as barriers to this supposed mobility. Furthermore, when literacy education is linked so closely with the development of citizenship the way it frequently is in prisons and the way Amy Wan found in her own case studies, "the burden of realizing citizenship remains on the individual rather than locating that burden within a larger system of inequality" (Wan 35). Ultimately, it functions as part of a larger discourse about individual "choice" that is frequently mobilized around issues of crime and punishment—you, incarcerated person, made "bad choices" that landed you in prison. I, person who has never been incarcerated, made "good choices." Under this ideological umbrella, education becomes the solution to make up for your "bad choices," never mind that many of my students grew up in neighborhoods ravaged by gentrification and subject to funding cuts for schools, where sometimes the best way to ensure that they were fed and clothed and housed meant joining a gang. The "second chance" that so many of these programs claim to provide is, for many, actually their *first* chance at education.

Jobs, reduced recidivism, cost savings to taxpayers, second chances—none of these is inherently negative. There is nothing wrong with making people more employable or keeping them from returning to prison. We *want* incarcerated people to stay out of the prison system. We *want* them to be able to financially support their families. And these descriptions were not written with radical activists in mind—they were written to be rhetorically persuasive to those who frequently have the power to make or break prison education programs: lawmakers and prison administrators. Cost savings, reduced recidivism, law and order—all of this is persuasive rhetoric in an era of mass incarceration, and a politics of presence requires that we acknowledge the power of the promises of prison education, especially for those who are incarcerated. The problem is that a focus on these factors presents a limited vision of citizenship for the formerly (or future formerly) incarcerated person. These programs seek to fill gaps in education and offer opportunities for incarcerated people, without acknowledging the systemic forces—poverty, racism, underfunded schools, homophobia, transphobia, etc.—that caused these gaps in education or the factors that render the incarcerated students in these programs non-citizens in the first place.

My analysis of these programs provides just a brief snapshot of the larger landscape that, while not comprehensive, does indicate patterns that repeat themselves across the country. After all, there are programs not included in this study because they operate with no mission statement or public materials at all. Even for those that do publish public materials, they may say one thing and do another, emphasizing particular ideologies in their public materials that may or may not manifest themselves in their curriculum and operations. Without further investigation, we have no way of knowing if they are presenting accurate portraits of the work going on, or if they are used to closely guide the programs. Regardless, they *do* shape the public narratives and images of incarcerated people, particularly since many of these programs publicize their work not just on institutional websites, but in local newspapers, where the representations circulate in the communities that surround the prisons, influencing the cultural discourses about incarcerated people.

Some programs do challenge this common framework by merging discussions of individual responsibility with arguments about strengthening communities, fostering life-long learning, or diminishing the stereotypes of incarcerated people. Third Mid-Atlantic Prison Program, for example, positions their teachers explicitly as "dedicated reformers who share a vision of social justice," who "also know that by expanding opportunities for college in prison, [they] reduce the rate of correctional failure, increase public safety, and in the long run reduce the costs of prison" to the taxpayers. These are gestures that challenge the normalized narratives of redeeming failed citizens through education, but this is done from within the same framework of individual responsibility. Most programs, however, do not acknowledge this tension between the limitations and possibilities of literacy education. A queer intervention—a queer perspective on prison education programs— can be sensitive to the most rhetorically persuasive arguments *and* begin to shift the conversation to the larger social forces that feed the prison-industrial complex in order to challenge the narratives we tell about incarcerated people. By maintaining an active tension between the politics of presence and the politics of critique, the systemic forces do not get ignored. A queer perspective can challenge the normalization of this particular vision of citizenship in these programs.

Toward a Queer(er) Vision of Prison Literacy Education: Constructing Alternate Visions of Citizenship at the CSCE

In an essay appropriately titled "Building an Abolitionist Trans and Queer Movement with Everything We've Got," Morgan Bassichis, Alexander Lee, and Dean Spade issue an urgent call for readers to imagine a radically different world. Drawing on the radical lineage of previous queer activism, they ask the reader to imagine a world without prisons, a world where solutions to social problems do not rely so frequently on incarceration. Their essay urges readers to do this work "with everything [they've] got," a project that is necessarily dispersed and fragmented in order to respond to the dispersed and fragmented organization of the PIC. This work, they argue, must begin by "speaking what we have not yet had the words to wish for," by imagining radically different alternatives to a system that has permeated (often invisibly) many aspects of everyday life (43). Finding and articulating these words to imagine new futures is a crucial project for literacy educators working on prison education projects.

The vision of citizenship that I have outlined in my case study, the one so prevalent in the guiding vales of prison education programs, has been normalized to the point of near invisibility: Take advantage of your "second chance" at education and make economic contributions to your community so you aren't a burden on the good, law-abiding taxpayers. Literacy educators must challenge the ways these narratives construct a problematic image of the incarcerated (un)citizen because the representations of our work not only shape what we do but also perpetuate particular images of incarcerated people to the public. These representations have a material impact because they get re-inscribed over and over in the larger narratives that support mass incarceration. If we do not intervene, this discourse about the work of literacy inside prisons will reproduce itself unimpeded. Identifying and challenging the ideologies of citizenship that underwrite our prison education programs is one queer and critical act that allows us to compose new visions for our work so that we may begin "speaking what we have not yet had the words to wish for." All across the country, important work is already underway in prison education programs, but if that work falls into a pattern of representing prison education and incarcerated students using bootstraps discourses, then we are shaping larger public perceptions of incarcerated people and placing limits on the work of the programs. However, when we challenge normative narratives of crime and punishment, we open up new possibilities for public representations of our work and for what the work of prison literacy programs can achieve. I end here with describing a few ways we can flip traditional scripts and offer one example of what this might look like in action.

What I offer here is, first and foremost, not a blueprint or a map. To argue for a stable and fixed set of guidelines or principles ignores local complexities and contextualized readings of resistant acts. Given the dispersed and fragmented organization and operations of the PIC, the work of negotiating between the politics of presence and the politics of critique must be contextual, constantly negotiated and renegotiated in ways that are provisional and always subject to constant revision. When taking into account the various stakeholders that influence the way we frame our programs, what looks like progress in one program is not in another. By negotiating local complexities and demands, literacy educators can push back against the problematic narratives that underwrite their programs, narratives that position incarcerated people solely as deviant citizens in need of redemption. We can critique these visions of citizenship by imagining our practices beyond the confines of individualism and by shifting our focus to practices that position incarcerated people as members of vibrant communities and as crucial components of a network of relationships.

Rather than offer a set of specific guidelines that may not address local rhetorical situations, I instead encourage literacy educators in prison programs to pay attention to three key areas of the representation of their work: the rationale and justification for the program, the stories we tell about our classrooms and our students, and the goals and projected outcomes of the program. When we provide a rationale to the many different audiences and stakeholders, we must find ways to push back against justifications for this work that are articulated solely in terms of the cost savings that can come from incarcerated people pulling themselves up by their bootstraps in order to (finally) take advantage of the educational opportunities that will (finally) shape them into good citizens. When we tell stories of success, we must imagine new possibilities for how those stories might be composed. Finally, when we articulate the goals for our programs, we must frame them in ways that do not position incarcerated people as deviant citizens in need of redemption through education, but as people whose relationship to the PIC has been shaped by a web of systemic forces. In doing so, we can continue to do the imaginative work that will increase the vibrant possibilities for how we can compose our stories that represent our work back to the world.

My own efforts to imagine a different vision of literacy education in prisons began when I was recently appointed as the director of the Center for the Study of Correctional Education (CSCE) at California State University, San Bernardino. In the mid-1990s, the CSCE was developed as a space for research, professional development, and building prison education programs. In taking on this role, I have the opportunity to shape the future direction of the CSCE's mission. As I work to get new programs off the ground and build partnerships with other educators, I begin by thinking about how to make actionable what I call for in this article. How do we communicate differently about our work, and how might this framework shape the efforts on the ground in our programs? What follows is a copy of the guiding values and questions we have developed in order to shape and frame the work that takes place under the CSCE's umbrella.

COMMUNITY WRING COLLECTIVE IN PRISON[4] GUIDING VALUES

- We value the voices, experiences, interests, and knowledge of incarcerated people.
- We believe that education is a human right. Education needs to traverse borders and boundaries, including prison boundaries, and so we seek to foster literacy practices that enrich lives both inside and outside the prison gates.

- We are committed to an intersectional approach to literacy education, one that recognizes the complexity of each person's relationship to power and privilege.
- We believe learning is a lifelong process and should be open to all people regardless of sentence length and status in the criminal justice system.
- We believe that education is reciprocal, meaning that everyone has something to teach and everyone has something to learn.
- We believe that educators should be prepared for the particularities of teaching in the prison system and should engage in continual professional developmentand reflection ontheir work.

Key Questions:
- What can we learn from each other?
- Who are our audiences?
- What materials and methods best relate our concerns and ideas?
- What can we *hear* from inside a prison? What can we *say* from inside a prison? What conditions shape our writing and thinking?

These values and questions are part of a working document, subject to revision and re-evaluation as the CSCE builds its work and engages with diverse audiences. What I have aimed for here is a set of principles that represents a more complex view of literacy practices within the confines of the prison walls, one that situates literate activity as a way of pushing back against and surviving within institutions that have caused a great deal of harm.

In these guidelines, the curriculum is shaped by values similar to those we have for the literacy and composition education we strive to offer students in our traditional university classrooms. Incarcerated people are positioned as members of a community of learners, as people whose literacy practices are part of an interconnected web of relationships both inside and outside the prison. These guidelines recognize that literacy practices are shaped by a person's position in the world and their relationship to power—no value-neutral literacy education is possible. Literacy allows for reflection—not in the traditional sense of reflecting on the need for redemption or in the tradition of personal expressivism but as a mode of action toward social change, where students are asked to participate in community conversations. It encourages all participants to ask questions about power and privilege, about what we can say and who hears what we say, and what the consequences of both might be, which is especially important in an institution defined by communicative constraint (e.g., Cavallaro, et al.) and inevitable complicity on the part of volunteers (Curry and Jacobi). Ultimately, of course, I would hope that these workshops help incarcerated people achieve a number of goals traditionally associated with prison literacy programs—if released, I hope they will find good jobs to support themselves and their families, and I hope they will never, *ever* return to prison. But these guiding values do not limit us to these future-oriented outcomes, and through being open to all people, including lifers, they attempt to recognize a much broader vision of what literacy can do in the world.

The tensions around citizenship that are illuminated by prison literacy programs point toward the need to bring the *public representation* of our work in line with the values that shape the long- standing tradition of scholarship connecting literacy to power, privilege, and potential social action (Cushman; Royster). Previous scholarship has broadened our understanding of the ways that socially and politically marginalized groups use literacy education both to achieve larger goals *and* to acquire specific kinds of education previously denied to them (Kates; Royster; Sharer). In the context of the prison, we extend this work by seeing how difficult it is "to separate literacy from the US nation- state's equal investment in disciplining individuals into becoming normative and socially respectable citizens-subjects" (Pritchard 25) and the simultaneous impossibility of ever recognizing that ideal if you are an incarcerated (un)citizen.

My goal in developing these guiding values and this larger framework has been to suggest a way for literacy scholars and educators to intervene in prison education narratives and to revise the typical stories that get told about the connections between literacy and citizenship. Of course, taking re- sponsibility for the narratives that we create is only a small portion of the larger problem that prisons present in our society. However, given the prominent place that literacy education has in the project of reform and punishment, this is an important site of intervention into a very complex problem. So- cial justice work around the PIC requires a diversity of tactics, multifarious acts of micro resistance that build a larger tapestry of work. My proposed approach and particular intervention is one such act of micro resistance, calling for literacy educators to participate in the project of un-making and un-doing the logics that have caused so much damage in the lives of so many people, the logics that have rendered a whole segment of our society disposable. Our field, in which so many are drawn to projects related to social justice, needs to contend with the difficult and uncomfortable questions that the prison generates for us.

As I sat down to write this conclusion, a short piece written by Elizabeth Gaynes, head of the Os- borne Association, came across my social media newsfeed. Gaynes highlights many of the problems with the ways we talk about mass incarceration that I found in my research, and one line in particular struck me: "We can only see people as the worst thing they have ever done if we don't *actually see them*" (n.p., emphasis mine). The millions of people who are incarcerated in our prisons are rendered invisible by the language we use to erase the multifaceted complexity of incarceration in this country. We continue to blame individual circumstances and promote individual stories of the redemption of formerly bad citizens into good, erasing the array of systemic factors that do far more to contribute to what we call mass incarceration. One crucial way that we can start to *see* incarcerated people is by reframing our work in strategic ways. I offer this queer literacy framework as but one of many entry points into a larger conversation, and it is my hope that other literacy educators will take up this framework and revise it and extend it as necessary. In order to queer our work, we must continue to ask—over and over again—the questions I propose, viewing our work as provisional and contingent in response to the complexity of the PIC. As I continue to pursue these questions, I am both guided by and haunted by a sentence from Thom Gehring, a long-time prison educator in California, a quote that shows me the enormous stakes of such work: "If we want to learn to be less brutal, we need to learn from those we have most brutalized."

Acknowledgments

I am deeply grateful to Jessica Cavallaro, Jasmine Lee, Karen Rowan, Samantha Looker (who read the earliest and messiest drafts), Roam Romagnoli, Mary Boland, Melissa Forbes, the gradu- ate students of ENG 634, and the two anonymous reviewers for their support and feedback on this project.

Notes

1. Current estimates place their numbers at more than 200 programs across the country ("Prison Program").

2. The list contained 149 entries as of January 2017; it is occasionally updated when the authors find new program information.

3. Throughout my analysis, I call these programs "prison *education* programs" instead of "prison *literacy* programs" in order to accurately capture their multifaceted focus, but each program I selected has a literacy component as part of their programmatic work. "Literacy," in this study, is defined as a range of practices that include reading, writing, speaking, and meaning making that play a role in the project of prison education.

4. I am grateful to Paul Beehler, Erie Leduc, and Ginger Walker for their feedback on the development of these values.

Works Cited

"12,000 Incarcerated Students to Enroll in Postsecondary Educational and Training Programs Through Education Department's New Second Chance Pell Pilot Program." *US Department of Education*. 24 June 2016. Web. 25 April 2017.

Alexander, Michelle. *The New Jim Crow: Mass Incarceration in the Age of Colorblindness*. New York: The New Press, 2012. Print.

Bassichis, Morgan, Alexander Lee, and Dean Spade. "Building an Abolitionist Trans and Queer Movement with Everything We've Got." *Captive Genders: Trans Embodiment and the Prison Industrial Complex*. Eds. Eric A. Stanley and Nat Smith. Oakland: AK Press, 2011. 15–40. Print.

Berry, Patrick W. "Doing Time with Literacy Narratives." *Pedagogy* 14.1 (2014): 137–60. Print. https://doi.org/10.1215/15314200-2348938

—. *Doing Time, Writing Lives: Refiguring Literacy and Higher Education in Prison*. Carbondale: Southern Illinois UP, 2017. Print.

Brandzel, Amy L. *Against Citizenship: The Violence of the Normative*. Urbana: U of Illinois P, 2016. Print. https://doi.org/10.5406/illinois/9780252040030.001.0001

Bryan, Victoria M., and Rebecca Ginsburg. "Higher Education in Jails and Prisons Programming List." Nov. 2017. Web. 15 Sept. 2016.

Cavallaro, Alexandra J., et al. "Inside Voices: Collaborative Writing in a Prison Environment." *Harlot: A Revealing Look at the Arts of Persuasion* 15 (2016). Web. 2 Oct. 2018.

Cohen, Cathy J. "Punks, Bulldaggers, and Welfare Queens: The Radical Potential of Queer Politics?" *GLQ: A Journal of Lesbian and Gay Studies* 3.4 (1997): 437–65. Print. https://doi.org/10.1215/10642684-3-4-437

Curry, Michelle, and Tobi Jacobi. "'Just Sitting in a Cell, You and Me': Sponsoring Writing in a County Jail." *Community Literacy Journal* 12.1 (2017): 5-22. Print. https://doi.org/10.1353/clj.2017.0020

Cushman, Ellen. *The Struggle and the Tools: Oral and Literate Strategies in an Inner City Community*. New York: State U of New York P, 1998. Print.

Davis, Angela Y. *Are Prisons Obsolete?* New York: Seven Stories Press, 2003. Print.

Gaynes, Elizabeth. "The Destructive Lie Behind 'Mass Incarceration.'" *Time*. 19 May 2017. Web. 20 May 2017.

Gehring, Thom. "Recidivism as a Measure of Correctional Education Program Success." *Journal of Correctional Education* 51.2 (2000): 197–205. Print.

Graff, Harvey J. *The Literacy Myth: Cultural Integration and Social Structure in the Nineteenth Century*. New Brunswick: Routledge, 1991. Print. https://doi.org/10.4324/9781315132969

Guerra, Juan C. *Language, Culture, Identity and Citizenship in College Classrooms and Communities*. New York: Routledge and NCTE, 2016. Print. https://doi.org/10.4324/9781315858081

Hinshaw, Wendy Wolters, and Tobi Jacobi. "What Words Might Do: The Challenge of Representing Women in Prison and Their Writing." *Feminist Formations* 27.1 (2015): 67–90. Print. https://doi.org/10.1353/ff.2015.0010

Jacobi, Tobi. "Speaking Out for Social Justice: The Problems and Possibilities of US Women's Prison and Jail Writing Workshops." *Critical Survey* 23.3 (2011): 40–54. Print. https://doi.org/10.3167/cs.2011.230304

Jacobi, Tobi, and Elliott Johnston. "Writers Speaking Out: The Challenges of Community Publishing from Spaces of Confinement." *Circulating Communities: The*

Tactics and Strategies of Community Publishing. Eds. Paula Mathieu, Steve Parks, and Tiffany Rousculp. Lanham: Lexington Books, 2012. Print.

Jacobi, Tobi, and Stephanie L. Becker. "Rewriting Confinement: Feminist and Queer Critical Literacy in SpeakOut! Writing Workshops." *Radical Teacher* 95 (2013): 32–40. Print. https://doi.org/10.5406/radicalteacher.95.0032

Kates, Susan. *Activist Rhetorics and American Higher Education, 1885-1937*. Carbondale: Southern Illinois UP, 2001. Print.

"Mass Incarceration Problems." *American Civil Liberties Union*. N.d. Web. 14 June 2017. Meiners, Erica R. "Building an Abolition Democracy; or, The Fight against Public Fears, Private Benefits, and Prison Expanstion." *Challenging the Prison-Industrial Complex: Activism, Arts, and Educational Alternatives*. Ed. Stephen John Hartnett, U of Illinois P, 2011. 15-40. Print.

Meiners, Erica R, and Roberto Sanabria. "On Lies, Secrets, and Other Resistant Autobiographic Practices: Writing Trauma out of the Prison Industrial Complex." *JAC: Journal of Advanced Composition* 24.3 (2004): 635–52. Print.

National Conference of State Legislatures. "Felon Voting Rights." 2016. Web. 18 Dec. 2018. Plemons, Anna. "Literacy as an Act of Creative Resistance: Joining the Work of Incarcerated Teaching Artists at a Maximum-Security Prison." *Community Literacy Journal* 7.2 (2013): 39–52. Print. https://doi.org/10.1353/clj.2013.0008

"Prison Program: Education, Research, Service." N.d. Web. 2 June 2017.

Pritchard, Eric Darnell. *Fashioning Lives: Black Queers and the Politics of Literacy*. Carbondale: Southern Illinois UP, 2016. Print.

Royster, Jacqueline Jones. *Traces of a Stream: Literacy and Social Change Among African American Women*. Pittsburgh: U of Pittsburgh P, 2000. Print. https://doi.org/10.2307/j.ctt6wrb9s

Schorb, Jodi. *Reading Prisoners: Literature, Literacy, and the Transformation of American Punishment, 1700-1845*. New Brunswick: Rutgers UP, 2014. Print.

Sharer, Wendy B. *Vote and Voice: Women's Organizations and Political Literacy, 1915-1930*. Carbondale: Southern Illinois UP, 2004. Print.

Spade, Dean. *Normal Life: Administrative Violence, Critical Trans Politics, and the Limits of Law*. Durham: Duke UP, 2011. Print.

Stanley, Eric A., and Nat Smith, eds. *Captive Genders: Trans Embodiment and the Prison Industrial Complex*. Oakland: AK Press, 2011. Print.

Villanueva, Victor. "Blind: Talking about the New Racism." *The Writing Center Journal* 26.1 (2006): 3-19. Print.

—. *Bootstraps: From an American Academic of Color*. Urbana: National Council of Teachers of English, 1993. Print.

Wan, Amy J. *Producing Good Citizens: Literacy Training in Anxious Times*. Pittsburgh: U of Pittsburgh P, 2014. Print.

Alexandra Cavallaro is Assistant Professor of English at California State University, San Bernardino and the director of the Center for the Study of Correctional Education.

Supplemental Material

"Making Citizens Behind Bars (and the Stories We Tell About It): Queering Approaches to Prison Literacy Programs"
Alexandra Cavallaro

Part I: Reflection on the Origins of the Article

Like most ideas of mine, this article has its origins in a coffee shop, in a moment of frustration, and required someone else to point out that what I just said was the basis for my next research project. I had just finished my dissertation on literacy and rhetorical education in the LGBTQ community, and I was sick of it. I had no desire to look at it ever again. "What I really want to do," I told my friend, "is focus on prisons. I wish that people in the field who work at the intersection of Rhet/Comp and queer studies also studied prisons, but I'm not finding anything." I had been volunteering for the Education Justice Project, tutoring writing in a men's prison and teaching two upper-division college writing courses. This work was so much more immediate to me, and I wanted to integrate it into my scholarship as I moved into my first faculty position. I found that the concerns and stories of the incarcerated men I worked with would not leave me alone, and I had no desire to set them aside. She looked at me in that way that only a good friend can and gently pointed out that I had just articulated my next project. "Um, *you* could do that work," she said. Oh. I could, couldn't I?

While this article came out of a desire to unite my research on queer literacies and prison education, without the often invisible labor of others—of friends, colleagues, and incarcerated people—this article would not have become what it is. From that first moment in a coffee shop to the final edits, I benefitted enormously from the generosity of others, people who read drafts in many forms, who listened while I talked through ideas, and who modeled the kind of scholarship I wanted to do. And while it is important I acknowledge all of these friends and colleagues, it is especially important to acknowledge that the origins of this piece are also linked to my connections with the many incarcerated people I have had the privilege of working with. Their invisible labor is particularly important to acknowledge because they are confined in a system that is designed to keep them silent and hidden and steals their labor in multiple ways. This happens with their wage labor (they generally make less than a dollar an hour) and in the restrictions on and theft of their intellectual labor. I am grateful for the readership of this piece, but I am saddened and angered that you will not get to read the work of so many others, like my former student, Rob, who responded to a call for journal entries from the Anne Frank Foundation. Internal Affairs confiscated his work, and he was given two choices: either destroy the journal or face additional investigation and disciplinary action (most likely, time in segregation). Days later, his journal was shredded. Such an experience is not an uncommon one for incarcerated people. These are the people and stories that formed the tapestry of this article, that prompted me to find ways that prison education could resist, rather than support, a violent prison system.

Part II: Description of Research Methods, Findings, and/or Pedagogical Impact

One of the challenges of studying prison education programs in any kind of systemic or comprehensive way is the lack of publicly available information and the wide variety in the type of programs offered. When I found Rebecca Ginsburg and Victoria Bryan's "Higher Education in Jails and Prison Programming List," it was a researcher's dream. At the time, it contained information on 149 programs across the United States. From that list, I selected 54 programs across 25 states for analysis, choosing programs with publicly available information and a literacy education component. My analysis was guided by queer critiques of the prison industrial complex, and I examined programs' language for where they put their focus: individual responsibility (through an emphasis on personal accountability and bootstraps narratives), a systemic critique (usually through an emphasis on the systemic inequalities that cause incarceration), or a combination of the two.

As I did this research, I found myself frustrated with the limited ways that prison education programs articulated visions for their work. The vast majority of programs focus on individual responsibility, rehabilitation, and recidivism. When they do, it limits what I know to be the more radical potential of prison education. Since taking on a new role as the director of a center that supports research on prison education, facilitates programming in prison, and hosts trainings for prison educators, I have used the findings that emerged from this research project to build the list of values that appears in the article and that have guided my work since.

Of course, applying these principles to educational programming in prison has not been without its challenges. These values emphasize reflection on power structures, agency for incarcerated people, and reciprocal/mutual learning, all things that the operations of the prison industrial complex does not value. For example, one of the values is that programming should be open to all people, regardless of length of sentence. As it currently stands, the facility we teach in does not allow those with a life sentence to participate.

They simply will not allow them into our classes. These tensions highlight my ultimate goal for prison education work—not to build better programs, but to make the need for this work, to borrow from the great Angela Davis, "obsolete" through prison abolition.

Part III: Discussion Questions

Many readers of this article may not work in prison contexts, but it is my hope that this work may prompt you to think about how you can extend this work into other contexts. The questions posed by this work need not be limited to prison education.

1. This article argues that the notion of citizenship is particularly fraught for incarcerated people because they are denied many of the things that we have come to associate with the privileges of citizenship. Where else do we see notions of citizenship similarly complicated outside of prison contexts?

2. The "Guiding Values" of the Community Writing Collective in prison poses several key questions: what can we learn from each other? Who are our audiences? What materials and methods best relate our concerns and ideas? What can we *hear* from inside a prison? What can we *say* from inside a prison? What conditions shape our writing and thinking? Think about the contexts where you write (in classrooms, in communities, at home). What do these questions illuminate for you?

3. Whose invisible labor shapes your own work? Why is that work invisible and what are the consequences of that work remaining invisible? What could and should we do to make it visible, and what would be gained by doing so?

PEDAGOGY

> *Pedagogy* is on the Web at http://pedagogy.dukejournals.org/

Pedagogy is a journal dealing exclusively with pedagogical issues. *Pedagogy* is intended as a forum for critical reflection and as a site for spirited and informed debate from a multiplicity of positions and perspectives. It strives to reverse the long-standing marginalization of teaching and the scholarship produced around it and instead to assert the centrality of teaching to our work as scholars and professionals.

The Adaptive Cycle: Resilience in the History of First-Year Composition[1]

Clancy Ratliff's "The Adaptive Cycle: Resilience in the History of First-Year Composition" appeared in a special issue of Pedagogy on "Resilience in the Age of Austerity." The essay is a new examination of the history of the first-year composition requirement using the "adaptive cycle" idea about the resilience of systems. Ratliff argues that we may be experiencing the collapse of required FYC and should look to other possible futures of college writing. While both Stroupe and Ratliff look to new "futures" for writing studies, they take very different approaches. We chose Ratliff's piece because he focuses on the profession as a whole, particularly the institutional position of first-year composition, through the lens of resilience science. Particularly now, in this moment of austerity and disruption in higher education, it is useful to understand the resilient history of rhetoric and composition in the university.

---

1. *Pedagogy*, vol. 19, no. 2 © 2019 by Duke University Press.

The Adaptive Cycle Resilience in the History of First-Year Composition

Clancy Ratliff

First-year composition (FYC) has been a resilient institution. It has remained a part of students' university education despite being a course that many students would rather not take and some instructors would rather not teach, plus a now 116-year debate in English studies about whether the universal requirement, or "compulsory composition," as Michael Harker (2015) puts it, should exist. Recent years, however, have seen a new test of FYC's resilience, this time an economic one: state cuts to higher education's budgets and the student debt crisis, both of which have called for colleges and universities to make getting a degree faster and cheaper. One way to shave off some time and cost has been to give more students automatic credit for FYC via high scores on standardized tests; another has been an increase in institutions' dual-enrollment course offerings, which provide credit for FYC classes for high school students. Competency-based education and prior learning assessment are other credit-granting mechanisms that are on the rise in the wake of the economic crisis. FYC has kept its position as a required course, or courses, despite occasional arguments that the requirement should be discontinued, but it may not be resilient enough to remain intact in the face of these challenges. In 2014, Joyce Locke Carter, then program chair of the Conference on College Composition and Communication (CCCC), wrote an email addressed to the Association of Teachers of Technical Writing listserv in which she encouraged that audience to consider attending CCCC, pointing out that "as dual-credit, AP [advanced placement], and other waivers to first-year writing requirements continue to deepen, I think it's clear that much of the activity of college writing instruction in the future will take place in technical and professional writing classes, as well as other sorts of upper-division writing classes." Eighteen months later, Carter (2015: n.p.) wrote to a broader audience in her CCCC chair's blog a post that reflects on challenges and opportunities for the future of CCCC: "Dual Credit and Advanced Placement are already eroding [FYC], and will probably succeed in moving all first-year writing instruction out of higher education within the next 10 years. Do we fight to retain this market, or do we pivot to others, such as WID [writing in the disciplines], advanced writing, writing in the workplace, etc.?" One of rhetoric and composition's best leaders has made, with good reason, the prediction that FYC will probably last only about one more decade, which suggests decreased resilience.

In this article I analyze the resilience of FYC by using both the history of the compulsory composition debate and ideas about resilience from environmental studies. However, I must first disambiguate four distinct ideas: (a) the FYC course or sequence, (b) the universal requirement, (c) the field of composition studies, and (d) composition studies' authority regarding the FYC course or sequence. The term *first-year composition* (FYC), as I use it in this essay, specifically means the experience of a dedicated writing course, or a two-course sequence, during the first year on a college campus, led by composition studies experts whose professional judgment about the course or sequence is respected. The resilience of this FYC experience is my primary concern here; admittedly, the universal requirement (which is generally what ensures the FYC experience) is not being waived but, rather, fulfilled by AP, dual enrollment, and the like, but the on-campus FYC writing experience is getting a de facto waiver, in many cases without regard for our field's knowledge and authority. Joyce Malek and Laura R. Micciche (2017: 86) give a thorough account of the threat to FYC in Ohio, arguing that

> the practice of exempting students from writing classes undermines conceptions of writing widely embraced by composition teachers: writing as a tool for active participation in democratic culture, writing as a way of composing selves as well as communities and cultures. Despite our efforts to design a curriculum that asks students to understand communication as a rhetorical practice that calls for careful understanding of self and other, individual and community, and our attention to research as an inquiry-based exercise in how to keep questions open and how to work responsibly with the words of others, AP scoring interpellates our composition course as equivalent to a minimally acceptable free response to three acontextual prompts for an unspecified audience. The notion that writing is something other than a measurable skill does not figure into the institutional credit apparatus.

Malek and Micciche add that the granting of precollege writing credit "takes for granted the idea that a way of advantaging students is to award them college credit for high school learning" and that, further, "we are to believe that providing students fewer opportunities for writing advantages them" (87). They are writing particularly about the Advanced Placement Program (AP) exam, but their argument applies as well to other automatic-credit mechanisms. Here I show how the erosion of FYC has been happening on my campus and in the state of Louisiana and elsewhere, and I suggest some ways that college writing, and the body of knowledge about teaching it that we have built, can remain resilient. To be sure, my argument for preserving college writing's resilience is not basic self-preservation; these issues matter to me primarily because I believe that writing is a mode of learning and that students flourish when their writing is given serious attention and encouragement, beliefs that rhetoric and composition studies has demonstrated and amplified through its theory and research.

Resilience Science and FYC

William Rees (2010: 2), whose research is in community planning, economics, and ecology (and who coined the phrase *ecological footprint*), defines *resilience* as "the capacity of a system to withstand disturbance while still retaining its fundamental structure, function, and internal feedbacks." He adds that "resilience science is based on the simple premise that change is inevitable and that attempts to resist change or control it in any strict sense are doomed to failure" (5). Using ideas from economics about resilience, Rees identifies four phases of the adaptive cycle: how resilience is built, maintained, threatened (and destroyed), and rebuilt:

- *Exploitation and growth phase:* This phase sees "establishment and rapid growth" of the industry or species.
- *Conservation phase:* Usually the "longest phase of the cycle," the conservation phase sees "consolidation and accumulation" of the opportunistic species or industry. Rees observes that "establishment firms become complacently unresponsive to changing market conditions or emerging new technologies."
- *Release phase:* This is also known as the collapse of the system. "With resilience at a minimum" in this phase, many possible events have the power to end the system.
- *Reorganization phase:* During this part of the adaptive cycle, "the chaos of release creates numerous opportunities for novelty and experimentation. . . . Events during the reorganization determine what species/corporations will ultimately dominate the subsequent growth phase." (7)

As a thought experiment about FYC's resilience, here I map these phases onto the history of required FYC, particularly the past challenges leveled against it by those calling for the discontinuation of the FYC requirement. This mapping is not strictly linear, and I purposely refrain from putting strict time boundaries around the phases. Still, the adaptive cycle schema offers us a new narrative of the history of required FYC that is worth telling; while I do not argue for the adaptive cycle in a foundationalist sense, I am convinced that it has some explanatory power when applied to the history of the FYC requirement.

As I explain below, higher education's current economic situation is an ongoing threat to the on-campus FYC writing experience in a moment when its resilience in many universities is low. Tony Scott and Nancy Welch (2016: 6) argue that, "in the age of corporatization and austerity, we now face the consequences of a field that has never established a scholarly habit of positioning composition scholarship in relation to the powerful political economic factors and trends that shape composition work." They provide an analysis of the post-2008 landscape for higher education: the "wage freezes, staff cuts, program retrenchment, class size increases" and the "cost-shift from public to private, with student debt by 2014 surpassing the $1 trillion mark" (9). They add that "higher education has not returned to pre-crisis levels of funding" and position "more defunding as the solution to problems of defunding," with "accountability and efficiency mandates that push foundational changes in curriculum" rather than reinvesting budget revenue in public higher education (9–10). In this context, we may now be in FYC's release phase.

FYC's Exploitation and Growth Phase

The early growth of FYC can be traced through enrollment numbers of colleges and universities. Citing Alexandra Oleson and John Voss, Harker (2015: 27) writes that "the number of undergraduates in American universities increased from 52,300 in 1870 to 156,800 in 1890; 237,600 in 1900; and 597,900 in 1920." It experienced another growth spurt with the introduction of open admissions institutions and the GI Bill, which supported many more students than had attended college previously. The rise of basic writing classes facilitated the growth of FYC as well. During this long period, some scholars in rhetoric and composition studies have critiqued the existence of compulsory composition on practical and ethical grounds. In 1996, Robert J. Connors wrote about what he called the "new abolitionists," arguing that the history of composition has seen "reformist periods" (led primarily by Dewey's ideas) and "abolitionist periods." According to Connors (1996: 48–49), who gives a detailed account of these periods, those who initially wanted to abolish the FYC requirement in the 1890s claimed that it "was never meant as a permanent English offering but was instead a temporary stopgap until the secondary schools could improve." Early arguments in the history of composition, from 1900 to 1915, called for raising admissions standards at universities to make FYC unnecessary, as well as to integrate writing into all courses (Connors 1996). One in particular, Thomas Lounsbury's 1911 article "Compulsory Composition in Colleges," argues that the FYC requirement should be discontinued due to its "drills and other repetitive exercises aimed toward teaching students to write themes" and its failure to make a real difference in students' written eloquence, pointing to examples of writers and orators who never had FYC such as Abraham Lincoln and Ulysses S. Grant (qtd. in Harker 2015: 19). Despite these limitations, the FYC requirement continued and expanded.

FYC's Conservation Phase

The compulsory composition debate subsides and resurfaces throughout the history of composition without affecting the existence of the requirement. In 1973, Ron Smith observed reforms in higher education that he argued would signal the end of the FYC requirement, such as "uniform equivalency testing, true three-year degree programs, the general elimination or streamlining of lower-division requirements, [and] performance or competency-based instruction" (qtd. in Connors 2003: 288). While Smith noticed the beginnings of the reforms we are now confronting on a larger scale, FYC stayed resilient for decades following. Rees (2010: 3) wrote that ecosystems "are self-organizing, self-producing systems in which each major component exists in vital relationship with other components. These relationships must be maintained if the components are to continue being able to produce themselves and the system is to retain its functional integrity." What components does FYC need to be resilient? I suggest knowledge; research; a place in the curriculum; faculty with enough job security and academic freedom to accumulate experience, expertise, and status; and students to serve.

Rees (2010: 4) explains that in ecosystems, "when humans maximize the harvest of a particular species . . . we inadvertently alter that species' relationships to multiple other species (e.g., predators and prey) in the ecosystem, setting off a cascade of feedback responses that can fundamentally erode the system's integrity." In higher education, the FYC requirement does not involve a simple, direct predator-prey dynamic, but we can make some connections between FYC labor and the resilience of the FYC experience. Rees continues: "Some species may be lost, others may be favored, and, ultimately, the system may cease to function in ways that are necessary to sustain either the target species or their human predators. In short, the evidence suggests that in addition to over-harvesting, efficiency-oriented maximum production strategies simplify both exploited ecosystems and the social systems they support. They eliminate important processes and redundancies, and make the socio-eco-system more vulnerable to additional stress. The system loses resilience" (4). It is not clear exactly who the predator is in the ecosystem of FYC—tenured research faculty or administrators—but the exploitation of the vast majority of composition teachers, who are contingent, part-time faculty and graduate students, has been well documented for many decades. If it is the case, as I claim, that a resilient program needs strong faculty with the requisite job security and academic freedom to grow as teachers and researchers, thus contributing to the longitudinal mentoring of students and making of knowledge in the discipline, then our system of required FYC is losing resilience.

Sharon Crowley (1998: 254) wrote that "post-Fordist institutions rely on part-time or other disposable faculty, such as graduate students, to do the teaching. The advantages of part-time faculty are economy (lower salaries, fewer benefits) and flexibility (layoffs in hard times are relatively simple)." These advantages are short term, semester to semester, year to year, and though FYC has admittedly held up regardless of its long history of outrageous labor practices, this precarious model of academic labor is a key weakness in FYC's long-term resilience, making it less able to withstand threats, which are an inevitable part of the adaptive cycle. James Sledd (1991: 271) argued that

> denigrators of composition and its teaching have often repeated the pretense that freshman English is indeed remedial, unnecessary for most college entrants, and therefore unfit for a college curriculum; but the pretense is dangerous, less because it is untrue (which it is) than because it invites the more exalted administrators to abolish the one course on which departments of English most depend for their existence. For the professoriate, the apparently safer argument, despite its own internal contradictions, is insistence both on the maintenance of the freshman course and on the wisdom of staffing it with the least experienced, least prepared, most poorly paid of teachers: the teaching assistants, who are essential if the research machine is to be kept rolling.

A quarter of a century later, we see even more clearly that the economic model of reliance on contingent academic labor—which, it should be said, includes faculty in all fields—is unlikely to change. Sadly, we are only continuing to lose resilience when it comes to the faculty's role in maintaining that model. The question now becomes what to do if we are, in fact, truly in the midst of the release phase, which would destroy the FYC ecosystem as we know it and force reorganization.

In 2001, Michael Moghtader, Alanna Cotch, and Kristen Hague replicated Ron Smith's 1973 study surveying colleges and universities about their FYC requirement. Smith (1974: 139) had found that 24 percent of institutions had no FYC requirement, 76 percent had at least one required course, and 45 percent had two or more required courses. Moghtader, Cotch, and Hague (2001) found that more schools had an FYC requirement in 2001 than in 1973. But, they also found, more schools are allowing exemption of the on-campus FYC writing experience, especially public schools. They prophetically warned: "It is deceptive to state that the growth in the composition requirement necessarily means that all is well with writing programs—particularly if this growth translates into an overreliance on a staffing population of part-time instructors who lack benefits, recognition, and long-term job stability. And it is from this position that any predictions of the future of the writing requirement must be made—regardless of the reformist or abolitionist side that one takes" (460). They correctly pointed out that the resilience of the on-campus FYC writing experience depends on having faculty with expertise teaching writing who have authority and status within the institution.

The conservation phase continued to see critiques of compulsory composition, notably Crowley's (1998) contention that FYC is based on a paternalistic discourse of needs: administrators determine that students need the service that FYC provides. This nebulous service is an introduction to academic discourse, including standard English. Crowley remarks that "the instrumental service ethic of the required composition course" is "to make student writing available for surveillance until it can be certified to conform to whatever standards are deemed to mark it, and its authors, as suitable for admission to the discourses of the academy" (253). The universal FYC requirement, she claims, disregards students' individual histories and cultures, leaving students "as people who exist only in the institutional present, and who perform exercises that meet the institutional needs to rank and exclude" (260). For Crowley, the whole endeavor is deeply flawed, so much so that the incidental good it may do for some students is outweighed by its abuses of both teachers and students.

Sledd agrees, and while he does not make a case at length to abolish compulsory composition, he notes what we may now call an unsustainable situation losing resilience. Sledd (1991: 279) argues that "the foofaraw about literacy and the shortcomings of higher education . . . make it presently impossible to abolish college composition altogether," meaning that the continual rhetoric in the media about declining literacy, combined with the lack of support at most institutions for writing across the curriculum (WAC) and robust upper-division writing in the disciplines courses, keeps required FYC in place, despite the shocking working conditions of its teachers. He adds that "to the argument that money [to compensate instructors properly] is unavailable, the answer is that inadequate support of an essential program is the most wasteful of possible alternatives" (279). From an economic perspective, Sledd may have a point: it is better to spend no money and have no writing program at all than it is to spend some money, even if relatively little, to have a program fraught with so many problems. It is this reasoning that reveals FYC's vulnerability to our current moment of austerity.

FYC's Release Phase

Brian Walker and David Salt make the point that "the longer the conservation phase persists, the smaller the shock needed to end it" (qtd. in Rees 2010: 7). This observation suggests that no system is infinitely resilient. I have hesitated to set strict time frames marking the beginnings and ends of FYC's exploitation and growth phase and its conservation phase, but the fact is that required FYC has existed for about two centuries, and the release phase of its adaptive cycle may be under way. We see a coordinated governmental and economic effort to bypass on-campus FYC, including national efforts such as the US Department of Education's College Scorecard, plus state-level automatic-credit and early-college initiatives that result in more students who arrive on campus with FYC credit. These initiatives, combined with state disinvestment in higher education and more competition for students among universities, result in added pressure on writing programs to accept precollege credit for FYC courses, which technically keeps the universal FYC requirement in place but effectively waives the immersive experience of writing for first-year students.

A 2015 ACT report claims that dual enrollment has grown by 75 percent nationally in the past ten years. Some states are offering college credit options to students as young as twelve. At Iowa State University, almost one-third of the students test out of FYC. The University of South Florida St. Petersburg recently went from 446 sections of FYC to 266, owing mostly to the explosion of dual enrollment. FYC occupied the top of the list of the Florida College System's ten most frequently taken dual-enrollment courses, with first-semester FYC as the most frequently taken, and second-semester FYC as the next most frequently taken. In the 2012–13 academic year, 19,545 students in the Florida College System took first-semester FYC (up 6.1 percent from the previous year); 14,389 took second-semester FYC (up 8.4 percent from the previous year) (Ratliff et al. 2017).

At the University of Louisiana at Lafayette, where I teach, the number of dual-enrollment sections of FYC offered by our department has increased

533 percent since 2010. Undergraduate enrollment has been increasing, with record-breaking numbers almost every fall, but enrollments in FYC have been decreasing steadily, from 2,100 students enrolled in FYC in Fall 2010 to just over 1,750 enrolled in FYC in Fall 2015. Louisiana has also started requiring large groups of students to take the AP and College-Level Examination Program (CLEP) college equivalency exams; the high schools are evaluated—and funded—based in part on how students perform on such tests and how many students participate in dual enrollment. Louisiana's state scholarship program, the Taylor Opportunity Program for Students, has had its funding cut, and the state board of regents has proposed further increasing dual enrollment to give more students the opportunity to enter college with fifteen credit hours, six of which come from FYC, and perhaps some that come from sophomore general education literature survey courses as well. Certainly there is a push on our campus to increase our sophomore dual-enrollment course offerings.

Before Louisiana opted out of the Common Core State Standards, it was a governing state in the Partnership for Assessment of Readiness for College and Careers (PARCC). I was asked to be on my university's campus leadership team for PARCC, which was tasked with providing feedback to the nonprofit organizations that were developing assessments for the Common Core State Standards. During this work, the state persistently asked us to list competencies that we wanted to see in college-level student writing, as if to pin us down, to identify how they might capture those competencies in a test (in an expected twist, they did not use our recommendations in their final reports). It would be hard to dispute Chris Gallagher's (2016) contention that competency-based education is the logical conclusion of outcomes assessment.

The existence of the on-campus FYC writing experience is being compromised not only in practical terms, as more students are arriving on campuses with FYC credit, but also in the co-optation of our rhetoric of pedagogy. Proponents of competency-based education, or prior learning assessment, have co-opted the rhetoric of critical pedagogy: of decentering teacher authority and empowering students to learn. Proponents of dual enrollment have co-opted the rhetoric of equity. To critique dual enrollment is to be against students' opportunity to go to college, to gain the confidence that they are capable of college-level work, to be adequately challenged in school, to go to college for a lower cost and thus take on less student loan debt (school districts help fund dual-enrollment courses and college equivalency tests).

Scholars in composition studies persist in critiquing the de facto waiver of the on-campus FYC writing experience. The Council of Writing Program Administrators' "Position Statement on Pre-college Credit for Writing"

(Hansen et al. 2014) notes that students often take the AP English Language and Composition Exam during the junior year of high school. The authors ask: "Should [FYC] credit be given for short, formulaic timed writing the student did two years prior to matriculating at college? If a student bypasses [FYC] on the strength of such a small amount of writing—even if it was rated highly by test scorers—might they be missing out on the developmental and socializing effects of more writing and of writing assignments that are designed for the curricular moment when they matriculate at college?" (189). The authors have similar concerns about dual-enrollment courses taken in high school classrooms. They suggest that an FYC course "is designed for students on a college campus, who are typically 18 and 19. Designers of college [FYC] courses generally plan the curriculum to challenge emancipated young adults who should be ready for the rhetorically challenging and perhaps morally and ethically challenging texts" discussed in the course, which students between the ages of fourteen and sixteen may be unprepared to do (195). The Two-Year College Association (TYCA) identifies six areas of concern about dual-enrollment credit for FYC in its "Executive Committee Statement on Concurrent Enrollment" (2012: 1): "quality control for courses," "environment on the high school campus," "the cognitive and affective readiness of students," "policies for handling parental involvement," "college support of high school faculty," and "college grades awarded to concurrently enrolled students." And yet, states continue to make decisions about awarding college credits without regard for our field's professional judgment. Malek and Micciche (2017: 88) challenge the community of composition studies teachers and scholars to reach out more to those outside the field, claiming, "We rely on rhetoric that communicates to insiders but fails to imagine a world in which writing is merely a measurable skill and a 3-credit course to check off, despite the fact that this view often wins the day." They call for raising awareness of the purpose and value of the on-campus FYC writing experience among university administrators, faculty in other departments, parents, and the business community.

Those who have argued for discontinuing the universal requirement tend to agree that the perpetual crisis rhetoric around literacy is what really keeps FYC going as an institution. What we have now, in what may be FYC's release phase, are standardized, high-stakes testing and cost cutting masquerading as increased rigor at the primary and secondary levels: the solution to the writing problem that had been sought all along. So students ostensibly graduate high school knowing writing once and for all, in many cases without having a designated place in the college curriculum for their continued development as writers.

Institutional Maneuvers to Counter the Release Phase

As more universities adopt budgetary models that require departments to manage their own tuition revenue, it is possible that they will recognize the threat to FYC, long considered the cash cow of English departments, and push back against the erosion of the universal requirement. Some universities are creating new second-year-level writing courses that have no means of exemption, such as Florida State University's sophomore-level writing course called Research, Genre, and Context. Others are integrating writing into first-year seminar courses, such as the seminars at the University of Richmond, which Carol Wittig has called "writing in a new wrapper" (Ratliff et al. 2017).

Another preservation model comes from Brigham Young University (BYU). In 2006, a whopping 35–40 percent of students at BYU received AP test credit for FYC (Hansen et al. 2006). Kristine Hansen and her colleagues at BYU conducted a study to evaluate the writing by students who had received credit for FYC via the AP exam. Hansen et al. (2006) explained that the state paid for students to take AP exams because it expects to save money later on: the state does not have to spend as many dollars per student for as long a time, and those students graduate and become taxpaying workers sooner. After evaluating student writing and surveys from students for self-perception and self-efficacy, Hansen et al. found, unsurprisingly, that "for entering college students, two general writing courses are better than one"— and much better than none (464). Students who had AP coursework in high school plus FYC in college were the strongest writers, and the weakest were those who had scored a 3 on the AP exam and opted not to take FYC.

Hansen et al. (2006) detailed the ways that FYC is preserved at BYU despite such a large percentage of students who enter with FYC credit. At the time of their study, BYU had three FYC courses, including honors courses, which students are free to take without any additional eligibility requirements. They write, "Despite having already earned credit for the requirement, about 40 percent of entering students with AP English scores of 4 or 5 choose to enroll in FYC, usually Honors 200. But only about 30 percent of students with AP scores of 3 choose to enroll in FYC" (468). The administration issued a recommendation, included with students' registration materials, that students take FYC even if they have credit for it. Hansen et al. add: "Some academic departments have also voiced their concern about allowing so many students to skip first-year writing, and three large departments— English, History, and Psychology—have recently begun to require their majors to take first-year writing regardless of AP status" (469). Additionally, the BYU Honors Program requires students to take FYC independent of

AP exam scores. While BYU is a private university, less beholden to performance-based state funding models and statewide articulation agreements, it does show a way to keep writing courses as an on-campus experience, while not necessarily a universal one.

FYC's Reorganization Phase

How, when the existence of the FYC requirement has always been contested, may we preserve college writing in the first year and beyond? For Connors (1996: 58), factors contributing to the FYC requirement's resilience have been open-admissions universities in the 1970s, sustained crisis rhetoric in mainstream media about illiteracy, and more professionalization of teachers via doctoral programs in composition to defend the requirement. The overreliance on contingent faculty has weakened FYC's resilience in the form of the "sustained action from teachers" that Connors cites as a means of keeping the requirement in place. The rise of austerity in higher education from 2008 to the present is unprecedented in the history of composition, and in an attention economy, crisis rhetoric about literacy must compete with all the other content on the internet.

If we are indeed in the release phase of FYC's adaptive cycle, it will be a years-long period during which the number of sections of FYC will slowly dwindle. Perhaps, in this thought experiment, the release and reorganization phases are overlapping. Rees (2010: 7) says that, in economic terms, the reorganization phase is a time when "new technologies and aggressive entrepreneurs can move in to fill niches left by failing firms." Crowley (1998: 265) advocates making FYC an elective course, which may call for some entrepreneurial thinking to persuade students to enroll in it, and she is confident that "there is a place for composition in the university, and that place does not depend upon Freshman English." She recommends "a vertical elective curriculum in composing" (262). For the past decade, some of these structural reforms have been taking place in college writing, and below I list some possibilities for adapting college writing to the present changes in higher education.

Take Ownership of Dual-Enrollment Programs

The term *credit laundering* exists for a reason. Colleges and universities form partnerships with high schools at a rapid rate, and these sometimes come with only a cursory consultation between a composition faculty member and the high school teachers who teach the dual-enrollment FYC courses. Some programs, to get around accreditation requirements for college-level instructors, list that composition faculty member as the instructor of record, serving as a "master teacher" of the dual-enrollment sections while the high school teachers are effectively considered teaching assistants. Because FYC is headed in the direction of high schools, it would benefit students, teachers, and the discipline if we turn our attention there as well. That means more mentoring of high school teachers in composition theory and research and active engagement with what is taught in high school English, adjusting FYC as carefully as possible so that when it is taught in a high school setting, it is as close to the course taught on the college campus as it can be. Malek and Micciche (2017: 92) make this recommendation as well, as they have mentored and trained dual-enrollment teachers in composition studies in their Graduate Certificate for Teachers of English program for high school teachers.

It also means more advocacy for dual-enrollment teachers. What happens when we include dual enrollment in the academic labor conversation? I think it's time to do it. When high school teachers are tasked with FYC, they are usually full-time employees with benefits who are paid a salary for teaching high school English along with the per-course payment that adjunct instructors receive. Still, there are problems with working conditions for secondary school teachers, particularly the lack of freedom to design curriculum and assessments. Teachers must be in a position of strength if we are to have a resilient FYC writing experience, and failing to support dual-enrollment teachers is a failure to learn from FYC's worst mistake.

Align with Campus Student Success Initiatives

The austerity movement has brought with it a renewed emphasis on retention, student success, and graduation rates. Writing has been recognized as a high-impact practice: creative and intellectual engagement that helps students learn, reflect on their learning, and stay in college. By helping students be persistent and resilient, which we want to do anyway, college writing as a learning experience and discipline of study becomes more resilient, the thinking goes. One caveat of this approach, though, is articulated by Crowley (1998: 257):

> When evidence about the retention of at-risk students is used to support the claim that minority students profit from required instruction in writing, at-risk status is equated with minority status—an equation that I resist. Indeed, it is my desire to resist equations like these that in part drives my resistance to the universal requirement, which tends toward standardization and away from the recognition of students' diverse abilities and desires. If I am right that the required introductory course remains in place in order to socialize stu-

dents into the discourse of the academy, to the extent that it succeeds in this it supplements or even erases students' relations to their home languages. The universality of the requirement suggests to me that this is, precisely, its point.

One response to Crowley's concern is the insistence on the important role of affect in FYC pedagogy. Steve Lamos (2016) argues for "affective-labor-in-pace": being encouraging, helpful, supportive, and collaborative, and doing so in a way that helps students engage with the space, including the classroom and the community. It rejects neoliberal emphases on standardization and automation, and it cleverly denies that side of the rhetoric of student success, which for Lamos is firmly the province of affective-labor-in-space.

Take Translanguaging Seriously

College writing, whatever form it takes, whether a required first-year course or something else, must embrace a wide variety of genres, discourses, creative and experimental ventures, and multiple ways of using language, including languages in addition to English. The last several years' work in translingualism have demonstrated that what we want writing pedagogy to do—help students communicate and make meaning within a variety of purposes, audiences, and contexts—is limited when we approach it from a monolingual orientation. Translanguaging opens up the rhetorical possibilities for students dramatically and contributes to linguistic social justice. Suresh Canagarajah (2016: 266) defines *translingual orientation* as "a perspective on languages as always in contact and generating new grammars and meanings out of their synergy. The term also posits language as a semiotic system, integrated with other visual, aural, and tactile modalities, to communicate meaning." *Translingual writing* is "situated literate practice where writers negotiate their semiotic resources in relation to the dominant conventions of language and rhetoric" (266). Jerry Won Lee's (2016) work on "translanguaging assessment" productively challenges the notion of universal writing competencies, which form the rationale of precollege credit for writing. The future is translingual, and resilient college writing must also be.

Integrate Two-Year Colleges and Their Faculty and Students More into Writing Studies

Most of the FYC classes in the United States are taught at two-year colleges (Hassel and Giordano 2013). John Lovas (2002: 276) argues that "you cannot represent a field if you ignore half of it. You cannot generalize about composition if you don't know half of the work being done. We need new and substantial forms of collaboration on a local and regional basis so that the quality of all writing programs can be improved." Two-year colleges are a major site of the FYC experience, and efforts to increase FYC's resilience must include them.

Engage in Writing about Writing

One example of a robust curricular reform is writing about writing, now in its second decade, which establishes FYC as Introduction to Writing Studies and ambitiously frames it as introducing a discipline by teaching the body of knowledge made by rhetoric and composition scholars, making it visible and available for undergraduate students to use and contribute to (Wardle and Downs 2007). This model is a strong counter to the least resilient FYC class: the one that repeats what students have already done in high school.

Pursue Writing beyond the First Year

Another site where resilience can be bolstered is college writing beyond students' first year. This includes the exemption-proof second-year writing course, but also other upper-division writing courses such as technical communication and advanced composition, which tend to be junior-level classes. The undergraduate writing major is an especially promising way forward for college writing for universities that have it. WAC is a particularly interesting and surprising case; it seems to have been resilient in the face of austerity. Shortly after the 2008 recession, Karen J. Lunsford (2009: 2) wrote that "funding for WAC/WID programs per se has softened. WAC and WID are no longer the Next New Things that draw grants. Rather, granting foundations currently are promoting technology initiatives that may or may not include writing instruction as an explicit component." Not long after that, Michael Pemberton (2010: n.p.) warned readers of *Across the Disciplines* that in this time of "budgetary cutbacks, cancelled programs, terminated searches, reduced or eliminated travel funds, expanded class sizes, and mandatory unpaid furloughs . . . the fate of WAC programs has to be considered uncertain at best. 'Hard' money, previously committed long-term to WAC/WID, is now under scrutiny, and new 'soft' money is almost nowhere to be found." However, Pemberton now is more optimistic about the stability of WAC programs. He recently wrote that "funding has become increasingly tight, especially with allocations to support public universities plummeting nationwide year by year, but on the other hand, I still have a sense that WAC programs are expanding, partly because they seem to have been the focus of a lot of institutional QEPs [quality enhancement plans] over the last five or six years" (e-mail message to author, 23 October 2017). WAC's resilience as attributable to its place in QEPs is an interesting notion, an idea explored in the collection *Reclaiming Accountability: Improving Writing Programs through Accreditation and Large-Scale Assessments* (Sharer et al. 2016).

Conclusion

While we may be experiencing the slow collapse of FYC and the reorganization of college writing, the discipline of rhetoric and composition is unlikely to start a new adaptive cycle and enter a new growth phase without improving working conditions for teachers. My opinion on how to move forward is that it is not feasible to act monolithically as a discipline in a particular direction—to preserve FYC or to direct energies to other writing courses in the university. We must act in our local settings and advocate for college writing in the forms that make the most sense for particular institutions. At some places, that will mean preserving the on-campus FYC experience by not granting credit from test scores or dual enrollment; at others, it must necessarily mean preserving college writing for as many students as possible in all the courses possible. Whatever happens, we can assume that the Trump administration will only accelerate already existing efforts to defund higher education and cut corners from students' learning experience, and if FYC is to remain a resilient student learning experience, we must redouble our efforts to share our knowledge as much as possible, with policy makers and with teachers and students at all levels.

Works Cited

ACT. 2015. "Using Dual Enrollment to Improve the Educational Outcomes of High School Students," www.act.org/content/dam/act/unsecured/documents/UsingDual
Enrollment_2015.pdf

Canagarajah, Suresh. 2016. "Translingual Writing and Teacher Development in Composition." *College English* 78.3: 265–73.

Carter, Joyce Locke. 2015. "Solstice." *Sailing the Four Cs: My Year of Living Dangerously as CCCC Chair* (blog), 21 December, Joycelockecarter.com/CCCC/solstice/.

Connors, Robert J. 1996. "The Abolition Debate in Composition: A Short History." In *Composition in the Twenty-First Century: Crisis and Change*, edited by Lynn Z. Bloom, Donald A. Daiker, and Edward M. White, 47–63. Carbondale: Southern Illinois University Press.

Connors, Robert J. 2003. "The Abolition Debate in Composition: A Short History." In *Selected Essays of Robert J. Connors*, edited by Lisa Ede and Andrea Lunsford, 279–94. New York: Bedford/St. Martin's.

Crowley, Sharon. 1998. *Composition in the University: Historical and Polemical Essays*. Pittsburgh: University of Pittsburgh Press.

Gallagher, Chris. 2016. "Our Trojan Horse: Outcomes Assessment and the Resurrection of Competency-Based Education." In *Composition in the Age of Austerity*, edited by Nancy Welch and Tony Scott, 21–34. Logan: Utah State University Press.

Hansen, Kristine, et al. 2006. "Are Advanced Placement English and First-Year College Composition Equivalent? A Comparison of Outcomes in the Writing of Three Groups of Sophomore College Students." *Research in the Teaching of English* 40.4: 461–501.

Hansen, Kristine, et al. 2014. "The CWPA Position Statement on Pre-college Credit for Writing." *WPA: Writing Program Administration* 37.2: 180–99.

Harker, Michael. 2015. *The Lure of Literacy: A Critical Reception of the Compulsory Composition Debate*. Albany: SUNY Press.

Hassel, Holly, and Joanne Baird Giordano. 2013. "Occupy Writing Studies: Rethinking College Composition for the Needs of the Teaching Majority." *College Composition and Communication* 65.1: 117–39.

Lamos, Steve. 2016. "Toward Job Security for Teaching-Track Composition Faculty: Recognizing and Rewarding Affective-Labor-in-Space." *College English* 78.4: 362–86.

Lee, Jerry Won. 2016. "Beyond Translingual Writing." *College English* 79.2: 174–95.

Lovas, John C. 2002. "All Good Writing Develops at the Edge of Risk." *College Composition and Communication* 54.2: 264–88.

Lunsford, Karen J. 2009. "Writing Technologies and WAC: Current Lessons and Future Trends (Editor's Introduction)." *Across the Disciplines* 6.2: 1–14.

Malek, Joyce, and Laura R. Micciche. 2017. "A Model of Efficiency: Pre-college Credit and the State Apparatus." *WPA: Writing Program Administration* 40.2: 77–97.

Moghtader, Michael, Alanna Cotch, and Kristen Hague. 2001. "The First-Year Composition Requirement Revisited: A Survey." *College Composition and Communication* 52.3: 455–67.

Pemberton, Michael. 2010. "Reflections on *Across the Disciplines*." *Across the Disciplines* 7.1, wac.colostate.edu/docs/atd/editor/editor2010.pdf.

Ratliff, Clancy, et al. 2017. "The Future of College Writing and How to Stop It." Presentation at the annual convention of the Conference on College Composition and Communication, Portland, OR, 15–18 March.

Rees, William. 2010. "Thinking 'Resilience.'" In *The Post Carbon Reader: Managing the Twenty-First Century's Sustainability Crises*, edited by Richard Heinberg and Daniel Lerch, 1–12. Watershed Media, www.postcarbon.org/publications/thinking-resilience/.

Scott, Tony, and Nancy Welch. 2016. Introduction to *Composition in the Age of Austerity*, edited by Nancy Welch and Tony Scott, 3–20. Logan: Utah State University Press.

Sharer, Wendy, et al., eds. 2016. *Reclaiming Accountability: Improving Writing Programs through Accreditation and Large-Scale Assessments*. Logan: Utah State University Press.

Sledd, James 1991. "Why the Wyoming Resolution Had to Be Emasculated: A History and a Quixotism." *JAC* 11.2: 269–81.

Smith, Ron. 1974. "The Composition Requirement Today: A Report on a Nationwide Survey of Four-Year Colleges and Universities." *College Composition and Communication* 25.2: 138–48.

TYCA (Two-Year College Association). 2012. "TYCA Executive Committee Statement on Concurrent Enrollment." 24 March, www.ncte.org/library/NCTE-Files/Groups /TYCA/Concurrent_Enrollment.pdf.

Wardle, Elizabeth, and Doug Downs. 2007. "Teaching about Writing, Righting Misconceptions: (Re)Envisioning 'First-Year Composition' as 'Introduction to Writing Studies.'" *College Composition and Communication* 58.4: 552–84.

Clancy Ratliff is an associate professor at the University of Louisiana at Lafayette. Her research and teaching focus on composition pedagogy, feminist rhetorics, and authorship and intellectual property. Her work has appeared in *Women's Studies Quarterly, Composition Forum,* and *Computers and Composition Online.*

Supplemental Material

"The Adaptive Cycle: Resilience in the History of First-Year Composition"
Clancy Ratcliff

Part I: Reflection on the Origins of the Article

Donald Murray has famously said that all writing is autobiography. I can see his point in all the writing I have done, but most of all in my work about writing program administration, which is thoroughly situated in time and place. I started teaching at the University of Louisiana at Lafayette as a pre-tenure WPA in fall 2007. The state's universities were still reeling from the damage caused by Hurricane Katrina and Hurricane Rita; the exodus of students in New Orleans's universities (University of New Orleans, Southern University New Orleans, Xavier University, Tulane University, Loyola University New Orleans, Dillard University, University of Holy Cross, and Nunez and Delgado Community Colleges) and sudden spike in enrollment at nearby Louisiana State University, Baton Rouge Community College, University of Louisiana at Lafayette, South Louisiana Community College, and other institutions meant that, at least at UL Lafayette, first-year M.A. students who hadn't yet met the SACS requirement of eighteen hours of graduate coursework in the discipline were enlisted to teach Basic Writing their first semester in the program, and enrollment caps in FYW increased from 25 to 27 in Fall 2005: a "temporary," "emergency" increase that was still in place in Fall 2007. It took us years to get it reinstated to 25. In sum, we experienced austerity early.

Then, that next semester--Spring 2008--the global market collapsed, and Louisiana suffered the most drastic budget cuts to higher education in the nation. The governor, state legislators, and administrators at the University of Louisiana system level and UL Lafayette university level were desperate to cut costs by any means necessary. The legislature passed the GRAD Act, which stood for "Granting Resources and Autonomy for Degrees," and it provided an opportunity for universities to replace the funding they lost from the state by increasing tuition. Because they had to increase the graduation rate to qualify for permission to raise tuition, they had an incentive to grant general education credit to more students so that they would be more likely to complete a degree, and to do so faster. Naturally, six of those general education credit hours were FYW, so I was close to ground zero of the austerity crisis of the last dozen years. I saw more and more students getting FYW credit. I read the collection *Composition in the Age of Austerity* with great interest, and when I saw a call for proposals for a special issue of *Pedagogy* on the theme of resilience, edited by the same editors of *Composition in the Age of Austerity* and seen as a next step from that collection, I believed I could contribute. I talked to my good friend from graduate school, Amy Propen, about theories of resilience from environmental studies, and she recommended an edited collection titled *The Post-Carbon Reader*. I read it, and in William Rees's chapter on resilience, I encountered the idea of the adaptive cycle as applied to both nature and economics, and I was struck by how plausibly it could be mapped onto the history of FYW. I'd like to take this opportunity to acknowledge the help of the reviewers and the editors, especially Chris Gallagher, who really put me through the paces with regard to revision, but who strengthened the essay immensely.

Part II: Description of Research Methods, Findings, and/or Pedagogical Impact

The experience of writing "The Adaptive Cycle" has had a lot of influence on my teaching and my thinking about FYW and college writing in general. In my reflections about FYW and all the reading and thought experiments and exercises I did while writing the article, it occurred to me that FYW classrooms are possibly the place with the most diverse group of students in higher education. Yet, in graduate faculty meetings, we cast about for ways to increase diversity in our M.A. and Ph.D. programs, in departments that have them. (I had a one-year interim stint as Director of Graduate Studies recently. Again, all writing is autobiography.) In other words, in English studies, we start out with the most diverse group of students in the university, FYW, and end up with one of the least diverse, graduate students. What we need to be doing is *keeping* the diversity *we already have* in FYW by sufficiently supporting and mentoring FYW students. We need to have a critical view of FYW's perpetuation of writerly whiteness and turn to the practices of *discursive homeplacing* and *safe harboring*, set forth by Karen Keaton Jackson, Hope Jackson, and Dawn Hicks Tafari. Their article was published after "The Adaptive Cycle," but I strongly believe that in the time FYW has left, we must be as kind, supportive, encouraging, and empowering as possible while we serve students. We must have full and radical faith, trust, and confidence in them as writers and intellectuals. That means practices like grading contracts, as well as thinking big about accessibility and inclusion for students with disabilities. I don't know if FYW is really going out of higher education or not, but in any case, we should learn from its successes and failures.

Part III: Discussion Questions

1. Are rumors of First-Year Writing's demise greatly exaggerated? What might be some arguments that more students are taking FYW?

2. If we are in the release phase, how much longer will it last? How might another recession in the wake of COVID-19 affect FYW's place in higher education?

3. How will these developments change composition research and its implications for pedagogy?

4. How has enrollment in Basic Writing and Second Language Writing courses been affected, if at all?

Works Cited

Jackson, Karen Keaton, Hope Jackson, and Dawn N. Hicks Tafari. "We Belong in the Discussion: Including HBCUs in Conversations about Race and Writing." *College Composition and Communication*, vol. 71, no. 2, 2019, pp. 184-214.

REFLECTIONS

Reflections is on the Web at https://reflectionsjournal.net/

Reflections: A Journal of Community-Engaged Writing and Rhetoric is a peer-reviewed journal published twice a year. The journal focuses on how community-based writing projects 1) contribute to our knowledge of theories, practices, and uses of writing and rhetoric; and 2) alter traditional pedagogy and research practices of composition and rhetoric and allied fields. We seek to publish the academic research that emerges from community-engaged writing projects as well as the non-academic genres produced by project participants—the poetry, essays, photographs, and memoirs that often emerge from such work. We invite submissions from anyone who has been involved in a service-learning, community literacy, or community writing project, including community members, university, college, community college, or public school faculty, students, and activists.

Learning to Value Cultural Wealth Through Service Learning: Farmworker Families' and Latina/o University Students' Mutual Empowerment via Freirean and Feminist Chicana/o-Latina/o Literature Reading Circles[1]

Georgina Guzmán's article stands out because it is both an important contribution to service learning with Latinx students in Latinx community settings, specifically, and a significant contribution to community engaged writing and rhetoric more generally, addressing reciprocity, one of the most relentless obstacles to productive partnerships. Guzmán analyzes a community-engaged writing project in her Chicana/o- Latina/o Literature course at California State University Channel Islands (CSUCI), in which students read and discuss Chicana/o-Latina/o literature with farmworker families living in low-income farmworker housing tracts in Oxnard and Camarillo, California. CSUCI is the only four-year Hispanic Serving Institution (HSI) to serve Ventura County; the student body is 53 percent Latino/a, and 59 percent first-generation college students.

---

1. *Reflections*, vol. 18, no. 2 © 2019 Georgina Guzmán. This article is licensed under the Creative Commons Attribution 4.0 International License (CC BY). For more information, please visit creativecommons.org.

Learning to Value Cultural Wealth Through Service Learning: Farmworker Families' and Latina/o University Students' Mutual Empowerment via Freirean and Feminist Chicana/o- Latina/o Literature Reading Circles

Georgina Guzmán

This paper traces strategies and successes—for both students and community partners—in the implementation of service learning within my English 353: Chicana/o- Latina/o Literature classes at California State University Channel Islands. In order to bridge university culture and the farmworker communities that work and live alongside the university, in consultation with community partners, we created bilingual reading circles where students went in to read and discuss works of Chicana/o literature with residents in low-income farmworker housing. Using a critical framework of Freirian pedagogical practice in the classroom and in the community, I explore how first- generation Latina/o students' participation in service- learning enabled them to counter a cultural deficit model of thinking about farmworkers. In the process, students learned how to value their own rich cultural wealth and the familial assets they bring to the university and society as a whole.

"There is a big difference between going to class and taking notes on the statistics of people trying to cross the border and actually hearing the voices of those statistics."

—Alejandra, CSUCI student

Fifty miles north of Los Angeles, California, our campus at California State University Channel Islands (CSUCI) is nestled amidst a veritable microcosm of California: Ventura County is a racially, culturally, and economically diverse semi- agricultural setting that supplies about one-third of the state's annual strawberry volume. One cannot drive to campus without witnessing firsthand the sight of Mexican farmworkers hunched over in the sun, harvesting strawberries and other fruits and vegetables. Witnessing this sight every day makes me ever-mindful of the social polarization that exists in our country—of the haves and have nots working across the street from each other in the fields and the university, whose days are spent in the same geographical space but whose life paths never cross.

Addressing this community and its institutional disconnection, difference in privilege, and unequal access to education has become a central part of my classroom and service learning pedagogies. In an attempt to bridge these divides, for the last two years I have developed and taught a Chicana/o-Latina/o Literature course at CSUCI and coordinated student-led reading circles within the farmworker community; this course requires students to read and discuss Chicana/o-Latina/o short stories, poems, novels, and autobiographies with farmworker families living in low-income farmworker housing tracts in Oxnard and Camarillo, California.

More than just incorporating community service into classroom learning to expand the students' understanding of course materials, these reading circles employ "critical service learning" pedagogies "purposefully infused with social justice components" to help both students and community members alike "interrogate systems of oppression, work to dismantle social inequities, and forge authentic relationships between higher education institutions and the community 'served'" (Portillo and Hickman 2011, xi). Student demographics at CSUCI create rich opportunities for critical service learning, providing models to bring forth more equitable collaborations that disrupt the traditional underprivileged-privileged binary that undergirds many service learning projects. CSUCI is the only four-year Hispanic Serving Institution (HSI) to serve Ventura County; our student body is 53 percent Latino/a, and 59 percent of our students are first-generation college students. In traditional paradigms of service learning, particularly at Predominantly White Institutions (PWI), more privileged students from higher socioeconomic stratums typically venture out to volunteer in underprivileged communities of color that are foreign to them. One example is J. Estrella Torrez's service learning project at Michigan State University, which facilitated an opportunity for white middle- class students to participate in dialogues with Latina/o farmworker students who were enrolled in a high school equivalency diploma program (2015). Scholars are mindful of how participating in service learning with such unequal dynamics can make it "difficult for students to avoid seeing themselves as saviors despite the emphasis on mutual learning" (Grobman 2005, 130) and can too easily degrade into a "liberal do-gooder stance" (Cushman 1999, 332). However, the majority of students who enroll in my

Chicana/o-Latina/o Literature courses at CSUCI are first-generation, bilingual children of Latina/o immigrants and/or children or grandchildren of farmworkers themselves who come from surrounding agricultural communities. Most of the students live at home with their parents and commute, so they themselves currently live or have lived amongst the underserved farmworker communities where they are participating in the reading circles. In this way, my students' experiences depart from traditional service learning models.[1]

This paper presents a case study of these reading circles, particularly the reciprocal exchange of knowledge and the benefits that reciprocity created for both the students and the community members. For, as I learned in final assessment meetings and students' final reflection papers, the mutual benefits were far greater than I had ever imagined or hoped for. Students were able to decolonize their minds by personally engaging with the very populations of whom they had learned to be ashamed; their unlearning of shame was one of the hallmarks of their liberatory education. Through dialogue, the farmworkers learned to own their culture as a productive site of learning. Moreover, one of the greatest benefits that I did not foresee was the power that we, as Latina academics, had to provide models of what Latinas could achieve. We served as mentors to Latina women and children who learned to see university students as peers and the university itself as a democratizing place where they were welcome—a space that now figured into their and their children's present and future reality.

This paper examines how the reading circles implemented feminist and liberatory pedagogies to achieve the following outcomes: 1) enable students and farmworkers to recognize a cultural deficit model and reject it for cultural wealth; 2) build mutual trust; 3) enable the students and farmworkers to become more politically aware and politically active; and 4) bridge the university and community to foster collaborations for lasting reciprocity. I share these narratives and outcomes to provide a model for a service learning course that helps democratize the university and culminates in the type of town- gown collaboration that social justice-minded professors aspire to achieve.

---

1. Special thanks to our community partners, Cabrillo Economic Development Corporation (farmworker housing sites: Villa Cesar Chavez in Oxnard, CA and Casa de Sueños in Camarillo, CA), Community Development Director Priscila Cisneros, Manager Dolores Rodiles, and residents from these housing tracts. Also, special thanks to Pilar Pacheco and Dennis Downey in the Center for Community Engagement at CSUCI, who granted us funds for the books used in the reading circles every semester. Thanks to more than 240 students from ENG/CHS 353 over the course of Fall 2014-Spring 2015 and Fall 2015-Spring 2016.

Pedagogical Approaches

These reading circles with farmworkers are not the first of their nature; my pedagogical approaches align with those undertaken by similar Freirean service learning projects, in particular, J. Estrella Torrez's project with her university students' participation in trust-building dialogues with Latino/a farmworker students who were enrolled in a GED program, especially in the way that her course "encouraged students to dialogue around issues of race, class, gender, and other forms of oppression" and "foster an exploration of big questions of social inequities dividing communities" (2015, 2, 8). As in Torrez's project, the reading circles created safe spaces and "it was within these particular spaces that students exchanged stories in the process of self-reflexivity" (Torrez 2015, 2). But what most distinguishes my case study is its focus on establishing connections between primarily Latina/o students and Latina/o community members and teaching service learning at an HSI rather than a PWI.

Teaching primarily working-class Latina/o students at an HSI provides rich opportunities for community building, but it also poses unexpected pedagogical challenges, different than those that arise when teaching middle-class white students at a PWI. Although my students are primarily Latina/o students, the range of their empathetic identification with Latina/o immigrant communities greatly varied. This is because first-generation Latina/o university students face specific challenges in self-valorization and cultural appreciation; they largely attend the university with hopes of attaining social mobility—of not working in the fields, like their parents or grandparents might have. Furthermore, given that the disparagement of their culture is normalized in the dominant popular discourse, identifying as coming from a Latina/o and/or immigrant background can be regarded as a social disability. For example, Dennis Romero's recent article in the *LA Weekly*, "In Order to Succeed at Work, Some Latinos Hide Their Heritage," reveals how Latinos on the job continue to hide their ethnic difference. Citing a report entitled "Latinos at Work: Unleashing the Power of Culture," which was released by the nonprofit think tank Center for Talent Innovation (CTI), the article states that "While Latinos will account for 80 percent of the growth of the U.S. workforce between now and 2022, three out of four of them say they 'repress their heritage in the office'" (Romero 2016). Hence, along with a college degree, the desire to minimize one's ethnic background is oftentimes deemed as the prime strategy for upwardly mobile success. As a literature professor, I have found that teaching students diverse literature that is culturally relevant and responsive to the surrounding community in and around the educational institution (in our case, a predominantly Mexican and farmworker community) is key in helping them unlearn these self- negating ideologies. But it is one thing to read about farmworkers in literature—it is another thing entirely to break bread and share life stories with them. Service learning is the key piece in catalyzing social consciousness. My pedagogical mission in the classroom is to enable students to unlearn this shame and be able to value and engage with community members as equals; in service learning, I want community members to learn to value themselves. My teaching is informed by a critical race theory lens, particularly Tara Yosso's concept of "community cultural wealth" (2005), because this paradigm-shifting concept enables both students and community members to counter a "cultural deficit" model of thinking about themselves, farmworkers, and their Latina/o culture. Moreover, Torrez's "reconceptualization of the idea of civic engagement by underscoring the consistent cycle of 'server' and 'served'" is particularly useful in understanding the mutually benefitting, non-hierarchical pedagogy undergirding the service learning goals in these reading circles (2015, 4). When she argues that "in transforming this binary into a cycle, students are confronted with the array of differing forms of capital possessed by marginalized communities" (2015, 4), our service learning course's social value takes on a greater valency. For the ultimate result of these reading circles is that both Latina/o students and farmworkers were able to value a cultural capital that they had previously deemed inexistent.

Before students go out into the community, we read the Brazilian educator Paulo Freire's book *Pedagogy of the Oppressed* (1970) in order to help them begin to reflect on their privileged social location and prepare them to be mindful community facilitators and teachers. What I want my students to gain from reading Freire is to unlearn the dominant view that their students—in this case, the farmworker families they will meet with—are not "empty vessels to be filled" with knowledge because they lack valuable knowledge of their own (Freire 1970, 79). Rather, I want students to go out into the community to engage in dialogue with residents from an equitable, non-hierarchical position—to become equal partners, facilitators, and co-creators of knowledge and critical thinking via the shared reading of literature. Ultimately, I want my students to create mutual trust, meaningful dialogue, and an investment in what Freire calls "horizontal relationships." The ultimate goal of education—as Freire states, is "to critique and transform the world [through] dialogue, critical questioning, love for humanity, and praxis—the synthesis of critical reflection and action" (1970, 80). These lessons have been reciprocal, as both Latina/o university students' and farmworkers' participation in the reading circles have enabled them to undergo a process of self and cultural affirmation—a true *concientización*—a critical social consciousness at the heart of liberatory education.

Because the reading circles are composed of female farmworker residents and mostly female students, the course also incorporates feminist pedagogical practices to create true Freirean circles where students are able to create mutual trust between women. I model feminist pedagogy through my own rigorous honesty and vulnerability with the hopes of creating a safe space to enable students to share their own stories, ultimately enabling them to then apply these skills with community members as well. In Chicana/Latina feminist theory, this pedagogical practice is called the sharing of one's *testimonio*—the telling of one's life story. It is "a form of expression that comes out of intense repression or struggle, where the person bearing witness tells the story to someone else" (The Latina Feminist Group 2001, 13). *Testimonio* also involves the unlearning of shame to overcome silence. Because the sharing of once hidden personal stories can develop trust between women, it is "the primary methodology for feminist praxis" that helps create "*comadrazgo*: the Latin American/ Latina tradition of women's kinship, reciprocity, and commitment" (TLFG 2001, 15).

To model feminist pedagogical strategies in developing *comadrazgo*, I use *testimonio* when reading Sandra Cisneros's *The House on Mango Street* in class. We close-read the story "Alicia Who Sees Mice"— which is about a young girl who is the first to attend college despite her patriarchal father's gendered expectations that she live a life of domesticity. In the story, Alicia's father exclaims that "a woman's place is sleeping so she can wake up early with the tortilla star" and we are told that "Alicia, who inherited her mother's rolling pin and sleepiness" takes "two trains and a bus because she doesn't want to spend her whole life in a factory or behind a rolling pin" (1984, 31-32). I share with my students that as the eldest daughter in a deeply patriarchal Mexican household, although my parents always encouraged my education, my father above all expected me to learn to perfect the art of cooking, cleaning, and child-rearing. My mother was very smart, but she never had the opportunity to attend college. She always did all the housework so that I could focus on my studies. I had never met anyone who had ever gone to college, much less a Latina woman who had done so, so when I went to college I saw myself as living out the dream that my mother never had the access to fulfill. Thus, I pair Cisneros's story with *my* story as a way to discuss the gendered roles that Latinas may grow up with at home and how we can use our education and oftentimes, our mother-daughter relationships, to surpass these limiting and debilitating expectations. After hearing my *testimonio* and reading the story together, many students open up about the patriarchal challenges they face at home. This is precisely why I chose to teach this book in the reading circles as well; the many feminist vignettes found within *The House on Mango Street* enable us to air out our families' "dirty laundry" in regards to fathers, husbands, and boyfriends. And the shared airing out of dirty laundry develops trust and kinship between women.

READING CIRCLES

CSUCI's Center for Community Engagement provided me with grants to purchase the books for the community reading circles. They also put me in contact with a community partner that had expressed a desire for community programming and would therefore be a great fit for our service learning: Cabrillo Economic Development Corporation (CEDC), which constructs and manages low-income and farmworker housing in Ventura County. Our students met with farmworkers who lived in CEDC's farmworker housing tracts.[2]

The key to developing and establishing reciprocity in service learning is to develop and establish a respectful relationship with the community partner. A lot of scaffolding is required in the first weeks to meet with the community members; I met several times over coffee with the apartment manager and the housing residents. It was crucial to listen to their needs and concerns—we needed to address the visions of the host community and then, from there, plan and structure our service learning program. Like other service learning facilitators, I believe that "host communities should control the services provided and have significant control over what is expected to be learned" (Stanton, Giles, and Cruz 1999, 3). After several meetings with farmworker families who lived in these housing tracts, together we identified their needs and concerns that could be addressed and enriched through student service and interaction: the need to promote 1) literacy amongst adults and children; 2) critical dialogue about pressing personal, familial, and social concerns; 3) English language skills amongst adults; and 4) afterschool mentorship, tutoring, and support for the children. Together, we planned and established weekly bilingual reading circles where students from my class would come to the farmworker family housing, split up, and

---

2. CEDC was incorporated in 1981 in order to revitalize former farm labor camps in Ventura County; to this day, it has built (and continues to manage) 32 major housing developments for low-income families in the county. Some of the housing tracts require that residents work in the fields in order to qualify for this low-income housing. For more background information, see http://www.cabrilloedc.org/history

read books with groups of adults or children. The readings would then segue into discussions of the community's experiences and concerns.

As part of the service learning project for the course, students pay weekly visits to two sites: Villa Cesar Chavez in Oxnard and Casas de Sueños in Camarillo. My Chicana/o-Latina/o literature class has about 30 students; 15 students attend service learning in the first site and 15 go to the second site, parceled out into three groups of five. Over the semester, each one of the three groups attend the service learning site four consecutive times, once a week. In regards to class assignments, every week each group develops their lesson plans in class before going to meet with the farmworker families, and students formally report on their service learning experiences in the next class meeting. More informally, and perhaps more excitingly, they also integrate what they learned in the field into class discussion.

The course readings I assign are critical in helping students "engage in the critical reflection necessary to understand their service learning experience in the larger context of issues of social justice and social policy—rather than in the context of charity" (Stanton, Giles, and Cruz 1999, 3). As stated earlier, in the first few weeks of class, we read Freire's *Pedagogy of the Oppressed* in order to help students become self-reflexive about their role as students and educators. But the works of literature we read are just as important in helping students value and understand the community and be better prepared to form respectful, socially responsible relationships. I carefully assign novels, short stories, and memoirs that will enable students to gain an understanding of the most pressing issues facing Latino/a communities in the United States—both historically, systemically, and presently. I introduce my students to works of Chicana/o- Latina/o literature written from the Farmworker Rights Movement and Chicana Feminist Movement in the 1960s to the present, with an emphasis on literature that examines Latina/o labor conditions, immigration experiences, gender dynamics, cultural and language identity, and race discrimination. We then use our dialogue about literature in class as a springboard for developing lesson plans that help facilitate discussions with the community about these topics, which are some of the most salient topics facing Latina/os in the United States today.

Together, students and farmworkers read one book per semester in the reading circles; to date, they have read the following works of fiction and non-fiction: 1) Tomás Rivera's *And the Earth Did Not Devour Him/y no se lo tragó la tierra* (1972), short stories about migrant farmworkers, systemic violence in the fields, and discrimination in the schools; 2) Sandra Cisneros's *The House on Mango Street* (1984), short stories about a feminist Latina girl growing up in an underprivileged community racked by poverty, domestic violence, shame, and the stresses of growing up bicultural; 3) *21st-Century*

Latino Leaders: Latinas and Latinos Who Are Transforming Society (2013), which is a collection of biographies of important Latina/o figures such as Sonia Sotomayor, Sandra Cisneros, and other politicians, writers, filmmakers, and artists; 4) Alejandro Morales's *Little Nation and Other Stories* (2014), a collection of short stories about Latina/o Los Angeles, urban development, and police brutality; and 5) Reyna Grande's *The Distance Between Us* (2012), a Mexican immigrant's memoir about challenges on both sides of the border, which includes discussions of domestic violence, transnational family dynamics, and being undocumented in the United States. The majority of the books we read are written by women, per the specific request of the female farmworkers. Such is their desire to feel represented in the literature.

Along with providing relevant topics of dialogue between students and farmworkers, the other major reason I selected the books we read together is because they are available in both English and Spanish, making them accessible to both English and Spanish speakers. We read these books in class together and analyze them for many weeks before students create their own lesson plans to lead discussion about the books within the community reading circles, which typically consist of four-to-six women. Because the students have to read the books in English during class time and read and teach the books in Spanish in the community, they also develop greater bilingual literacy.

Appropriate assessment of the service learning experience for both students and community partners is also a crucial part of the project—it is how we came to learn about the outcomes of reciprocity and the mutual benefits that both parties have gained. In the last reading circle of the semester, we held an assessment meeting where all the students, community member participants, the CSUCI Center for Community Engagement Director, and I partook in a capstone celebration and a *"conviviencia"* (collective, social gathering) where we shared food and heard about everyone's experience in the service learning for the semester. The farmworker women's narratives discussed in this essay stem from the reflections they shared in that final meeting. Finally, as the final assignment of the semester, students were required to write a four-to-five page final reflection paper that connected what they learned in service learning with what they learned in the class. Most of the student reflections I include in this paper stem from that final assignment.

Outcomes: Reciprocity and Mutual Benefits through Unlearning the Cultural Deficit Model

As students shared in their reflection papers, participating in the reading circles with farmworker families enabled them to experience a series of paradigm shifts in the way that they perceive farmworkers, the Spanish language, Latina/o parents and Latina/o culture, the society in which they live, the value of literature, and their education. Likewise, in the final assessment meetings, farmworker participants also shared that they experienced the very same paradigm shifts, especially regarding their culture and their relationship to students and educational institutions. The reciprocity and mutual benefits brought forth by these reading circles, as Torrez notes, is precisely what distinguishes critical service learning: "the consistent cycle of 'server' and 'served' moving throughout the project" (2015, 4)—the equitable, non-hierarchical exchange of knowledge between students and community members. Together, students and farmworkers were able to counter what Yosso terms a "cultural deficit" model of thinking about themselves and were able to own their culture as a site of productive learning (2005, 72).

Indeed, this is what my students immediately learned upon meeting with the farmworker women. They were above all surprised by how much *they* unexpectedly learned from the farmworkers. One student wrote, "Before starting service learning I was really excited about going out into my community and being able to share some of the knowledge that we learned in class. What I did not anticipate, however, was how much these women were going to teach me" (Alejandra, CSUCI student). The usual paradigm that students had bought into was that university students are more learned, that they are imparters of knowledge in relation to the common, uneducated folk. In the case of reading with Mexican farmworkers, these feelings of superiority might be heightened because of the community's marginalized race, class, gender, occupation, and legal status.

Part of the reason that students like Alejandra are so amazed "to be taught something" by farmworkers is that, typically, students' education up to that point has taught them to regard these Mexican farmworker communities through a "cultural deficit" model of thinking. They have learned that people like them have nothing to teach anyone, not even their own children. According to Yosso (2005), "one of the most prevalent forms of contemporary racism in

U.S. schools is this deficit mode of thinking" (70):

> In attempting to explain the widespread underachievement among students of color and students from lower socioeconomic strata

in schools, many teachers, and administrators locate the problem within the students, their families, and communities. This "cultural deficit" model attributes students' lack of educational success to characteristics often rooted in their cultures and communities (ie. that families, communities don't value education and don't help their children succeed). Research grounded in a deficit perspective blames the victims of institutional oppression for their own victimization by referring to negative stereotypes and assumptions regarding certain groups or communities. This perspective overlooks the root causes of oppression by localizing the issue within individuals and/or their communities…Under the cultural deficit model, schools are absolved from their responsibilities to educate all students appropriately, and the blame is shifted almost entirely to students and their families. (2005, 72)

Under this cultural deficit logic, the dominant view holds that Mexican farmworkers in Ventura County find themselves at the bottom of the U.S. socioeconomic ladder because of their lack of determination to invest in and value education in their countries of origin and in the United States. Indeed, that is the dominant view that most students (even Latina/o students) have acquired throughout their education. Negative stereotypes abound in class when I ask, "what prevents Latina/os from succeeding in school?" It's usually the same litany of stereotypes: the parents don't care about education—they value work, the students are apathetic, they never learn English correctly, etc. As part of their education, Latina/o students have come to believe that their people do not have any useful skills or knowledge that they can pass on to their children to enable them to succeed in school; their culture, their language, and values represent deficits in terms of what is required to succeed in the United States. My students admitted to having bought into this cultural deficit model in regards to their preconceptions about farmworker Latino families and Latino families in general. In the words of one student: "I learned that although I am Chicana, I too am susceptible to biases and stereotypes about my own community that are not true such as these women being illiterate because they do not have a formal education" (Jenny, CSUCI student).

While listening to farmworkers' *testimonios*, however, students realized that the stereotype that Latina/os do not value education is untrue; they learned that these women longed for the education that had eluded them because of their disadvantaged means. One student wrote:

> As for the ladies, I was surprised they actually read the book, not in the sense that I thought they were dumb or anything

but surprised in the way that they were eager to learn. I hear a lot of negative stereotypes that field workers are people that are there because they don't want to learn, who didn't want to go to school. These ladies shared their stories as well as relatives of theirs that really would have loved to continue school but because of life they were not able to. But they do not give up on learning and they showed that by being there despite their age and the negative stereotypes. One of them said that some people would tell her why would she want to go read a book for an hour that it was just a waste of time, despite that she was still there. (Maria, CSUCI student)

Students' participation in these reading circles helped them self-reflect and break the cycle of (self-) prejudice against Latino communities: "meeting these women made me grow as a person because it made me realize that I was following the trend people with power often fall in, oppressing communities that are denied the resources to obtain a better education or in most occasions are offered the resources but are forced to prioritize employment to support themselves financially" (Cinthia, CSUCI student). The women's tenacity to keep on reading books and attending the reading circles served as an inspiration for the students to reflect on their educational privileges and keep on going forward with their own education: "These women inspired me to *"echarle ganas"* [work hard, put lots of effort] in my education. They all would reiterate about how they wish they could have continued with their own education" (Bridget, CSUCI student).

In many cases, by learning to value Latina/o farmworkers' stories, students came to value their own parents and their culture—a culture of which they had oftentimes been taught to be ashamed. My first-generation/minority/working-class students learned to value and embrace what Yosso (2005) terms their "community cultural wealth"— the "rich cultural wealth and the assets they bring to the university and society as a whole" (Yosso 2005, 72). Students no longer saw their culture as putting them at a disadvantage, but instead, as bestowing them with assets—language skills, cultural values, feminist ideals, and ethics of hard work ("*echarle ganas*") that would help ensure their success in higher education and in life. And they became ever-grateful and appreciative of their parents' hard work. Said one student, "my experiences in service learning gave me the opportunity to reflect on the sacrifices my parents have made for me to gain an education" (Sandra, CSUCI student). One of the things that students kept highlighting about their service learning experience was that farmworkers "reminded them of their parents," referring to "a feeling of family again," "a second family," and "a second home." Some students might have felt like they were getting a second chance to start over with their parents—and in learning to value the service learning residents' stories and sacrifices, students came to value their own.

Students also learned the moment they stepped into the community that their Spanish-language proficiency, despite its usual perception of being a deficit, is actually an asset that helps them engage with the world around them. Students in the class had varying degrees of Spanish proficiency; some are fully fluent speakers and readers and some understand the language but cannot speak it. In some cases, students admitted to not being taught Spanish by their parents and/ or not wanting to learn Spanish while growing up in order to become "more American." Therefore, having to use (and in some cases, revive) their heritage language created a paradigm shift in the way they perceived and carried out their education. As one student noted, "my Spanish turned out to be a desirable skill. This service learning experience made me proud to put my Spanish to use" (Sandra, CSUCI student). Fluent Spanish-speakers were able to take on leadership roles, lead discussions, ask complex questions, and better engage with the farmworkers. It even let them in on jokes and personal stories (non-Spanish speakers remarked that they sometimes heard the group laugh but didn't understand why and felt left out). Bilingual speakers, for once, got to feel validated for their assets—they could finally use their bilingual skills to bridge the university and community.

The farmworker women also learned to value their "community cultural wealth" by overcoming feelings of low self-worth as uneducated immigrant women. Like the students, these women had also inherited these negative beliefs about themselves—they too had subscribed to the cultural deficit model. Because they were poor and undereducated in Mexico (a very class-conscious, socially stratified society) and were agricultural workers in the United States, the women had normalized being treated condescendingly by the educated class in both countries (treated as *"gente sin importancia"*— people who lack importance). They therefore expressed surprise that the students and I, as Latina academics, "were so smart and educated and yet very humble." One farmworker said "it was really nice to see educated women like yourselves be so kind and inviting. You never made us feel that you were different from us." The women's equitable interaction with the students helped them overturn social hierarchies they had previously learned to internalize. In regards to their culture, the farmworker women had once tended to believe that they had nothing to offer their children—they were grateful to educational institutions, which they then regarded as filling up their children, who they perceived as empty vessels in need of enlightenment. They initially had a passive view of their role in their children's education; however, the reading circles changed that.

In the final assessment meetings, the women shared with us that the literacy building skills they acquired through the reading circles enabled them to become better-equipped to advocate for themselves and their children in school. Many farmworker women told us that the books they got to own and read in these reading circles were the only books they had ever owned in their lives; they had no prior experience reading a text and discussing it. They shared with us that the practice of dialogic reading with CSUCI students enabled them to better help their children with their homework. The students modeled how to ask critical questions and have critical discussions about written materials.

The students served as role models that enabled the women to gain agency in their children's educations. The fact that most of the students were Latinas too made the women feel that their culture or gender were not hindrances in being able to engage with or participate in educational institutions. For example, one mother—Maricela— was able to overcome the embarrassment that had prevented her from attending her children's school meetings. She stated, "meeting all these young Latinas attending the university really inspired me and gave me confidence in myself. *Aprendí a desenvolverme con gente de la escuela*" ("I learned how to engage with and participate with people from school.") The translation of this phrase is very symbolic, though, in relation to the process of feminist empowerment. For, *"aprendí a desenvolverme"* literally translates as: "I learned how to 'unfold' myself, 'unpack' myself with people at school"—it describes the metaphorical blooming of a flower or the unwrapping of a gift. As spending time with Latina students gently eased her into overcoming her feelings of shame and learning to step into her role as her child's advocate, Marisela was able to bloom with the confidence she gained by opening that gift of agency within her. Befriending empowered students from her culture enabled her to use her culture as a source of strength.

A grandmother—Lourdes—also shared that participating in the reading circles encouraged her to become better educated and learn English so that she could also *"desenvolverse"* and set an example for her grandchildren. But in this nation of immigrants, she became a cultural ambassador as well. Lourdes stated:

> Here I was, encouraging my grandkids to *'superarse'* (to better oneself) and I wasn't doing anything to improve myself. I hadn't learned English despite all my years here in the U.S. So I made it my goal to attend ESL classes at the public library. I met lots of immigrants from all over the world—from the Middle East, Ethiopia, India. I made lots of friends from different cultures. We were all there learn-

> ing how to speak English. I learned a lot from them, too. And I taught them about my Mexican culture, too. Every Friday we bring food from our countries, even though we are learning to be American (laughs).

Even at her old age, Lourdes is learning English to be able to engage and participate in the public sphere. But she also draws from her Mexican culture and proudly shares it with students and immigrants from other countries in order to show them that "the Mexican culture is rich and beautiful, no matter what 'El Trump' says."

In a true circle of reciprocity, just as the women's living culture had helped decolonize students' minds, once students were able to decolonize themselves, they in turn were able to help the farmworkers' children begin to do the same. For example, one of the stories that my students read and discussed with the farmworkers' children is "My Name" from *The House on Mango Street*. In that story, narrator Esperanza bemoans the fact that her name sounds too ethnic:

> At school they say my name funny as if the syllables were made out of tin and hurt the roof of your mouth. But in Spanish my name is made out of a softer something, like silver, not quite as thick as sister's name—Magdalena—which is uglier than mine. Magdalena who at least can come home and become Nenny. But I am always Esperanza. I would like to baptize myself under a new name, a name more like the real me, the one nobody sees. (Cisneros 1984, 13)

As part of their lesson, students had the children write about their name and reflect on it. They asked: "Where does your name come from? Do you like it? Why or why not?" Students were surprised to see that many kids whose names were more Latino-sounding, like Esperanza, felt more ashamed of their name and wanted to choose a different one. A seven-year-old girl named Guadalupe said that she didn't like her name. She couldn't articulate the reason for her dissatisfaction, but just kept saying, "I don't know why. I just don't like it. It's just different." In class, students remarked that they were surprised to see how, from a very young age, Latina/o children learn to be ashamed of their culture and aspire to better fit into American society. In little Guadalupe, students saw reflections of their past selves, of the long since forgotten injuries that had led them to learn to devalorize their culture. In the reading circle, students were able to tell little Guadalupe that her name was beautiful, that it was the name of a famous religious figure, and that she should be proud of her name. By helping Guadalupe heal from shame and see her culture as an asset, the students reified these lessons within themselves.

MUTUAL TRUST: FEMINIST PEDAGOGY IN PRAXIS

At first, we were disappointed that only a few men from the community attended the first session and that after they saw that the attendees were mostly women, they never came back. This provided us with an opportunity to create an organically feminist circle. For, above all, the farmworker women remarked that they liked having a weekly hour where they could leave behind ("*el marido*" [the husband]) and their domestic drudgery to do something that was just for them. They liked reading and sharing viewpoints with the female students during what they called their "feminist hour." Guided with feminist pedagogies of *testimonio* (testimony) and *comadrazgo* (women's kinship), this women's space helped create a site for mutual trust and empowerment through reciprocal storytelling. Just as I had modeled *testimonio* by sharing my personal stories while teaching literature in the classroom, students used these strategies to become exemplary facilitators of mutual trust in these community reading circles. My student Vanessa shared how, after reading stories about domestic violence in *The House on Mango Street* in the reading circle, she was inspired to share her and her mother's poignant story with the women. She shared that at the age of 15, she helped her mother kick out her emotionally and physically abusive, adulterer father out of their apartment. After being fed up with his violence, they packed up his things in boxes and threw them out the window. She and her mother got several jobs to support the family without the father's help. Vanessa was courageous, both in what she did and in sharing that story. Her ability to find her voice and rile up her courage— to stand up against patriarchal violence—inspired other women to share.

With this trust-building honesty, many farmworker women overcame their initial fears of public storytelling; students stated that they learned to see women like these farmworkers and their mothers as valiant warriors in the face of "immigration and women's battles against machismo" (Vanessa, CSUCI student). After Vanessa shared her story, Maria—a woman from the community—shared how one day she was fed up with her husband's demands and she had to teach him the hard way that she was not his maid. She grabbed a newspaper, pointed to the wanted ads, and asked him, "Do you want a servant? Because if you do, you can find one here in the job ads. I am not your maid!" My student Alejandra noted: "the women's ability to share their experiences, which I'm sure were not easy to relive, was very inspiring. These women who are often looked down upon for their cultural and language differences earned my admiration in ways that I did not expect. Coming from a patriarchal society, these women have proven to be pioneers, defying gender roles and paving the way for all women to say not to oppression." There was certainly no deficit of feminist beliefs among the community women—the safe space we created simply enabled them to articulate and voice them. Inspired by "Freire's practice of *concientización*, in which communities construct self-reflective political consciousness, [these] Latinas contributed to empowerment efforts through literacy and giving voice, documenting silent histories" (TLFG 2001, 3). In the developing of *comadrazgo* (women's kinship), both the farmworkers and students learned to appreciate the value of female friendships and relationships, which tend to be undervalued in the face of a heteronormative world that teaches women to value above all their relationships to men.

Students' and Farmworkers' *Concientización*: Political Consciousness and Activism

The more students discussed literature and exchanged stories with the farmworkers, the more they reached a *concientización*—a political consciousness—that enabled them to voice critiques about social inequality, self-reflect on their educational privilege, and envision their role in combating systems of oppression. The reading circles truly demonstrate that "literary texts and community service can work reciprocally to heighten (and in some cases introduce) awareness of the complexities of race, gender, and class as they intersect in people's lives—in literature and in the real world" (Grobman 2005, 133). Literature and community engagement served as the conduits between theory and praxis.

For example, reading literature about undocumented people's lack of access to education, combined with speaking to undocumented women, enabled students to acquire a sense of social responsibility—a desire to use their education to work on behalf those who are less privileged. Students and farmworkers reflected on their shared reading of Reyna Grande's *The Distance Between Us* (2012). In regard to a quote about the importance of Latinos pursuing education in the United States, Grande says, "Me and my siblings had been given the opportunity of a lifetime. How could we let it go to waste? ...We owed it to them, our cousins, our friends, to do something with our lives. If not for us, then for them, because they would never be able to" (280, 282). Students shared that reading these heartbreaking passages alongside undocumented farmworker women and hearing these women's poignant testimonies of glass ceilings and shattered dreams in the United States, of low-paying jobs and no way out, made them "reflect on [their] responsibility to take full advantage of the opportunities and resources available to [them]" (Alejandra, CSUCI student). One woman shared that "she had left the fields but now had two other jobs: she worked as a janitor at a gym and at a restaurant." She said that her work was exhausting and not valued, "but no matter what, she always took pride in her work and did her very best job no matter the nature of it." She would have liked to get a job in another line of work, "but given her status, that's all she can work in for now." As Alejandra stated, "Before the semester began, I was unaware of how much legal status matters in this country and what it means to not have status." Reflecting on their privileges (citizenship, access to college) motivated students to use that privilege to work towards social justice for undocumented families.

While reading a short story from Alejandro Morales's book *Little Nation* (2014), entitled "Los Jardines de Versailles" ("The Gardens of Versailles"), the women and students critiqued issues of urban development, displacement of the disenfranchised, disregard for Mexican communities, and gentrification. "Los Jardines de Versailles" is a story set in 1920s Los Angeles that tells the tale of a couple whose beautiful adobe home is destroyed by the city due to oncoming modernization and the building of an electrical grid and infrastructure. When students read the story with the farmworker women, they were able to learn more about how even today, in their own city, poor communities of color are displaced to build freeways that serve the more privileged:

> Service learning taught me a lot about the history of the city of Camarillo. After we finished reading the story "Los Jardines de Versailles," the group told us that a similar story had happened to several Latino families about 10-15 years ago when the Lewis exit off the 101 was constructed in order to create an off-ramp to access the university. I found it surprising to discover how the city similarly tore down a little community in Camarillo essentially to expand the freeway. Now that I live in Camarillo, I didn't realize the history or the events that have happened in this city. Apparently, just like the mayor who wanted to take the property of the couple in the story we read, that is what they did to the Latinos here in this city. (Maria, CSUCI student)

Through speaking to the farmworkers who live in their community, students were able to unearth hidden histories of inequality and educated their classmates when they shared those stories in class. They learned that transportation and access to the university came at the cost of displacing the poor farmworker community who already lacked access to affordable housing. These discoveries led students to ask a series of social justice-oriented questions: How does the city of Camarillo treat its farmworkers today? What else had they done to them? Are farmworkers given access to affordable housing today? What other barrios were destroyed? How is the university implicated in all of this? Students realized that, just like in the story that we had read, these farmworker women were the very people who did not have political representation or a voice in the town hall meetings where city developers laid out their plans for expansion. Thus, the students sought to advocate for these women and their children. One student stated: "I found the dates of town hall meetings and I hope to attend and create a voice for this community that shouldn't be left in the shadows" (Lizbett, CSUCI student).

Faced with the realities of injustice, many students committed to becoming activist-scholars. They began to research and apply to graduate school programs that would enable them to further work on behalf of these communities. My student Jacinta was so moved by what she learned in service learning that she applied and was accepted into an M.A. program in public service and social justice. Jenny is currently getting her Master's in social welfare and Maria is entering a Ph.D. program in clinical psychology; they both plan to work with undocumented families as therapists. Erika began an M.A. program in migration studies. Liliana just received her M.A. in Mexican American studies and is applying to jobs to become a university professor. Students truly acquired a social consciousness about how race, class, citizenship, and gender structure and impact one's social location, experiences, and access to justice in the world. Many are currently seeking to further dismantle these social inequities.

The farmworker women told us that these Latina activist-scholars truly made an impact on them as rising activist-mothers and on their children, who now had college-student mentors to look up to. As my student Karla recalled:

> Marisela said that she brings her children to these reading circles because she wants them to see Latino students that go to college. To have them be inspired by role models and know that it is possible to get a higher education. They aspire to go to college because they see someone of their culture, of their family being able to do it. (Karla, CSUCI student)

One farmworker woman said that "it was really helpful and eye- opening to have discussions of education with Latina/o university students," who themselves have navigated and are navigating the educational pipeline. Above all, the farmworkers truly valued having Latina/o university students as mentors for their children. The children looked up to the students and felt proud to know that they had a friend who attended the university. None of the children had ever met anyone who attended the university, so they looked up to the students who visited their homes on a weekly basis.

After gaining agency through their interactions with these Latina role models, some of the farmworker women have sought to further their education and have become activists in various ways in order to better advocate for themselves and their families. One *señora* is now part of a mother activist group called *"Madres Promotoras"* (Mother Liaisons/ Outreach Workers) that advocates for bilingual instruction in her son's school district. I recently invited her to speak at our university's Center for Community Engagement's "Celebration of Service" event. She said she'd be happy to attend but asked if it was okay to come a bit later since she had a speaking engagement on the local radio station earlier that day. Another woman is part of the non-profit organization House Farm Workers and attends city council meetings to advocate for low-income housing for farmworkers because she says that though she may be fortunate to have low-income housing, most workers like her do not. Lourdes—the grandmother I mentioned earlier—is attending ESL classes and becoming a nascent Latina activist, while two other mothers are now attending community college with the goal of transferring to CSUCI. Thus, from the fields to community college and beyond, we are effectively creating an activist-scholar educational pipeline in the community. In this way, our service learning program carries out values of mutuality and collaborative vision, with "social justice being the logical extension of this mutuality" (Baker-Boosamra, Guevara, Balfour 2006, 481).

The women have effectively learned to see their life stories as sites of valuable knowledge-production. As we plan future collaborations with them, the women have stated that "although they really enjoyed reading stories, they'd now like to start writing their own." Just as interacting with the women helped students feel empowered to seek out social change via graduate school, talking to the students and hearing their stories has helped farmworker women fuel a desire and discover an agency to tell their once-marginalized stories and bring their and their children's lives from out of the shadows. Our next steps are to continue this community partnership with faculty and students in the Spanish department who can enable the women to write and perhaps publish their own *testimonios* about surviving and thriving as farmworker women.

University-Community Partnerships: Fostering Collaborations for Lasting Reciprocity

Our greatest achievement is that over the course of two years of service learning, we have created a lasting, reciprocal, and sustainable community partnership and a diverse educational pipeline that has placed the university within reach for the community. The Chicana/o-Latina/o literature reading circles have effectively bridged the university-community divide: since the program's inception, farmworker adults and their children, who had never stepped foot on campus (even though it is five minutes away), now feel welcome and regularly attend and participate in campus events. I share our experiences and lessons in order to help other teachers develop similar town-gown collaborations and reciprocity through service learning.

The greatest lesson I have learned is that the formula to developing collaboration is creating a respectful and equitable relationship with the community: demonstrating care and appreciation for what they have to say—attentively listening to their stories, letting them know that they have important things to contribute to the university, and encouraging them to share their wealth of knowledge and lived experience within that institution. That recognition and acknowledgment, though it may seem simple and thus easily overlooked, is the true basis for mutual trust and kinship. All of these personal gestures help make community members feel invited, empowered, and acknowledged, and once they feel that the appreciation is genuine, they may feel more comfortable coming to the university because they see it as a place that might in fact value them. That is how we open the doors and create a true university-community partnership.

As a result of the interaction between community and university students that we facilitated through this service learning project, farmworker adults and their children have attended author readings (Luis Alberto Urrea, author of *The Devil's Highway*, a non-fiction book about the U.S.-Mexico border), film screenings (the documentary *Harvest of Empire*), family festivals (CSUCI Science Fair), and forums (on topics such as U.S. policy in Puerto Rico and the aftermath of Hurricane Maria). I have found that the key to having community members attend campus events is extending them a personal, cordial, and sincere invitation that reiterates to them that their stories matter and that their voices, perspectives, and participation are not only important but absolutely necessary to help better educate university students and staff. If they feel valued, they will indeed come. For example, when the parents of forty-three missing students from Ayotzinapa, Mexico visited the CSUCI campus to raise awareness about state-sanctioned violence against poor students in Mexico, I personally called community members and told them that as former residents of Mexico, their perspectives were sorely needed at this event in order to create a more informed dialogue with the Ayotzinapa parents. The *señoras* and some of their husbands came to campus and met with these parents—they conversed with their compatriots within the walls of our university and later shared the insights of their conversations with our students in service learning. Ultimately, through the partnership we established through service learning, we are fulfilling the mission of the university as a site for critical dialogue and social justice within both the local and the larger, international educational community. Perhaps the least expected way that we were able to establish lasting connections and reciprocal affection was through food. The last lesson I learned in the final assessment meetings was that sharing a meal between farmworker families and students helped cement a lasting friendship that has endured over the years. In our last meeting, we organized a potluck with the women: students brought pizza, cake, and cookies for the kids. But *las señoras* surprised us by cooking and bringing traditional Mexican dishes: *ollas de pozole* (beef and hominy soup) and *tamales*. Many of the students, particularly those who lived in student housing, were very emotional because it had been so long since they had had a home-cooked Mexican meal that reminded them of home and "fed their soul." In addition, CSU students regularly experience food insecurity, so they were extremely thankful to be fed and taken care of by the women. The women's generosity and the hard work despite having little financial means really made the students appreciate the community members and all they had done for them. It was a truly reciprocal moment, for the *señoras'* gesture of hospitality was their way of thanking the students for the humility, mentorship, and educational empowerment they brought to their community. As we shared a delicious meal and laughed and cried at the sometimes poignant, sometimes funny stories we shared, we created lasting, reciprocal, loving memories together. And those connections have never faded.

Technology has also really helped in this regard: through various social media platforms, the students, the farmworker women, their children, and I are able to stay connected and continue our partnerships to this day. Several farmworker women also regularly text me for advice such as what to ask their child's high school counselor or what classes to take at the community college.

Ultimately, the service learning that we are carrying out in these community reading circles provides a real-world opportunity to address the realities of demographic change in the United States and improve educational access. Given that Latina/os are the fastest- growing population in the United States and Latino/a students account for the largest growth of college students today, there is a growing need for educational institutions to address the expanding population's educational needs (Fry and Lopez 2012). Moreover, as educators, "we need to equip students with bilingual and bicultural skills to foment stronger relationships within and among these communities" (Torrez 2015, 9). This service learning experience has renewed my belief in the emancipatory, educational, and community- building power of literature, for our experience showed us that reading and discussing stories written by Latina/o authors enabled students and community members to share their own stories and participate in transformative dialogues about gender, race, class, language, and immigrant experiences in the United States. Literature was the catalyst that sparked students' and community members' liberatory education; coupled with dialogue, it enabled them to strive to improve and achieve educational access and social justice for all. At a time when the humanities are seen as expendable and funding for them has decreased, our reading circles prove those ill-informed policies wrong. Even as anti-immigrant sentiments are growing and gaining steam, our reading circles provide a bold contestation against such racism and prejudice. We are developing activist-scholars, community activists, and culturally proud young generations that will serve as future leaders and role models in their own right. In the face of an ever-increasing, hegemonic, state-sponsored hate, we have effectively developed a resistance that is transforming the academy and the nation—one student, one farmworker, one mind at a time.

REFERENCES

Baker-Boosamra, Melissa, Julia A. Guevara, and Danny L. Balfour. 2006. "From Service to Solidarity: Evaluation and Recommendations for International Service Learning." *Journal of Public Affairs Education*. 12 (4): 479-500.

Barber, Benjamin and Richard Battistoni, eds. 1993. *Education for Democracy: Citizenship, Community, Service: A Sourcebook for Students and Teachers.* Dubuque: Kendall.

Cisneros, Sandra. 1984. *The House on Mango Street.* New York, NY: Vintage Books.

Cushman, Ellen. 1999. "The Public Intellectual, Service Learning, and Activist Research." *College English* 61: 328-36.

Freire, Paulo. 1970. *Pedagogy of the Oppressed.* Bloomsbury Academic; 30th Anniversary edition, 2000.

Fry, Richard and Mark Hugo Lopez. 2012. "Hispanic Student Enrollments Reach New Highs in 2011." Washington, D.C.: Pew Research Center, Pew Hispanic Center. Retrieved from http://www.pewhispanic.org/2012/08/20/hispanic-student- enrollments-reach-new-highs-in-2011/

Grande, Reyna. 2012. *The Distance Between Us.* Washington Square Press.

Grobman, Laurie. 2005. "Is There a Place for Service Learning in Literary Studies?" *Profession*: 129-140.

Morales, Alejandro. 2014. *Little Nation and Other Stories.* Houston, TX: Arte Publico Press.

Porfilio, B and Hickman, H., eds. 2011. *Critical Service learning and Revolutionary Pedagogy.* Charlotte, NC: Information Age.

Rivera, Tomás. 1970. *Y no se lo tragó la tierra/And the Earth Did Not Devour Him.* Houston, TX: Arte Público Press.

Romero, Dennis. 2016. "In Order to Succeed at Work, Some Latinos Hide Their Heritage." *LA Weekly*, September 21, 2016. https:// www.laweekly.com/news/in-order-to-succeed-at-work-some- latinos-hide-their-heritage-7408594

Shwartz, Marcy. 2012. "Public Stakes, Public Stories: Service Learning in Literary Studies." *PMLA* 127(4): 987-993.

Schweitzer, Ivy. 2015. "Completing the Circle: Teaching Literature as Community-Based Learning." In *Service Learning and Literary Studies in English*, edited by Laurie Grobman and Roberta Rosenberg. New York, NY: The Modern Language Association of America.

Stanton, T, D. Giles, and N. Cruz. 1999. *Service Learning: A Movement's Pioneers Reflect on Its Origins, Practice, and Future*. San Francisco: Jossey-Bass.

The Latina Feminist Group. 2001. *Telling to Live: Latina Feminist Testimonios*. Duke University Press.

Torrez, J. Estrella, Santo Ramos, Laura Gonzales, Victor Del Hierro, and Everardo Cuevas. 2017. "Nuestros Cuentos: Fostering a Comunidad de Cuentistas Through Collaborative Storytelling With Latinx and Indigenous Youth." *Bilingual Review/Revista Bilingüe* 33(5): 91-106.

Torrez, J. Estrella. 2015. "Construyendo Comunidad: Developing a Bilingual and Bicultural Framework for Community Building." In *The SAGE Sourcebook of Service learning and Civic Engagement*, edited by Omobolade Delano-Oriaran, Marguerite W. Penick- Parks, and Suzanne Fondrie, 67-74. Thousand Oaks, CA: SAGE Publications.

Yosso, Tara. 2005. "Whose Culture Has Capital? A Critical Race Theory Discussion of Community Cultural Wealth." *Race, Ethnicity, and Education* 8(1): 69-91.

Yosso, Tara. 2005. *Critical Race Counterstories along the Chicana/ Chicano Educational Pipeline (Teaching/Learning Social Justice)*. Basingstoke, United Kingdom: Palgrave Macmillan.

Georgina Guzmán is Assistant Professor of English at California State University, Channel Islands. A daughter of Mexican immigrants, she received her Ph.D. in English at UCLA. Her research and teaching interests explore the intersections of social identities, affect, and political consciousness-raising in Chicana/o- Latina/o Literature, U.S. Working-class Labor Histories, Latina Feminisms, and community-based service learning. She received the Community Engaged Faculty Award from the Center for Community Engagement at CSUCI as well as the Classroom Excellence Award from the *California Association of Teachers of English* (CATE). Selected publications include "Healing the Affective Anemia of the University: Middle-class Latina/os, Brown Affect, and the Valorization of Latina Domestic Workers in Pat Mora's *Nepantla* Poetry" in *Latino Studies*, vol. 15, no. 4, 2017, and "The Twenty-first Century Politics of *Latinidad*: Decolonizing Consciousness, Transnational Solidarity, and Global Activism in Demetria Martínez's *Mother Tongue*" in *(Re)mapping the Latina/o Literary Landscape: New Works and New Directions*, Palgrave Macmillan, 2016.

Supplemental Material

"Learning to Value Cultural Wealth Through Service Learning: Farmworker Families' and Latina/o University Students' Mutual Empowerment via Freirean and Feminist Chicana/o- Latina/o Literature Reading Circles"

Georgina Guzmán

Part I: Reflection on the Origins of the Article

This essay is the product of over 200 California State University Channel Islands students' service-learning efforts leading bilingual reading circles with Latina/o farmworkers in Ventura County, CA. My roles in this service-learning project were as planner, mediator, midwife, and scribe, and these experiences changed my life and career forever. Indeed, as I sat in my folding chair in the community room inside the farmworker family housing projects, the words of Mark Twain rang in my head: *"the two most important days in your life are the day you are born and the day you find out why."* That day I found out what I was born to do--bridge the university and the community and help empower students and farmworkers alike. This essay encapsulates everything I hoped to achieve when I took this job as an English professor at a Hispanic-Serving Institution (HSI) surrounded by agricultural fields and workers. I wanted to be of service to the Latina/os working in the fields (whom I witness laboring under the sun while on my way to my air-conditioned office). And I wanted to be of service to my mostly Latina/o students who must also navigate systemic racism despite having made their way into the university.

As an English professor, I strive to use literature as a vehicle to enable people to arrive at social consciousness and begin to imagine--begin to believe in their agency-- to change the world. The very reason I wrote this essay was precisely to document how literature and dialogue enabled my students and our community members to attain profound awakenings into consciousness. I wanted to capture their powerful stories and provide a model of service learning that could be replicated in other parts of the country with the aim of contributing to a larger social movement that seeks to interrogate systems of oppression and dismantle social inequalities.

As a literary scholar, I had never written anything like this essay—I had never written about real-time teaching on the ground. But as I saw community members become activists and my students fired up and going on to graduate school programs, the impact of our reading circles became so glaringly powerful. We had attained something here and I realized that if I didn't write these stories down, they would evaporate into forgotten history. It was upon reaching this realization that the words came in torrents; it was then that the writing came effortlessly and organically, as if my brain and body just needed to let everything out-- to tell the whole world what we had accomplished and how they could do it too. I strived to tell our story in efforts of disseminating its power.

Re-reading this essay in June 2020, in the wake of the heinous murder of George Floyd by Minneapolis PD and the communal uprisings against systemic racism and police brutality against people of color everywhere that it sparked--from Minneapolis to Oxnard, CA-- I believe it was small acts of raising consciousness at the community level such as ours that enabled us to arrive at this larger social movement today. And I am proud of that.

Part II: Description of Research Methods, Findings, and/or Pedagogical Impact

In this essay, I draw from several critical frameworks in order to analyze my students' service-learning experiences: 1) Paulo Freire's theorization of developing non-hierarchical, "horizontal relationships" between teacher and student, 2) Tara Yosso's concept of "community cultural wealth," which counters notions of deficit-thinking about minority communities, and 3) Latina Feminist pedagogical strategies of *testimonio* to develop a safe space in the classroom by modeling vulnerability and creating trust, kinship, reciprocity, and commitment. My rigorous and sustained examination of these three critical pedagogies in this essay led me to be more mindful and intentional about implementing them within my classroom.

For me, writing this essay taught me the importance of listening to every student's story (in the classroom and in the community) and empowering them to create, transmit, and facilitate knowledge-production that is socially relevant to their lives. In class, I am more mindful now about modeling how I would like my students to teach their future students, whether they be in the community or an educational institution: I encourage them to lead book discussions and prompt them to share their own stories. I ask students to write their own questions and concerns about the readings on the whiteboard during the first five minutes of class. I then let those questions guide our conversations. When we discuss class readings, I ask them, "how would you lead a discussion of this text if you were teaching it to your 80-year-old Mexican grandmother? What are some key themes or concepts you need to explain and go over in order to discuss the readings with her?" This is also my subtle way of helping bridge the classroom with the family living room and helping my first-generation college students overcome the alienation that they can sometimes feel at home and at school. Plus, placing the onus of pedagogy on the students helps them develop their own self-esteem and strength as pedagogues in their own right.

I have also found new meaning in the power of *writing* our stories. Listening to the farmworker women, we learned so many of their impactful life stories. I wish we had the capacity to write them down in Spanish, but that is a task in the works. However, what I have been able to do in my Chicana/o-Latina/o Literature class is create a critical autoethnography writing assignment for my students. They must tell their personal stories with a critical lens in order to not just tell their life narrative, but also analyze the significance of their formative life experiences. This writing assignment has been very fruitful and cathartic for students. It oftentimes helps them value their lives, their parents, and their communities. Or not. Sometimes in the process of writing, students learn to critique the patriarchy, racism, colorism, mental colonization, and homophobia that has afflicted them their whole lives.

By reading my students' life stories, I have also grown to develop a pedagogy of compassion and empathy. Students today have overcome life obstacles that I could not even imagine having to go through, and yet, they persevere and shine bright; they inspire me to keep on going. With the COVID-19 pandemic, what has been hardest for me is not being able to be in the classroom creating community with them. And the future of service-learning is uncertain amidst the pandemic. But I find optimism in remembering that our communities have survived many painful historical events and we will continue to survive and thrive no matter what.

Part III: Discussion Questions

1. How can service-learning provide students unique opportunities for meaningful writing, thinking, and reflection in a way that non service-learning classes cannot?

2. Why wouldn't Latina/o college students from farmworker or working-class backgrounds necessarily jump at the opportunity of participating in service-learning with the farmworker community? What does this reflect about their ideas about college?

3. There are many excerpts from student reflection papers included in this essay. Which reflections did you find most moving? Why? How did students' views of the farmworker women change and why?

4. How can service-learning practitioners ensure that service-learning is reciprocal, non-hierarchical, and benefits both parties involved?

5. After reading this essay, what kinds of service-learning partnerships can you envision creating? What community needs are you interested in addressing? Why? Is there any institutional support you can tap into?

RHETORIC OF HEALTH & MEDICINE

Rhetoric of Health and Medicine is on the web at http://journals.upress.ufl.edu/rhm/index

Rhetoric of Health & Medicine (RHM) is a multidisciplinary journal publishing original rhetorical studies (e.g., studies that use theories of rhetoric or persuasion) of health and medical practices involving communication. By rhetorical studies, we mean work that entails more than examining the language or discourse involved in health and medical issues, but that also uses theories of rhetoric to guide inquiry and arrive at nuanced observations about how persuasion works (or could/should work) in discourse and practice. Such studies can combine rhetorical analysis with any number of other humanistic or social scientific methodologies, including critical/cultural analysis, ethnography, qualitative analysis, and quantitative analysis; indeed, RHM seeks to encourage scholarly conversations about health and medicine across fields of inquiry and spheres of practice, in part by publishing inter- and trans-disciplinary research.

'All Smell Is Disease': Miasma, Sensory Rhetoric, and the Sanitary-Bacteriologic of Visceral Public Health[1]

This article by Emily Winderman, Robert Mejia, and Brandon Rogers investigates how sensory engagement (sight and smell) is used to mobilize publics against perceived health threats, these authors offer a strikingly original comparative analysis of public health images from two different points in history. Their analysis builds on a theory of visceral publics to problematize the longstanding raced, classed, and gendered consequences of miasmic thinking.

---

1. *Rhetoric of Health & Medicine*, vol. 2, no. 2 © 2019 by the University of Florida Press.

"All Smell Is Disease": Miasma, Sensory Rhetoric, and the Sanitary-Bacteriologic of Visceral Public Health

Emily Winderman, Robert Mejia, and Brandon Rogers

In this essay, we interrogate the power of sensory rhetorics to craft what Jenell Johnson (2016) defines as a "visceral public": a public bound by intense, shared feeling over a perceived threat of boundary violations. Specifically, we situate miasma—that environmental degeneracy produces bad smells carrying disease— as a historical disease etiology overtaken, but not fully displaced, by the insights of germ theory. This sanitary-bacteriological-synthesis is capable of constituting visceral publics so adeptly because germ theory's explanatory power as a disease etiology continues to rely on the rhetoric of sight and smell as a set of publicly accessible sensory engagements. To illustrate the raced, classed, and gendered consequences of this sanitary-bacteriological-synthesis, we offer a comparative analysis of two images of disease capturing the public imagination: the early 20th century typhoid fever and the 2015–2016 Zika virus outbreak.

On November 4, 1854, Florence Nightingale arrived at the makeshift British Army Hospital in Constantinople, Turkey with almost 40 nurses and nuns. British soldiers were suffering from disease, deplorable conditions, and high mortality during the Crimean War (Bostridge, 2008). Nightingale's report, that the hospital buildings "were in a terrible state of disrepair, with contaminated water supplies and malfunctioning drainage systems," catalyzed the March 1855 Sanitary Commission (Aravind & Chung, 4). The Commission "unclogged drains and removed debris from water pipes. They improved air circulation by installing windows and vents in the roof and washed the walls and floors of the hospital with lime" (p. 4). Nightingale's remarkably effective strategy to address the mortality rates by intervening with the hospital's environment (rather than its inhabitants) was shaped by her allegiance to the sanitary reform movement, a public health intervention that emerged in the early 1800s and peaked mid-century. Connecting poverty and poor sanitation, sanitary reform strategies were undergirded by the now-disproven theory of *miasmatism* attributing disease causation to "harmful odors, mists, or substances (for example, pollution), particularly resulting from organic matter in the environment" (Macdonald, 2004, p. 382). As an olfactory pedagogy, *miasmatism* trained the senses to recognize environmentally produced bad smells as threats to individual and collective health. For instance, in the hot, dry summer of 1858, the River Thames gave off a noxious odor (Halliday, 2001). Rather than assess the smell as simply a nuisance, *miasmatism's* rhetorical connection between smell and disease rendered the Great Stink a public health emergency.

In this essay, we interrogate the power of sensory rhetoric to craft what Jenell Johnson (2016) defines as a "visceral public": a public bound by intense, shared feeling over a perceived threat of boundary violations. We argue the visceral configuration of a public is based upon its rhetorical participation in the sensorium; what Debra Hawhee (2015), citing Joseph Dumit, defines as "the sensing package that constitutes our participation in the world" (p. 5). To advance this theoretical amplification, we situate *miasmatism*—the idea that environmental degeneracy produces bad smells that carry disease—as a historical disease etiology overtaken, but whose logics were never fully displaced, by the insights of germ theory. As a visual and olfactory mode of detecting circulating disease, miasmatic sensory logics were incorporated into germ discoveries to create what David Barnes (2006) names as a public "sanitary-bacteriological-synthesis," allowing *miasma* to retain cultural resonance despite obsolete scientific underpinnings. This transition is important because it established distinct sensory-based knowledge boundaries between public health experts and non-expert publics; the incomplete displacement of miasmatic thought dissociated germ-oriented, scientific publics from miasmatic-oriented, lay publics.

This essay proceeds as follows: we situate the development of public health practice as a constant epistemological negotiation between experts and lay publics and demonstrate how visceral publics become distinguished by unique forms of visual and olfactory sensory rhetorical engagement. We then introduce sanitary-bacteriological-synthesis by explaining why *miasmatism* retains resonance before presenting our comparative visual-olfactory rhetorical analysis of two journalistic representations of diseases capturing the public imagination: early 20th century images of "Typhoid Mary" Mallon and stock photography of Brazilian national Tianara Lourenco that circulated during the 2015–2016 Zika outbreak. From an epidemiological standpoint, we select these diseases because of their comparative asymptomaticity. While typhoid fever usually presents symptoms, "Typhoid Mary" Mallon famously did not (Leavitt, 1996). Similarly, when Zika is sexually transmitted, it often does so while infected persons do not display symptoms

(CDC, 2017). Viscerally alerting and managing those who might be affected by such asymptomatic diseases requires rhetoric. Each disease required a public rhetorical intervention to symbolize an asymptomatic threat. Each also operated according to a raced, gendered, and classed sanitary-bacteriological-synthesis for defining the victims and perpetrators of disease and thus provoked fear based upon physical and national boundary anxieties. Both Mallon and Lourenco were framed as non-native agents of infection. Mallon operates in metonymic terms to enable Irish immigrants to obtain membership as legitimate "white" Americans, whereas Lourenco operates in synecdochal terms to shore up whiteness by excluding infected, Latinx bodies. We close our essay with a discussion about visceral publics and managing fearful threats in public health rhetoric.

Sensory Knowledge Contestation in Visceral Public Health

Circulating definitions of public health often implicate the shifting relationship between scientific paradigms, expertise, and lay public knowledge. During the mid-1800s, public health included the spatial interventions of sanitary reform to meet the demands of explosive urban population growth. This period was also accompanied by a significant consolidation of health knowledge into the domain of professional organizations. For example, the American Medical Association legitimized itself by systematically disrupting midwives' experiential knowledge (Lay, 2000). With the development of germ theory in the 1860s, public health initiatives turned toward community health through projects such as widespread vaccination campaigns (World Health Organization [WHO], 1996). During the Progressive Era, scientific and medical experts began to enjoy unprecedented authority in the production of knowledge and administration of health policy. However, experts such as Dr. Ella Flagg Young, who needed to overcome cultural morality constraints when advocating sexual health education, often appealed to lay experience to resonate with audiences (Jensen, 2007). Instead of intervening with the environment or the community, over the course of the 20th century the third phase of public health attended to curative practices. Mid-20th-century academic hospitals privileged scientific and technological treatments of the governing elite over the widespread distribution of healthcare (WHO, 1996, p. 13). In 1996, the WHO (1996) proposed a fourth phase called "the new public health," concentrating on "equitable access to health services as well as related issues concerning the environment, political governance, and social and economic development" (p. 2).

Global public health professionals' focus on vulnerable communities has been scrutinized for its static, empirical conceptualization of community membership (Montgomery & Pool, 2017). If the promotion of collective health and mitigation of disease is a community effort, then questions of who belongs to the community are central and defining. Indeed, retaining the term "community" is problematic because "communities are assumed to preexist the research, to be timeless, and to be a whole" (Montgomery & Pool, 2017, p. 51). In that static formulation, lay knowledge from disenfranchised "communities" are often culturally stereotyped or dismissed.

Without having to rely on the pitfalls of engaging public health with a locus on a potentially exclusionary concept of "community," rhetoricians of health and medicine have theorized publics as both local and vernacular in order to expand what counts as a public as they adopt, resist, and transform expert knowledge from the ground up (Spoel, Harris, & Henwood, 2014). Rhetorical studies of health have intervened into the theory and practices of publics, drawing out the decidedly contingent, dispersed, and civic dimensions of public health. This holds important implications for how public health conceptualizes the bodies of concern and their capacity to influence recalcitrant, expert knowledge. By conceptualizing publics through a rhetorical perspective, public health stakeholders can displace simplified notions of a singular, monolithic public in favor of a more vibrant, participatory model marked by geographically dispersed and self-organized civic concerns (Keränen, 2014). Robin Jensen (2007) argues that there has long been a complex relationship between scientific experts and the public, and that "lay experiences remain crucial to understanding how health operates and how the people understand their relationship to health and the experts that generate that knowledge" (p. 219). Rhetorical scholars have adeptly accounted for how laypeople and those whose health has been positioned at the margins of society absorb, contest, and resist public health efforts (Bennett, 2015; Malkowski, 2014). When considering the bodies of public health, we must account for the mutually constitutive relationship between discursively molded bodies and specific experience of living in one's embodiment (Scott, 2014).

Johnson's (2016) theory of visceral publics merges considerations of publics as constituted by both discursive bodies and contextually locatable embodiment. Describing a mid-20th-century Massachusetts fluoridation controversy, Johnson extends the definition of what counts as historical discourse and argues that the emergence of publics cannot be explained solely by ideological adherence to scientifically sanctioned knowledge. Rather, visceral publics have two pillars: "they emerge from discourse about boundaries and they cohere by means of intense feeling" (Johnson, 2016, p. 2). The human body and anxieties about its boundaries are crucial because a public's "intense feelings cannot be dismissed as a lack of scientific literacy" (p. 14). Importantly, for global public health concerns, visceral publics are relevant when considering fearful negotiations over *national* boundaries, wherein a "threat is usually imagined in the figure of the faceless stranger" (p. 14). Comparing the visual rhetoric of typhoid and Zika speaks to the threat of both corporeal *and* national boundary violations: Irish immigrant Mallon brought typhoid fever across national, racial, and class-based boundaries in her role as a cook; Zika communication often appears in airports, tourist destinations, or other porous transitional spaces that structure mobilities and ultimately shape relationships between national boundaries.

Amplifying Johnson, we foreground how sensory rhetoric constitutes a visceral public and legitimates their operative health knowledge. Public health is inherently visceral insofar as public health rhetoric appeals to a contextually situated participation in the sensorium. Hawhee (2015) encourages scholars to consider the sensorium as "a bundle of constitutive, participatory tendrils, [that] may help to [. . .] think about the connective, participatory dimensions of sensing" (p. 5). The shared sensory experience necessary for the visceral understanding of public health need not encompass corporeal bodies' physical proximity to one another. Rather, rhetoric can draw out and direct the sense perception of individual bodies into a larger formation of a visceral public. Metaphor, synecdoche, and metonymy amalgamate individual sensing bodies into visceral publics because they offer perspective (metaphor), present a manageable, representative experience (synecdoche), or reduce complex experiences to a perceived essence (metonymy) (Burke, 1945/1969). In comparing the early 20th-century reaction to typhoid and contemporary public reaction to Zika, we heed Hawhee and Christa Olson's (2013) call for pan-historiography, or the practice of writing histories across spatial and temporal generational confines to supplement synchronic deep dives into an important rhetorical moment.

Tracing the rhetorics equipping a visceral public with sensory knowledge can prove daunting, especially when engaging with historical materials. First, we cannot assume the sensory rhetorics galvanizing a public within our current contextual configuration would have done so in the early 20th century. Alain Corbin (2005) cautions researchers to avoid denying the historicity balancing the "configuration of the tolerable and intolerable" (p. 130). For example, bathing is a relatively recent phenomenon, rendering Western contemporary olfactory capacities less willing to find body odors tolerable (Bushman & Bushman, 1988). Second, we must also grapple with what Corbin (2005) calls the "transience of evidence," or researchers' inabilities to ever fully recreate a past sensory experience through textual description alone (p. 131). Despite our inability to fully connect a sensory experience to a larger, public emotional transformation, sensory rhetoric remains potent nonetheless; while we can never be absolutely certain whether the document or event served as the cause or "more simply the crystallization" of new visceral rhetorics, their presence nonetheless helps to shape subsequent behavior (Corbin, 2005, p. 135). This matters not only because our sensory encounters can shape our behavior, but also because they can function as affective constitutive rhetoric to viscerally mold the boundaries of a shared national identity (Gruber, 2014). The sensory dimensions of rhetoric constitute the viscerality of public health, especially when the boundaries of expertise are at stake.

This essay examines how the olfactory and visual elements of the sensorium ground what Davide Panagia (2009) calls the "'sensible,' mean[ing] both 'what makes sense' and 'what can be sensed'" (p. 3). For a visceral public uninitiated into technical health expertise, a miasmatic disease explanation largely *makes sense because it can be sensed* via sight and smell, specifically. Thus, representations of noxious smells and visual decay can warn of a miasmatic presence that must be avoided at the risk of infection. Therefore, although Hawhee (2015) reminds us to consider the sensorium as a totality, not mechanized into discretely intelligible senses, the majority of our investigation centers around the roles of sight and smell pervasive within miasmatic disease etiologies.

Seeing Smell

Smell has not enjoyed nearly as much scholarly attention as visuality in rhetoric and media studies, likely due to the fleeting nature of olfactory evidence that Corbin (2005) observes. Nevertheless, the human olfactory capacities hold profound power to move individual and collective bodies. Spatial theorist Yi-Fu Tuan (1977) argues, "[o]dors lend character to objects and places, making them distinctive, easier to identify and remember" (p.11). Similarly, Constance Classen, David Howes, and Anthony Synnott (1994) argue olfactory norms constitute power relationships between different social groups across the West. Specifically, olfactory disgust can reduce the sociopolitical ensemble of disease to a private visceral reaction of something to be avoided (Cloud, 2014). For example, in the aftermath of the 2010 Haiti earthquake, Oprah Winfrey implored her viewers to imagine the "smell of decomposing bodies" (Cloud, 2014, p. 48). Olfactory rhetorics are central to disease rhetoric because disgust evoked by "diseased" smells can encourage visceral publics to avoid or demonize bodies visually represented as occupying disgusting spaces.

Circulating visual rhetoric implicating smell is central to the sensory transformation of disease systems. Rhetorical theorists have long accounted for the role of visual rhetorical representation and circulation in constituting, managing, and transforming publics (Finnegan, 2010). While Laurie Gries' (2015) work on visual circulation and virality speaks specifically to a contemporary context marked by rapid circulatory power afforded by new media technologies, her framework still resonates with how historical images of disease and contagious bodies moved through divergent "spatiotemporal flows" such as journalistic representation. While circulation is crucial to understand the spatiotemporal movement of images, examining visual composition, including color, light, and spatial arrangement within images helps to understand the sensory rhetorical appeals operative in cases of epidemic disease (Finnegan, 2010).

Visual rhetorics of smell are a rich analytic reservoir for interrogating the sensorial texture of visceral public health because the visual freezes an olfactory scene. Olfactory rhetoric enthymematically instantiated in an image functions as a public health pedagogy, instructing a visceral public to engage its senses to identify "miasmatic" individuals and remain on guard for their unwelcomed "invasion" (Omaar & de Waal, 1993; Sturken, 1997). Problematic images of disease reinforce preexisting biases and forms of systemic discrimination (Omaar & de Waal, 1993; Sturken, 1997). Taken together, when analyzing visual rhetoric, a consideration of rhetorical olfaction requires a thorough understanding of the contextual anxieties about bad odors and environmental degeneracy circulating at the time.

The historical transition from miasma to germ disease etiologies illuminates how public health has *always* been visceral, awaiting activation by the sensory rhetoric circulating throughout public culture. This transformation demonstrates how the sensorium has been imbricated in collective disease definition. We next historically contextualize and explicate *miasma* by positioning its implication in social issues and the construction of health-related moral standing. This moral dimension is crucial to understanding how the social judgments made possible by *miasmatism* were never fully abdicated, but instead blended into germ theory to create what Barnes (2006) has called a "sanitary-bacteriological-synthesis."

Epidemiological Transformations: Miasma, Germ Theory, and Sanitary-Bacteriological-Synthesis

Miasma has been a part of cultural lexicon since ancient Greece. The *OED* traces the term to the notion of *staining*: "to stain, sully, defile." In *Miasma:*

Pollution and Purification in Early Greek Religion, Robert Parker (1983) notes, the *mia-* prefix refers to a sense of "defilement, the impairment of a thing's form or integrity" (p. 3). Miasma referred to the following features of Greek life: "it makes a person affected ritually impure, and thus unfit to enter a temple: it is contagious: it is dangerous, and this danger is not of a familiar secular origin" (pp. 3–4). Miasma remains tethered to the notion of pollution and impurity, with its presence implying immorality and requiring social isolation for the infected.

Miasma has come to focus on how disease can spread through the olfactory capacities of humans and animals. The *OED* further defines miasma as "noxious vapour rising from putrescent organic matter, marshland, etc. Also in extended use, formerly believed to be the carrier of various infections." As Barnes (2006) summarizes, "the claim that foul-smelling odors caused emanations that spread disease is quintessential *miasmatism*" (p. 44). Edwin Chadwick's *Report on the Sanitary Condition of the Labouring Population of Great Britain* (1842) famously attributed cholera—which Michael McCarthy (1987) argues is a "cousin of typhoid"—to urban miasmas brought on by influences from the industrial revolution (p. 24). Chadwick wrote, "All smell is, if it be intense, immediate acute disease; and eventually we may say that by depressing the system and rendering it susceptible to the action of other causes, *all smell is disease*" (Halliday, 2001, p. 1469, emphasis added). While Chadwick's aphorism "all smell is disease" circulated widely, his extended claim revealed miasmas were capable of transgressing the borders of the body, rendering them susceptible to environmental influences. This aligns both with Johnson's (2016) argument about visceral publics constituted through a perceived threat of boundary violation *and* Brennan's (2004) theory of affective transmission positing that unconscious olfaction "alters the biochemistry and neurology of the subject" (p. 1). Chadwick similarly described affective transmission, stating "smell is disease" because a *miasma* acts on the body, depresses it, and opens it up to the proximal environmental influences. Germ theory, in contrast, argued the reverse: "fermentation, putrefaction, and infectious disease were caused by specific microbes found in the air and on surfaces" (Magner, 2005, p. 310).

While germ theory began disseminating internationally after 1864, it never fully overtook theories of *miasmatism*. Despite a rising scientific consensus of germ theory, the two paradigms overlapped because, for lay publics, there was little meaningful difference between diseases caused by microbes and miasmas. Indeed, "for most [19th-century] observers, there was no clear and practical distinction between miasmas and microbes" as the distinction "made no apparent difference in the everyday effort to prevent or cure human disease" (Barnes, 2006, p. 45). Miasma functioned as a ubiquitous, but ephemeral rhetoric that considered threats to collective health in terms of their sensory and spatial characteristics. Miasma remained compelling for it "allowed one to work at the impasse of environmental and biological etiology" whereas "bacteriology insisted it was all just germs" (Lessy, 2008, p. 4).

Despite eventual consensus around the veracity of Pasteur's developments, germ theory has always been haunted by specters of *miasmatism*, as Barnes (2006) argues in his "sanitary-bacteriological-synthesis" framework:

> Sanitary-bacteriological-synthesis brought the common sense cultural appeal and broad applicability of the old knowledge (for example that foul-smelling substances are bad for one's health) into harmony with the specificity and scientific mastery inherent in the new knowledge of microbes. This integration took place through the language of bacteriology, with a persistent overlay of moralizing disgust, and gave rise to a new set of meanings and practices that have shaped the understanding of disease to this day. Although it is now put to use for different diseases and in different settings, the sanitary-bacteriological-synthesis governs responses to infectious disease in the early twenty-first century even more powerfully than it did in 1900. (p. 3)

To explicate this blended theory, Barnes examines two important French public health events: The Great Stinks of 1880 and 1895 where "more than a mere annoyance, the stench that gripped [Paris] between late July and early October of 1880 represented a genuine public menace" (p. 12). While Pasteur was famous for his work with Silk Worms at the time and had inklings of what would eventually become a solidified germ theory, he had not concluded this principle with the utmost certainty. Considering the foul air was articulated to a decline in public health, miasmatic explanations of the Great Stink of 1880 were unsurprisingly the common refrain. By 1895 "all but a few hold outs" were on board with germ theory (Barnes, p. 2). Whereas almost anyone could once smell the purported danger of miasma, germ theory required the lay public to abdicate faith in their own sensory knowledge in favor of faith in the sensory equipment of scientific experts. Yet, miasmatic logics still crept into characterizations of the second Great Stink, demonstrating a more gradual and messy shift between bacteriology and sanitary imperatives.

The narrative capacity of *miasmatism* has enabled it to retain such a viscerally potent cultural and scholarly trace, even after the miasmatic approach to disease was fully disproven. For instance, contemporary organizational miasma theory describes "a contagious state of pollution— material, psychological, and spiritual—that afflicts all who work in certain organizations that undergo sudden and traumatic transformations" (Gabriel, 2012, p. 1137). Environmental themes also permeate Yiannis Gabriel's understanding of organizational miasma:

> [Miasma] is a state of rottenness for which individuals may be responsible [. . .], but that infects the entire state. A fundamental property of miasma is that it is highly contagious [. . .]. Once unleashed, the miasma is capable of afflicting everyone. (p. 1145)

This fundamental pollution of the organizational environment cannot be fully traced back to an individual, solidifying miasma as a diffuse, yet dangerous force.

Because miasma and its perceived effects are not always visible (due to asymptomatic carriers, for instance), miasmatic traits are easily inscribed onto the community spaces of which the "other" is a part. Typhoid fever and Zika offer two additional cases to examine how public health imperatives are viscerally marked by the blurring of the disciplinary boundaries between bacterial and miasmatic disease logics. Next, we illustrate how the sanitary-bacteriological-synthesis Barnes discusses is operative in the public frenzy surrounding the case of "Typhoid Mary" Mallon. We follow this section by analyzing the portrayal of Lourenco in contemporary Zika coverage. Although Zika coverage overwhelmingly features infants affected by microcephaly, our juxtaposition of Lourenco (who was frequently featured as the face of Brazilian Zika) with Mallon allows for us to illustrate how poor, ethnic women have been and continue to be understood primarily as vectors of disease transmission as opposed to victims of disease systems in their own right. By situating Mallon and Lourenco in terms of miasmas *and* germs, each image directs the olfactory imagination of the public toward contagion and population control. Through visual-olfactory rhetorics, Mallon and Lourenco come to viscerally represent what it means for a body *and* a nation to be healthy or diseased. Both women we examine, in disparate spaces and times, therefore contribute to sensorially grounded U.S. visceral publics based on their respective threats to public health.

"Typhoid Mary" Mallon: Visualizing Miasmas and Germs

Typhoid fever can be traced back to 430 BCE. Comprised of the bacteria e. Salmonili, typhoid attacks the intestines and spreads through bodily contact with infected feces (CDC, 2014). Typhoid decimated the Jamestown colonies between 1607–1624 and killed far more Civil War soldiers than combat wounds (McCarthy, 1987, pp. 53–57). With the disease's lengthy historical record, it has been unsurprisingly associated with *miasmatism*. Even after germ theory gained popularity in France, many insisted typhoid was of a miasmatic origin. In Bogota, "Colombian doctors showed little interest in the new theory of germ identity of typhoid during the 1880's" (García, 2014, p. 29). Rather, a number of physicians offered a miasmatic explanation, consolidating attention on "besieged cities, in prisons and camps, that is, places where people accumulated" (pp. 31–32). In a true sanitary-bacteriological-synthesis, physicians "mixed the old miasma terminology with germ terminology until the end of the [19th] century" (p. 42). Even with the 1897 Bogota typhoid surge, public health officials relied upon miasmatic explanations.

Rather than assuming that cultural differences kept Colombian health officials from adopting germ theory, we can observe how public health rhetoric during France's Great Stink of 1880 elucidates the blend of *miasmatism* and germ theory in Pasteur's own backyard. Germs associated with typhoid around 1880 meant "'germ' in the older, more general sense—a seed of disease [. . .]. This early case provides a clear and straightforward example of how the new germ theory was linked with and integrated into the old etiology of filth and transgression" (Barnes, 2006, p. 203). Despite the increasing hegemony of germ theory, *miasmatism* retained cultural currency. There is perhaps no better case study to examine *miasmatism*'s obstinacy than in the early 20th century U.S. case of "Typhoid Mary" Mallon.

The name "Typhoid Mary" articulates a history of public health, scientific discovery, cultural memory, racial negotiation, and epidemiology at the beginning of the 20th century. As the first reported North American "healthy" typhoid carrier, Mallon threatened distinctions between sick and healthy bodies and acted as a transitional object for negotiating the theories of germs and miasmas (Leavitt, 1996, p. 14). In transforming Mallon into Typhoid Mary, public health officials created an ethnic, gendered, and classed metonymic understanding of disease transmission. Blurring meaningful distinctions between differences, "[m]etonymy [. . .] allows us to use one entity to *stand for* another" (Lakoff & Johnson, 2003, p. 36). This makes it difficult to recognize the entity that has been replaced, as there is no longer any second entity. As such, the metonymic transformation of Mallon into Typhoid Mary threatened to subsume the ethnic, gendered, and classed essence of Irish immigrants writ large, and it operated as a visceral public health pedagogy about corporeal and national boundaries. Olfactory engagement with visual representations of Typhoid Mary enabled this operation. To illustrate this claim, we next examine Mallon's transformation into Typhoid Mary.

Born in Ireland in 1869, Mallon immigrated to the United States as a teenager. Mallon made a name for herself as a talented New York cook who served the city's elite families. By 1907, she had infected around twenty people with typhoid (Leavitt, 1996). The New York City Health Department forcibly retrieved Mallon's fecal samples and isolated her for three years in Health Department custody (Leavitt, 1996). In 1910, Mallon was released from her quarantine provided she never cook again. When health authorities found her cooking in 1915, they returned her to isolation for the rest of her life. By the time Mallon died in 1938, she had been "a special guest of the city of New York" for twenty-six years (Oliver, 1941, p. 266).

Mallon emerged at a kairotic moment in U.S. history when the emerging legitimacy of public health expertise intersected with the significant transformation of American racial politics. According to Marouf Hasian (2000), "At a time when bacteriology needed legitimation and 'public health' sought public recognition, 'Typhoid Mary' was a rhetorical vessel that invited various publics to see the importance of giving medical power to health officials" (p. 128). Simultaneously, the perception of Irish immigrants transitioned from a "looming threat to U.S. civilization and to Anglo-Saxon reproduction" to conditional members of the "American Race" (Roedigger, 2008, p. 137). Sara Josephine Baker (1939/2013), Mallon's physician, could thus view the Irish as simultaneously "incredibly shiftless, [. . .] wholly lacking in any ambition and dirty to an unbelievable degree" *and* "altogether charming in their abject helplessness" (p. 57). These exigencies—the medical community's need for public legitimation *and* the shifting U.S. racial politics—contextualized how Mallon gave bacteriologists the publicity they needed to legitimate themselves. For Priscilla Wald (2008), "accounts of Mallon suggest that ethnicity, class, and occupation, combined with her condition, ensured her transformation into an object of disgust and reprobation in the public-health and medical literature of the period. [ ]

She seems startlingly typecast for her role in the narrative" (p. 96).

Typhoid Mary's status as a transitional object for miasmatic and bacteriological logics emerged through vivid representations of her contagiousness. In the April 1, 1907 edition of *The Evening World*, reporters identified Mallon as a "walking typhoid fever factory." A day later, their rival the *New York American* described Mallon as a "Human Typhoid Germ." The original use of the term was more descriptive than pejorative because doctors and other investigators actually did not know the name of Mallon and used "Typhoid Mary" as a means to refer to a "Mary" who had typhoid. This alter ego eventually transformed Typhoid Mary into an epistemological transitional object for bacteriology (Leavitt, 1996). Typhoid Mary could then become a caricature and container of bacteriology that simultaneously localized and domesticated the germ within her (Gilman, 1988, p. 1).

Even with such headlines that referenced Mallon as a bacteriological entity (for example, a walking typhoid fever factory, a human typhoid germ, a living human culture tube, etc.), newspapers described Typhoid Mary in terms of a sanitary-bacteriological-synthesis. Specifically, they framed typhoid as a miasmatic disease wafting through the city's public spaces. In Mallon's first media portrayals, New York newspapers such as *The Evening World* ("Woman 'typhoid factory,'" 1907) and *The New York American* ("Human typhoid germ," 1907) characterized typhoid—and by extension Typhoid Mary—through both miasmatic and bacteriological logics.

In June of 1909, around the same time as Mallon's first plea for release from quarantine, the *New York American* ("Typhoid Mary," 1909) debuted a memorable illustration of Typhoid Mary (see Figure 1). Mallon's caricature stands in light clothes and an apron as she drops small, egg-sized skulls into a dark skillet. The 1907 and 1909 newspaper articles emphasize moral ambiguity and the lack of agency in Mallon's autonomous process of breathing. In particular, *The Evening World's* 1907 article specifically addresses her miasmatic elements: "She is immune, though with every breath she takes she draws in and exhales a cloud of dreaded bacilli" ("Woman 'typhoid factory,'" 1907, p. 8). In this context, Mallon is unwittingly a mobile diffuser of contagion—a woman who miasmatically taints every kitchen she occupies. An olfactory representation of typhoid fever as an airborne disease also manifests in the cooking-skulls illustration through the vapors moving from the skillet to Typhoid Mary's mouth or nose (and vice versa). The fumes do not originate from a heated skillet, but from Mallon and the skulls themselves. The miasma moving between Mallon and the skulls viscerally signifies an olfactory danger to the ostensibly healthy Anglo-Saxon bodies viewing the image, reminding them that typhoid threatens the boundaries of their bodies and homes through their domestic workers.

After Mallon's first quarantine, this illustration faded from the popular press, but it resurfaced after public health authorities isolated Mallon for the second time. In the July 11, 1915 *Richmond Times*, the image reappeared with text vilifying Mallon's "ignorance" and inability to respect public health expertise ("Microbe Carriers," 1915, p. 42). After her second quarantine, the authors direct attention towards Mallon's agential acts of malediction. The accompanying text focuses on her hands dropping skulls into the skillet: "These 'microbe carriers, almost always perfectly healthy themselves, exist by the hundreds. They are the most dangerous when they prepare food. It is then that they unwittingly 'season' with the germs of deadly disease—dropping, indeed, death into the cooking vessels" ("Microbe Carriers," 1915,

p. 42). Here, the hands, not the mouth or nose, produce contamination, foregrounding Mallon's spreading of germs. Unlike the autonomous nature of the diaphragm, the hand requires agential movements to drop or spread death. While the image of Mallon remained the same in both articles, the descriptions oscillated between foregrounding miasmas and germs as public health threats.

Figure 1. "Typhoid Mary," *New York American*, 1909.

The endurance of the fumes within the illustration combines—rather than transitions or separates—the miasmatic and germ epidemiological paradigms. Be it through her malevolent, agential fingers or the wafting dangerous air, Mallon's disease infects the corporeal boundaries around her and is thus a threat to be sequestered. As her lifelong quarantine attests, Typhoid Mary is a diffuse contamination and a pointed contagion; she must be removed from the public to ensure collective health. Isolating her on New Brother's Island facilitates miasmatic and bacteriological responses from the visceral public that her figuration constitutes.

Although the language about typhoid transmission shifts over time to more closely align with the disease's contemporary epidemiology, the cooking-skulls illustration recirculates a visual metaphor of contagion in which typhoid contaminates the very air we breathe. The 1915 text does not describe Mallon as a miasma, but her quarantine and the circulation of the 1909 image speaks to her role as a sanitary-bacteriological object. Her synthesized epistemological function manifests through this illustration and changing in-text descriptions. The cooking skulls image presents Typhoid Mary as a transitional figure and personification of a miasmatic microorganism. Like a bacterium, she infects whatever she touches; like a miasma, she sweeps disease from kitchen to kitchen around the city. If one follows the smoke in this image, the origin of the noxious fumes is unclear. So too is the ontology of and response to typhoid fever. Is Typhoid Mary exhaling or inhaling the "bad air"?

Considering early twentieth century racial politics, such a question may not have mattered. At the time, Irish immigrants were one step removed from miasmic conditions and were themselves a miasma to white communities. The Irish were viewed as vying with "the Russian Jews [. . .] for the distinction of living in the most lurid squalor [. . .] out of a mixture of discouragement and apparent shiftlessness" (Baker, 1939/2013, p. 70). Typhoid Mary cautioned Anglo Americans *and* Irish Americans, the latter as conditional Americans. For although Irish immigrants were beginning to be perceived as legitimate members of the "American Race" (Roedigger, 2008), "all forms of media from the period [characterized Irish women servants as] lazy, slovenly, dirty, [and] unskilled (especially at cooking)" (Wald, 2008, p. 97). Likewise, medical description of Mallon "consistently underscores her departure from conventional norms of white femininity, as, again, is consistent with depictions of Irish women servants generally" (Wald, 2008, p. 97).

In this regard, Typhoid Mary became a visceral metonymic caricature of racial anxiety. For Anglo-Saxon Americans, Typhoid Mary served as a reminder of the kind of immigrant one should avoid; for Irish Americans, Typhoid Mary served as a warning against the kind of immigrant one should avoid *becoming*. Nonetheless, it is precisely because Typhoid Mary operated metonymically (as a potential type of Irish immigrant) as opposed to synecdochally (as a representation of *all* Irish immigrants) that popular perception remained optimistic of the Irish pulling "themselves up out of the ruck" (Baker, 1939/2013, p. 70). Not all ethnic communities are so fortunate.

Comparing typhoid and Zika illuminates the public health consequences of figuring the miasmatic as a synecdochical representation of the whole. Just as our analysis of typhoid illustrates how germ theory operates as an extension—as opposed to a replacement—of miasmatic theory, the history of Zika illustrates how the gendered, raced, and classed politics of this epidemiological extension operate in contemporary terms.

Zika: Miasmatic Bodies and Infected Innocents

Although identified in 1947, medical interest in Zika remained sporadic until 2013 when a large outbreak occurred in French Polynesia, Easter Island, the Cook Islands, and New Caledonia (Kindhauser et al., 2016). Zika did not emerge as a sustained global concern until Brazil reported the first confirmed case of Zika in the Americas (on May 7, 2015) *and* a notable increase in newborns with *microcephaly*, severely small heads, which often hinders brain development (on October 30, 2015) (Kindhauser et al., 2016). Only at this point did the WHO's epidemiological interest in Zika increase from 18 entries (1947 to April 2015) to 68 entries (May 2015 to February 2016 [last updated February 2016]) (Kindhauser et al., 2016). While this accelerated rate of global response seemingly speaks to the previously unknown epidemiological severity of Zika, its prior outbreaks were under-investigated due to its clinical similarity to and frequent co-occurrence with outbreaks of other "mild" flaviviruses, such as Dengue, Chikungunya, and Yellow Fever (Kindhauser et al., 2016). These diseases often manifest in conjunction with Zika precisely because they share the same vector: the *Aedes Aegypti* mosquito (Pan American Health Organization & WHO, 2015). Zika can also be sexually transmitted, implicating the relational politics of race, gender, and sexual morality into its epidemiological discussions. After Zika was associated with infant microcephaly, the WHO declared Zika to be a Public Health Emergency of International Concern (Kindhauser et al., 2016). This timeline emphasizes how concern about disease is driven by which bodies are considered victims and vectors. Similar to Typhoid Mary, a sensory-driven, sanitary-bacteriological portrait of a Brazilian national, Tianara Lourenco, configures and collapses the relationship between victim and vector, generating visceral publics fearful of Zika and the bodies marked as capable of spreading it.

Focusing on the seemingly innocuous images of Lourenco, next we demonstrate how, just as with Mallon, journalistic representations of poor, non-Western women can activate a visceral public when figured as vectors of disease transmission. Although our interest in Lourenco's images may appear odd when contrasted against the ubiquitous circulation of images of infected infants born with microcephaly, the comparative invisibility of Lourenco warrants our attention precisely because circulation indicates an image has successfully met composition, audience, and formal needs (Smith, 2012, p.84). Our analysis of Typhoid Mary illustrates that the power of modern epidemiology, when filtered through journalistic media, is in its ability to act as a sensory pedagogy for non-expert publics to detect threats. By texturing a space as a miasmatic reservoir of disease and by simultaneously defining a body, behavior, or even population as a germ of disease transmission, sensory-driven health rhetoric is capable of activating visceral public health threats. Mallon's transformation into Typhoid Mary served as a metonymic warning of a specific ethnic essence needing to be sacrificed if the Irish were to fully become members of the white race. In contrast, Lourenco's images circulated in an environment where Latinx communities have long been perceived as always-already infected (Molina, 2011). Hence, Lourenco's relatively unacknowledged circulation vis-a-vis images of microcephalic infants, and in contrast to Mallon's hypervisibility, can be explained by a visual-olfactory instantiation of Lourenco's synecdochical relationship with the problematic history of Latina representation.

Isabel Molina Guzmán and Angharad Valdivia (2004) argue that "dominant representations of Latinas and African American women are predominately characterized by an emphasis on the breasts, hips, and buttocks. These body parts function as mixed signifiers of sexual desire and fertility as well as bodily waste and racial contamination" (pp. 211–212). If *miasmatism* has never fully departed, Latinx corporeal representation as waste clarifies the threat of their bodies spreading disease to Nations and publics anxious about porous boundaries. Each photograph of Lourenco features her wearing only a sports bra and cutoff shorts (see Figure 2).

Figure 2. Photo credit: Felipe Dana. This screenshot of *The Seattle Time*s (Barchfield & Savarese, 2016) illustrates how Lourenco's body has been incorporated into Zika coverage. (Screenshot by Authors)

These images are indicative of the mixed signifiers associated with Latinx representation, for a Google reverse image search (conducted on August 12, 2018) reveals Lourenco's image has circulated beyond Zika-related websites and onto several pornographic and sex trafficking websites. Without even referencing Zika, one non-pornographic website features Lourenco's image for an article on how "the sexual objectification of Brazilian women hurts" (Axelrod, 2017).

Contrasting Lourenco's images to the stock photograph in *Fortune*'s article about a CDC Zika travel warning (Mukherjee, 2016 [see Figure 3]), some of the basic features of *miasmatism* emerge and deftly blend with germ logics. Unlike the cleanliness of the Fortune photograph— which features full lighting and the subject wearing laundered workplace attire, Lourenco is intricately part of the damp, musty scene (see Figure 2). The poor lighting and uneven contrast renders the space productive of a noxious olfactory atmosphere. Lourenco's body is embedded within the miasmatic environment, indivisible from the scene of abject poverty, and fully subject to the environmental decay surrounding her. Because Zika is also sexually transmitted, Lourenco's body is also intelligible as infectious to sexual partners and future generations of children.

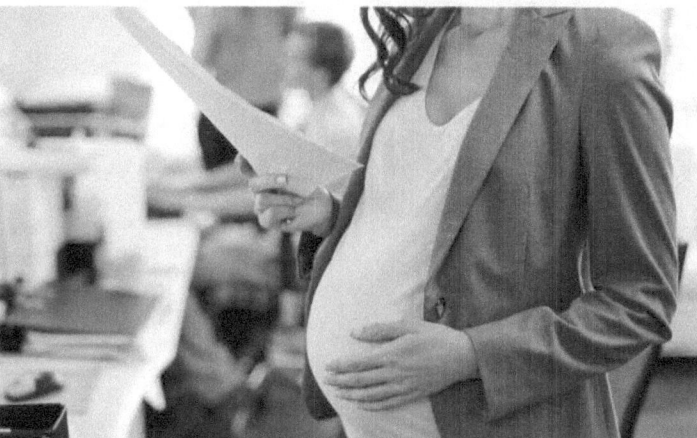

Figure 3. Photo credit: Paul Bradbury. This screenshot of *Fortune* (Mukherjee, 2016) illustrates how white bodies have been incorporated into Zika coverage. (Screenshot by Authors)

Her face, breasts, and stomach are highly contrasted, but the poor lighting casts a long shadow that blends her sexual figure with the abject background. Although no articles identify her as having Zika, Lourenco embodies a sanitary-bacteriological-synthesis engaging rhetorical olfaction to figure her body as both the victim and vector of the Zika virus. While this first image of Lourenco demonstrates the sanitary-bacteriological-synthesis, another Lourenco image amplifies viewers' miasmatic olfactory pedagogy.

On February 2, 2016, *The Guardian* featured a compilation of images for its article "Zika virus spreads across Americas—in pictures" (Rees-Bloor, 2016). In this photographic series, two images of Lourenco are featured among images of parents holding babies with microcephaly, pregnant women, public health workers spraying mosquito repellant, and pictures of environmental decay. In Figure 4, the long-shot image of Lourenco talking with two boys outside of a home is captioned: "Homes on stilts above the dirty water in Recife. Some of the slum's streets are flooded with sewage" (Rees-Bloor, 2016).

Figure 4. Photo credit: Felipe Dana. This screenshot of *The Guardian* (Rees-Bloor, 2016) illustrates how Lourenco's image is embedded within miasmatic rhetoric.

Bowing stilts precariously support the dwellings. The dirty water and accumulated sewage below activate the olfactory dimensions of a viewer's sensorium. The opaque visibility of the space under the dwellings appears as an environmental hazard potentially containing countless threats. The anchoring caption instructs a public to be fearful of Zika and people living in the Global South because these spaces flooded with sewage can be visually assessed as smelling bad and endangering the globe. Lourenco's figuration as synecdoche intertwines with the sanitary-bacteriological-synthesis framework to problematically figure her and other Latinx women of childbearing capacity akin to a miasma of infectious, Zika carrying mosquitos. Zika's asymptomaticity and capacity for unwitting sexual transmission positions women as infectious germs. When brought into conversation with issues of mosquito control in miasmatic environments, the collapse between woman and mosquito is then capable of being projected onto *all* Latinx women. *National Geographic* published an article featuring Lourenco's image, which notably reads "Like many of Brazil's estimated 400,000 pregnant women, Tainara Lourenco of Recife can't afford mosquito repellent" (Howard, 2016). If readers missed the significance of this synecdochical collapse, the article clarifies:

> The Zika virus is spreading "explosively" across Latin America and the Caribbean, and the city of Recife in northeastern Brazil remains a hotbed. [ ]
> *About 80 percent of Zika victims show no symptoms at all, but that's little consolation for Brazil's estimated 400,000 pregnant women.* (emphasis added, Howard, 2016, paras. 1–2).

For non-Latinx readers, it would be difficult not to perceive these 400,000 pregnant women—of which Lourenco has become the synecdochical public face—as Zika-infected miasmas emerging from the city of Recife.

Images ostensibly taken to emphasize the medical plight of poor Brazilian women positions them as both victims *and* vectors. This boundary matters, for the fear of disease often translates to the fear of the diseased. The difference between victim and vector classification is contingent upon racial, sexual, and classed assumptions. Of these, race transforms the "unfortunate victims of a serious disease into active transmitters of deadly germs, thus adding a medicalized dimension to existing nativism" (Molina, 2011, p. 1026). Just as not everyone who is afflicted is infected, so too is the corollary true: *not everyone who is unafflicted is uninfected.*

Featuring Lourenco's body to represent an infected body (politic) operates as a sanitary-bacteriological-synthesis because she is framed as *infected* by the stagnant, humid atmosphere conducive to mosquito proliferation. Simultaneously, she is always already *infecting* due to the combination of her sexualized appearance and her capacity to sexually transmit Zika to others. While viewers cannot smell, taste, or touch the scene, the harsh lighting, uneven contrast, sharp focus, and off-kilter angle of Lourenco's portraits combined with the scenic shots of Lourenco's house and floodwater creates a disconcerting scene and scent of poverty of which Lourenco is the center. Viewers are positioned in a relationship of disgust towards the subject of this visceral spectacle, and consequently the "captured" subject is reduced to a "non-agentive body" (Cloud, 2014, p. 49). The viewer is repositioned as the true victim of the representation (Chouliaraki, 2006).

The disconcerting features of Lourenco's images are not inherent in Lourenco herself nor the scene but rather are byproducts of the photographic framing. As Rakiya Omaar and Alex de Waal (1993) argue in their discussion on the pornography of disaster: "anyone who has watched a Western film crew [. . .] will know just how much effort it takes to compose the 'right' image." Indeed, Omaar and de Waal's (1993) term "disaster pornography" for understanding the spectacle of suffering is perhaps too appropriate as it pertains to the imagery of Lourenco: a Bing reverse image search for Lourenco standing in her doorway (see Figure 2) produces *only* pornographic photos as "similar images" (see Figure 5). This is not an accident but rather a byproduct of design: choices about lighting, pose, and framing.[1] So although this representation is *real*, insofar as the photograph is taken outside of Lourenco's home (Barchfield & Savarese, 2016), the aestheticization of disaster reinforce the themes of tropicalism that haunt Latinx representation (see Molina Guzmán & Valdivia, 2004).

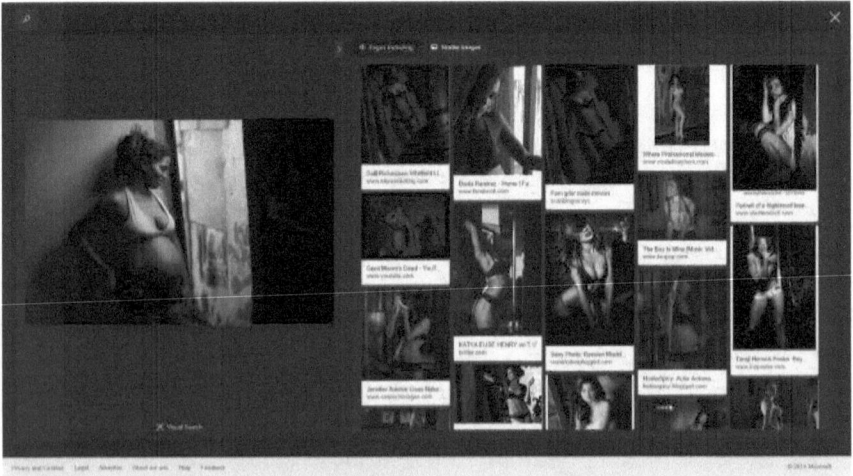

Figure 5. This screenshot of Bing's "visual search" illustrates how the formal attributes of Lourenco's image (e.g., lighting, pose, framing) resonates with the formal characteristics of pornography. (Screenshot by authors, taken on December 22, 2018)

---

1. We exclude clothing from this equation as a reverse image search of other women photographed in similar clothing but under different conditions (for example, brighter lighting) results in non-pornographic images of women in bathing suits or swimming. Hence, that a Bing reverse image search of Lourenco's image returns only pornographic results is not due to any inherent attribute within Lourenco herself (for example, her choice of clothing) but rather a direct result of the choices made by the photographer (for example, lighting, pose, and framing).

If Typhoid Mary served as the archetypal "healthy carrier," Lourenco and Latinx women operate as the archetypal always already infected healthy carrier: 80% may show no symptoms, but their racial, classed, and gendered configuration intersects with sensory rhetoric enough that *100% show sanitary-bacteriological symptoms*. Indeed, a February 9, 2016 article by *CNN* titled "Zika virus: What are the chances I'll get it (and other Q&As)" features images of slums, Lourenco, and other Latinx victims alongside images of the *Aedes Aegypti* mosquito, the virus, and public health officials attempting to contain the virus's spread (Tinker & LaMotte, 2016). Amongst the 29 photos is one of a woman (not Lourenco) surrounded in mist as "health ministry employees fumigate" the area (Tinker & LaMotte, 2016). No mosquitos are visible—only the woman and the repellant. The sanitary-bacteriological-synthesis is complete. Eight-months later, Lourenco's image is used without attribution (on September 8, 2016), for an article by *Breitbart News* refuting the link between microcephaly and Zika (Berry, 2016). Lacking context, the decision to feature Lourenco's image is puzzling, as the article is primarily about the Zika virus. From the larger perspective of the image's rhetorical circulation, however, it unfortunately makes sense: within the contexts of a sanitary-bacteriological-synthesis, even when the bacteriological threat of disease is minimized, the sanitary threat of the body remains.

Germ theory incompletely displaced miasmic theory not because germ theory rid epidemiology of the socio-symbolic "taint" characteristic of miasma, but rather because sensory rhetorics translate this miasmatic spatial pollution into a public, visceral relationship to the contagion. A sensorially acquired disgust thus becomes socially and epidemiologically justified because the disease is routed through biologics. Modern societies can be at peace with their discrimination because this intolerance is towards the germ, and not the person—except, as our analysis illustrates, the germ *both* symbolically and biologically replaces the person. Germ theory treats (some) infected individuals as a proxy of disease by discussing these infected outcasts primarily as vectors of disease transmission (Sturken, 1997). Which individuals are portrayed as victims and which are portrayed as vectors is contingent upon the treatment of race, class, gender, and other identity markers in miasmatic terms. This is not because socio-symbolic biases continue to plague modern epidemiology; rather, the success of modern epidemiology is due precisely to this merger of the socio-symbolic with the biologic. Because infection is no longer confined to a particular place (miasma), the "bio-logic" of germ theory necessitates the sociological analysis of the vector: "a living intermediary that carries an agent from a reservoir to a susceptible host" (CDC, 2012, p. 22 [glossary]). Reservoir, vector, host, mode of transmission, susceptibility, each of these fundamental epidemiological terms are as much socio-symbolic as they are biological (cf. CDC, 2012).

Conclusion: Miasmatic Expectations

Miasmatism remains central to the visceral formation of public health practices, even within disparate historical contexts. This argument holds implications for both health historians and contemporary public health practitioners. To define a disease necessitates first considering what causes physical and visceral disease. Because a (fear of) disease is inherently visceral, rhetoric is crucial to any public management of disease. This does not mean historical or modern medicine is *mere* rhetoric—as if rhetoric was any *mere* thing—but rather rhetoric is a fundamental part of medicine's method of inquiry and implementation. As Latour (1993) argues, the myth of modernity is predicated on the arbitrary division of the world into human and nonhuman arenas. Medical science portrays racism, sexism, and classism as ideological impurities—socio-symbolic breaches into the scientific system—as opposed to mutually constitutive tendrils of experts and lay publics negotiating the meanings and fears of disease.

In contrast, we have argued that racism, sexism, and classism are embedded within public health practices through visceral sensory engagements with disease rhetoric. Because diseases are biological counterparts to sociological unease, operating on one necessarily means operating on the other. Intensely visceral reactions of disgust can appear to gain scientific legitimacy as rhetoric connects miasma to the threat of contagious ethnic, non-natives, such as Mallon or Lourenco. Hence, modern medicine's desire to illustrate the efficacy of germ theory further inscribes fears rooted in racism, sexism, and classism within the understanding of disease itself. By transfiguring Mallon from person to disease, public health experts, with the assistance of a journalistic medium, flexed biological and sociological power. Mallon embodied the public's fear: a poor, immigrant woman capable of silently infecting upper-class Anglo-Saxon families. Consistent with germ theory, Mallon was figured as a foreign infection. Indeed, Mallon was detrimental to the health of the nation, as germs were detrimental to the health of the body. This metonymic interplay between the two—Mallon as germ, germ as Mallon—meant public health rhetoric raced, classed, and gendered the germ. The influence of this "socio-logic" of disease continues with the public representation of Zika. If Mallon illustrated how public health was prefigured with miasmatic suspicion of the vector—the raced, classed, and gendered reservoir of disease, whether healthy in appearance or otherwise—Lourenco illustrates the consequences of this miasmatic suspicion. While identification and subsequent policing of Mallon's body was hailed as a victory of modern public health, the miasmatic suspicion governing Lourenco's body illustrates a failure of contemporary public health. Because germ theory translates miasmatic logic from the language of exposure into the language of contagion, disease becomes mobile, intentional, imagined through the senses, and deeply visceral. Mallon's transfiguration resulted in quarantine and was considered a public health success; the germ was extracted from the public body. Lourenco, however, was never "here," and thus no "public" is threatened by her absent presence.

When discourse equates some bodies as vectors of disease transmission, then positioning these individuals vis-à-vis public interests functionally removes their well-being from public health concerns. Mallon was quarantined due to this logic. In contrast, Lourenco was never defined as a part of the public; much like the dangerous vapors of miasma, she is transitory and forgotten. Ironically, Lourenco herself should be included as an in-group member of a visceral public fearful of Zika, as it is never clear if Lourenco is actually infected with Zika; Natasha Rees-Bloor's (2016) report in *The Guardian*, suggests Lourenco did not have Zika: "she became pregnant at the start of the outbreak and fears catching the virus." Instead, she is positioned as a threat from the Global South. Consistent with the historical representation of "infectious foreigners" (Molina, 2011), the designation excludes her from the range of feeling and resources afforded to those who are constituted as a legitimate member of a visceral public of concerned future parents. Whereas typhoid was controlled at the cost of Mallon, Zika has been forgotten at the cost of Lourenco. Forgetting Lourenco is not a public health accident; Lourenco was always meant to be forgotten, as from the beginning she was meant to serve as an extra operating in the shadows of public health—close enough to serve as a fearful resource of disease, far enough to not prove any real threat of disease transmission. With our memory of Lourenco fading, public health efforts suffer. For example, Zika vaccine trials are at risk due to the decline of public interest (and corresponding funding) (Chen, 2018).

Finally, this essay throws into sharp relief the tensions that have historically existed between public health experts and the lay publics upon which they seek to intervene. As our analysis demonstrates, lay publics have historically and will continue to engage their sensory equipment to make sense of disease and fortify their own corporeal, affiliative, and national boundaries in response. Moreover, media outlets have continued to utilize the sensory rhetoric of *miasmatism* well after its epidemiological decline. Public health officials should be well aware of how popular journalistic outlets can sustain visceral publics and antiquated disease etiologies like *miasmatism* through vivid sensory descriptors. While *miasmatism* is able to intervene in the spatial context within which bodies move, it may also direct sensory perception to regressive public ends. Ultimately, rather than draw a firm boundary between public health experts and the lay publics they serve, experts should take stock of the complex visceral weave—rooted in the human body's sensory capacity—constituting public health strategy and outreach.

References

Aravind, Maya & Chung, Kevin C. (2010). Evidence-based medicine and hospital reform: Tracing origins back to Florence Nightingale. *Plastic and Reconstructive Surgery, 125(1):* 403–409.

Axelrod, Ilana Z. (2017). The sexual objectification of Brazilian women hurts. *Calabar Youth Council for Women's Rights*. Retrieved from https://cycwr.org.ng/the-sexual-objectification-of-brazilian-women-hurts-by-ilana-zelmanovitz-axelrod/

Baker, S. Josephine. (1939/2013). *Fighting for life*. New York: New York Review Books Classics.

Barchfield, Jenny, & Savarese, Mauricio. (2016, January 31). For Brazil's rich and poor, disparate response to Zika. *The Seattle Times*. Retrieved from https://www.seattletimes.com/nation-world/for-brazils-rich-and-poor-disparate-response-to-zika/

Barnes, David S. (2006). *The great stink of Paris and the nineteenth-century struggle against filth and germs*. Baltimore, MD: John Hopkins University Press.

Bennett, Jeffrey A. (2015). *Banning queer blood: Rhetorics of citizenship, contagion, and resistance*. Tuscaloosa: University of Alabama Press.

Berry, Susan. (2016, September 9). Massive study casts doubt on Zika as cause of microcephaly. *Breitbart*. Retrieved from http://www.breitbart.com/big-government/2016/09/09/massive-study-casts-doubt-zika-cause-mic rocephaly/

Bostridge, Mark. (2008). *Florence Nightingale: The making of an icon*. New York, NY: Farrar, Strauss & Giroux.

Brennan, Teresa. (2004). *The transmission of affect*. Ithaca, NY: Cornell University Press.

Bushman, Richard L., & Bushman, Claudia L. (1988). The early history of cleanliness in America. *Journal of American History, 74*(4), 1213–1238.

Burke, Kenneth. (1945/1969). *A grammar of motives*. Berkeley: University of California Press.

Centers for Disease Control and Prevention. (2012). *Principles of Epidemiology in Public Health Practice*: Centers for Disease Control and Prevention. Retrieved from https://www.cdc.gov/ophss/csels/dsepd/ss1978/ss1978.pdf

Centers for Disease Control and Prevention. (2014). Typhoid fever: General information. Retrieved from https://www.cdc.gov/typhoid-fever/sources.html

Centers for Disease Control and Prevention. (2017). Zika virus for healthcare providers. Retrieved from https://www.cdc.gov/zika/hc-providers/preparing-for-zika/clinicalevaluationdisease.html

Chadwick, Edwin. (1842). *Report on the sanitary condition of the labouring population of Great Britain: Supplementary report on the results of special inquiry into the practice of interment in towns* (Vol. 1). London, UK: HM Stationery Office.
Chen, Eli. (2018, January 17). Future of SLU's Zika vaccine trials remain uncertain as public interest and funding decline. *St. Louis Public Radio*. Retrieved from http://news.stlpublicradio.org/post/future-slu-s-zika-vaccine-trials-remain-uncertain-public-interest-and-funding-decline#stream/0
Chouliaraki, Lilie. (2006). Spectatorship of suffering. London, UK: SAGE. Classen, Constance, Howes, David, & Synnott, Anthony. (1994). *Aroma: The cultural history of smell*. London, UK: Routledge.
Cloud, Dana L. (2014). Shock therapy: Oprah Winfrey, celebrity philanthropy, and disaster "relief" in Haiti. *Critical Studies in Media Communication, 31*(1), 42–56.
Corbin, Alain. (2005). Charting the cultural history of the senses. In David Howes (Ed.), *Empire of the senses: The sensual culture reader* (pp. 128–139). Oxford, UK: Berg.
Dumit, Joseph. (2006). Neuroexistentialism. In Caroline A. Jones (Ed.), *Sensorium: Embodied experience, technology, and contemporary art*. Cambridge, MA: MIT Press.
Finnegan, Cara A. (2010). Studying visual modes of public address. In Shawn J. Parry Giles & J. Michael Hogan (Eds.), *The handbook of rhetoric and public address* (pp. 250–270). Hoboken, NJ: John Wiley & Sons.
Gabriel, Yiannis. (2012). Organizations in a state of darkness: Towards a theory of organizational miasma. *Organization Studies, 33*(9), 1137–1152.
García, Monica. (2014). Typhoid fever in nineteenth-century Colombia: between medical geography and bacteriology. *Medical History, 58(1)*, 27–45.
Gilman, Sander L. (1988). *Disease and representation: Images of illness from madness to AIDS*. Ithaca, NY: Cornell University Press
Gries, Laurie. (2015). *Still life with rhetoric: A new materialist approach for visual rhetorics*. Logan: Utah State University Press.
Gruber, David R. (2014). The (digital) majesty of all under heaven: Affective constitutive rhetoric at the Hong Kong museum of history's multi-media exhibition of terracotta warriors. *Rhetoric Society Quarterly, 44*(2), 148–167.
Halliday, Stephen. (2001). Death and miasma in Victorian London: An obstinate belief. *British Medical Journal, 323*(7327), 1469.
Hasian, Marouf A. (2000). Power, medical knowledge, and the rhetorical invention of "Typhoid Mary." *Journal of Medical Humanities, 21*(3), 123–139.
Hawhee, Debra. (2015). Rhetoric's sensorium. *Quarterly Journal of Speech, 101*(1), 2–17. Hawhee, Debra & Olson, Christa J. (2013). Pan-historiography: The challenges of writing history across space and time. In Michelle Ballif (Ed.), *Theorizing Histories of Rhetoric* (pp. 90–105). Carbondale: Southern Illinois University Press.
Howard, Brian C. (2016, February 5). Photos reveal impact of Zika on Brazil's streets. *National Geographic*. Retrieved from https://news.nationalgeo graphic.com/2016/02/160205-zika-photos-recife-brazil/
Human typhoid germ. (1907, April 2). *New York American*.

Jensen, Robin E. (2007). Using science to argue for sexual education in schools: Dr. Ella Flagg Young and the 1913 "Chicago Experiment. *Science Communication, 29*(2), 217–249.

Johnson, Jenell. (2016). "A man's mouth is his castle": The midcentury fluoridation controversy and the visceral public. *Quarterly Journal of Speech, 102*(1), 1–20.

Keränen, Lisa. (2014). Public engagements with health and medicine. *Journal of Medical Humanities, 35*(2), 103–109.

Kindhauser, Mary K., Allen, Tomas, Frank, Veronika, Santhana, Ravi, & Dye, Christopher. (2016). Zika: the origin and spread of a mosquito-borne virus. World Health Organization. Retrieved from http://www.who.int/bulletin/online_first/16-171082/en/

Lakoff, George, & Johnson, Mark. (2003). *Metaphors we live by*. Chicago, IL: University of Chicago Press.

Latour, Bruno. (1993). *We have never been modern*. Cambridge, MA: Harvard University Press.

Lay, Mary M. (2000). *The rhetoric of midwifery: Gender, knowledge, and power*. New Bruswick, NJ: Rutgers University Press.

Leavitt, Judith W. (1996). *Typhoid Mary: Captive to the public's health*. Boston, MA: Beacon Press.

Lessy, Rose E. (2008). *"This mysterious miasma": Environmental risk, Edith Wharton, and the literature of bad air* (Doctoral dissertation). Cornell University, Ithaca, NY. Retrieved from eCommons.

MacDonald, Marjorie A. (2004). From miasma to fractals: The epidemiology revolution and public health nursing. *Public Health Nursing, 21*(4), 380–391.

Magner, Lois N. (2005). *A history of medicine*. Boca Raton, FL: CRC Press.

Malkowski, Jennifer. (2014). Beyond prevention: Containment rhetoric in the case of bug chasing. *Journal of Medical Humanities, 35*(2), 211–228.

McCarthy, Michael P. (1987). *Typhoid and the politics of public health in nineteenthcentury Philadelphia* (Vol. 179). Philadelphia, PA: American Philosophical Society.

Microbe Carriers—The newly discovered danger to everybody's health—and there's no remedy for it. (1915, July 11), *Richmond Times-Dispatch*. Retrieved from https://virginiachronicle.com/cgi-bin/virginia?a=d& d=RTD191 50711.1.42

Molina, Natalia. (2011). Borders, laborers, and racialized medicalization: Mexican immigration and US public health practices in the 20th century. *American Journal of Public Health, 101*(6), 1024–1031.

Molina Guzmán, Isabel, &. Valdivia, Angharad N. (2004). Brain, brow, and booty: Latina iconicity in U.S. popular culture. *The Communication Review, 7*(2), 205–221.

Montgomery, Catherine M., & Pool, Robert. (2017). "From 'trial community' to 'experimental publics': How clinical research shapes public participation." *Critical Public Health, 27*(1), 50–62.

Mukherjee, Sy. (2016). The Government Just Issued Two Big Zika Warnings for Men and Women. *Fortune*. Retrieved from http://fortune.com/2016/09/30/zika-southeast-asia-travel-advisory/

Oliver, Wade W. (1941). *The man who lived for tomorrow: A biography of William Hallock Park, M.D.* New York, NY: E. P. Dutton & Co.

Omaar, Rakiya, & de Waal, Alex. (1993). Disaster Pornography from Somalia. Center for Media Literacy. Retrieved from www.medialit.org/reading-room/disaster-pornography-somalia

Panagia, Davide. (2009). *The political life of sensation.* Durham, NC: Duke University Press.

Pan American Health Organization, & World Health Organization. (2015). Epidemiological alert: Zika virus infection. Retrieved from http://www.paho.org/hq/index.php?option=com_docman&task=doc_view&Itemid=270&gid=30075=en&lang=en

Parker, Robert. (1983). *Miasma: Pollution and purification in early Greek religion.* Oxford, UK: Clarendon Press.

Rees-Bloor, Natasha. (2016, February 2). Zika virus spreads across Americas in pictures. *The Guardian.* Retrieved from https://www.theguardian.com/world/gallery/2016/feb/02/zika-virus-spreads-across-americas-in-pictures

Roediger, David. (2008). *How race survived U.S. history: From settlement and slavery to the Obama phenomenon.* London, UK: Verso.

Scott, J. Blake. (2014). Afterword: Elaborating health and medicine's publics. *Journal of Medical Humanities, 35*(2), 229–235.

Smith, Christina M. (2012). Theorizing circulation in visual rhetoric through Dorothea Lange's images of Japanese American internment. *Journal of Visual Literacy, 31*(2), 71–89.

Spoel, Philippa, Harris, Roma, & Henwood, Flis. (2014). Rhetorics of health citizenship: Exploring vernacular critiques of government's role in supporting healthy living. *Journal of Medical Humanities, 35*(2), 131–147.

Sturken, Marita. (1997). Tangled memories: The Vietnam War, the AIDS epidemic, and the politics of remembering. Los Angeles: University of California Press.

Tinker, Ben, & LaMotte, Sandee,(2016, February 2). Zika virus: What are the chances I'll get it? (And other Q&As). *CNN.* Retrieved from http://www.cnn.com/2016/02/09/health/zika-symptoms-vaccine-tests-questions/index.html

Tuan, Yi-Fu. (1977). *Space and place: The perspective of experience.* Minneapolis: University of Minnesota Press.

Typhoid Mary: Most harmless and yet the most dangerous woman in America. (1909, June 20). *New York American.* Retrived from https://commons.wikimedia.org/wiki/File:Mallon-Mary_01.jpg

Wald, Priscilla. (2008). *Contagious: Cultures, Carriers, and the Outbreak Narrative.* Durham, NC: Duke University Press.

Whipple, George C. (1908). *Typhoid fever: Its causation, transmission and prevention.* Hoboken, NJ: John Wiley & Sons.

Woman 'typhoid factory' held as a prisoner. (1907, April 1), *The Evening World.* Retrieved from https://chroniclingamerica.loc.gov/lccn/sn83030193/1907-04-01/ed-1/seq-3/

World Health Organization. (1996). New challenges for public health: Report of an interregional meeting. Retrieved from http://apps.who.int/iris/bitstream/handle/10665/63061/WHO_HRH_96.4.pdf?sequence=1

Emily Winderman is assistant professor of Communication Studies at the University of Minnesota, Twin Cities. Her research examines how reproductive health concerns are negotiated through rhetorics of public emotion. Her work has been published in *Rhetoric & Public Affairs, International Journal of Communication, Feminist Media Studies,* and *Communication Quarterly,* among others.

Robert Mejia is assistant professor of Communication at North Dakota State University. He researches how the political, economic, social, and cultural logics of race, gender, and class are embedded within and operate through communication technologies. His work has been published in *Communication and Critical/Cultural Studies, Critical Studies in Media Communication, New Philosopher,* and other outlets.

Brandon Rogers is a Ph.D. student in the Communication, Rhetoric, and Digital Media (CRDM) program at North Carolina State University. His research primarily intertwines media studies with critical health studies. In particular, he focuses on how popular media mediate masculinity to the benefit or detriment of men's health.

Supplemental Material

"'All Smell is Disease'; Miasma, Sensory Rhetoric, and the Sanitary-Bacteriologic of Visceral Public Health"

Emily Winderman, Robert Mejia, and Brandon Rogers

Part I: Reflection on the Origins of the Article

We are delighted to reflect upon the origin of this piece because the serendipity of its creation stands as a productive model for cross-disciplinary engagement and co-authored scholarship. In November 2016, Emily Winderman and Robert Mejia were participants in a National Communication Association discussion panel grappling with the rhetoric and politics of the Zika virus. Between 2015 and 2017, the Zika virus was dominating U.S. news, largely because of pervasive images of infants born with microcephaly. After the 2016 discussion panel was positively received, plans for a 2017 reunion emerged. For 2017, each panelist was randomly buddied up with another panelist to complete a comparative historical analysis of Zika and another epidemic. Emily and Robert were assigned a typhoid/Zika comparison and immediately went to work.

Following our presentation that had many of the seedlings of the essay in its current form, we applied for our paper to be considered for publication in the "Public Health" special issue of *Rhetoric of Health & Medicine*. At that point, Brandon Rogers was Emily's graduate assistant and provided such important contributions to the piece that we gladly invited him aboard as a co-author.

Ultimately, this piece serves as a testament to the virtues of co-authorship in the humanities. Passing the piece back and forth over several rounds of revision made the essay stronger because we had to grapple with our divergent theoretical equipment as we worked to fulfill the editorial guidance. Ensuring that the essay read in a somewhat unified voice required frequent conversations and trust in one another's vision. We are so grateful that our essay was selected for inclusion in this collection because writing it is now a fond memory that marks the beginning of a friendship and, hopefully, future essays.

Part II: Description of Research Methods, Findings, and/or Pedagogical Impact

As a cross-disciplinary collaboration between media studies and rhetoric of health and medicine, our methods were both critical and rhetorical. For a theoretical framework, we fused Jenell Johnson's visceral publicity and David S. Barnes' sanitary-bacteriological synthesis in order to situate and explain the circulation of public health related messages.

There were a number of methodological challenges that we faced in our task of comparing typhoid with Zika. In order to productively compare two disease epidemics separated by a century, we leaned on Debra Hawhee and Christa Olson's work on panhistoriography, which allows scholars to account for phenomena separated by even several centuries. Furthermore, because olfaction is difficult to capture in textual form, our analysis examined olfaction through the visual print medium and attended to compositional elements of the frame and the avenues of the image circulation.

The connective logic between typhoid and Zika is the sanitary-bacteriological synthesis, by which a certain sensation was the primary means for observing whether or not someone had a disease and were therefore dangerous. The same kind of logic inheres in the way we continue to talk about people affected with Zika. The sanitary-bacteriological synthesis functions within the context of systemic racism in global health efforts and therefore traffics in racist, classist, and gendered stereotypes, regardless of the time period we were examining.

Writing this essay has impacted our pedagogy by allowing us to be more creative with our comparative analyses. It is important that the comparison be careful and apt, but we should also not shy away from juxtaposing phenomena that are seemingly too divergent. This did not make for a more holistic piece (as in an additive interpretation) which is perhaps how a scientist or social scientist would perceive collaboration; rather, it made for a more nuanced piece (as in a dialectic interpretation), which attempted to recognize the similarities and differences between two epidemics.

For instance, the historical and geographic contexts surrounding Typhoid and Zika affected the racial rhetorics that are evinced through the iconography of Mary Mallon and Tianara Lourenco. Typhoid emerges in that historical moment when the Irish are becoming White. "Typhoid Mary" Mallon is thus figured metonymically as a potential threat to this racial transformation. Tianara Lourenco is thus figured synecdochally as a representation of the perceived medical threat of racial difference. What Mallon and Lourenco thus illustrated for us is that for matters of public health, poor, ethnic women are figured as vectors of disease transmission, in contrast to wealthier white women who are figured as victims of disease. These insights were made stronger because of our collaborative scholarship and thus pedagogically have taught us to think more purposefully about the benefits and processes of collaborative work.

Part III: Discussion Questions

1. How can smell be rhetorical? What role does smell play in rhetorical processes of racialization?

2. The authors rely on visual rhetoric to trace olfactory rhetoric. Can you think of some other rhetorical ways to analyze olfaction without relying on the visual?

3. How does the claim that the social judgments made possible by miasmatism (a historical disease rhetoric) was never fully abdicated, but instead blended into germ theory (a contemporary disease rhetoric) help us to understand why an understanding of history matters for the analysis of contemporary social problems (p. 122)? What other social problems (whether health or otherwise) would benefit from the insight of historical knowledge?

4. As a disease that also spreads asymptomatically, what types of sensory rhetoric are found in public discussions of COVID-19?

THE WAC JOURNAL

> WAC Journal is on the Web at http://wac.colostate.edu/journal/ and parlorpress.com/wacjournal

The WAC Journal is an open-access, blind, peer-viewed journal published annually by Clemson University, Parlor Press and the WAC Clearinghouse. It is published annually in print by Parlor Press and Clemson University. Digital copies of the journal are simultaneously published at The WAC Clearinghouse in PDF format for free download, http://wac.colostate.edu/ journal/. Print subscriptions support the ongoing publication of the journal and make it possible to offer digital copies as open access. *The WAC Journal* publishes WAC-related articles on WAC techniques and applications; WAC program strategies; WAC and WID; WAC and writing centers; interviews and reviews; and emergent technologies and digital literacies across the curriculum.

Building Sustainable WAC Programs: A Whole Systems Approach[1]

This article expertly blends history, theory, and practice in making the case for using complexity / systems theory in thinking through the various obstacles to developing sustainable WAC programs. The authors provide a novel approach that evaluates ways to understand the material and organizational conditions that allow WAC programs to start and sustain themselves. The authors create useful heuristics for programs to establish and maintain their fledgling programs. Additionally, during the WAC Summer Institute, this article inspired a discussion on sustainability, which participants ranked as the most valuable activity of the session.

---

1. *The WAC Journal*, vol. 29. © 2018 by Clemson University.

Building Sustainable WAC Programs: A Whole Systems Approach

Michelle Cox, Jeffrey Galin, and Dan Melzer

> From: Katherine T. Bridgman
> Date: 02/19/2016
> To: Jeffrey Galin
> Subject: Question about WAC consultation
> Hi Jeffrey,
>
> I am currently the Writing Center Director at Texas A&M-San Antonio, and I have been tasked with helping our relatively new university start a WAC program. So far, we have established our WAC committee as a subcommittee through our Faculty Senate that includes representatives from our colleges as well as the WAC director (me). . . . We are also getting ready to downward expand this coming fall and admit our first classes of first and second year students. We currently serve only third and fourth year students as well as graduate students. A primary task of our WAC committee will be to begin outlining policies for faculty support, student support, and expectations for writing-intensive courses. Writing-intensive courses are one of the four high-impact practices that we are targeting with our downward expansion.
>
> * * *
>
> As I plan our first meetings – which will be condensed into two "retreats" this semester – I was thinking about the possibility of inviting a guest speaker to speak with my colleagues. While I have a small budget to work with, my budget would not allow us to bring someone to campus. Do you know of consultants who would be willing to Skype in for a session with our faculty?
>
> Thank you for your time,
> Katherine

We open with this message sent to Jeff because, as co-chairs of CCCC's WAC Standing Group, we continue to be impressed by the number of WAC programs just getting started. We often hear from those launching programs or re-starting dormant programs at the annual CCCC's WAC meeting or through requests for consultations, such as this one. In their 2008 national WAC/WID survey, Christopher Thaiss and Tara Porter (2010) partly based their claim that the WAC movement is "alive and well" on this continued launching of new programs. In their survey, more than a third (36.3%, n = 206) of the institutions that identified as having a WAC program either have a program that is "just starting" or has existed for 1–5 years (p. 542). In addition, 152 institutions reported having plans to start a WAC program (p. 541).

We also open with Katherine's email because it represents the kinds of institutional challenges that WAC programs face, such as how to create institution-wide initiatives, plan for program growth, sustain program momentum, and prioritize strategic reforms over short-term fixes. These challenges often lead to program failure. Thaiss and Porter point out that "well over half of the 418 programs identified in [McLeod's] 1987 survey either no longer exist or have been 'restarted' in the years since" their 2008 survey (p. 558). Such a significant failure rate of WAC programs warrants serious attention.

In response to queries like Katherine's and out of concern for the writing programs we direct, we developed a systematic approach for building sustainable WAC programs. In this article, we provide an overview of our whole systems approach, offering a comprehensive theoretical model, which is derived from theories of complexity, systems, social network, resilience, and sustainable development. From these theories, we derive a set of principles and ground this theoretical framework in a WAC program-building methodology and corresponding set of strategies. Throughout this article, we return to the WAC program at Texas A&M-San Antonio (TAMUSA) to demonstrate how the theoretical framework works to develop a WAC program from the ground up. Although we present TAMUSA as a concrete application of our theoretical framework, our primary purpose is theory building: to lay out the broad strokes of the whole systems approach to initiate new ways of conceiving WAC program formation. More detailed applications of our theoretical framework to various WAC program contexts can be found in our monograph *Sustainable WAC: A Whole Systems Approach to Launching and Developing WAC Programs* (2018).

Why Theorize WAC Program Development?

In WAC literature, theory tends not to focus on the complexities of higher education or program administration, but rather on the writing pedagogies that are at the heart of WAC programs. This point is exemplified in "Theory in WAC: Where Have We Been, Where Are We Going?," in which Thaiss (2001) provides a comprehensive review of the writing theories that have informed WAC practice but does not touch upon theories related to WAC leadership or program development. This is not an oversight by Thaiss, but emblematic of a field that focuses more on theorizing WAC instruction than the administration of WAC programs. This focus on pedagogy may be inherent to the ways the field of WAC has developed and defined itself. Russell (2002) attributes the success of the WAC movement to its focus on pedagogy, as faculty are asked to commit to a "radically different way of teaching" that offers "personal rather than institutional rewards" (p. 295).

When the literature does focus on WAC program administration, it tends to emphasize program description and advice rather than building a theory of administering and building WAC programs. The WAC literature describes individual programs (Fulwiler & Young, 1990; Segall & Smart, 2005; Thaiss et al., 2012); provides advice for developing specific program elements, such as faculty workshops or writing fellows initiatives (Mcleod, 1988; McLeod & Soven, 1991; McLeod et al. 2011; International Network of WAC Program, 2014); and describes challenges to WAC programs and steps WAC directors may take so that their programs persist (Townsend, 2008; Young & Fulwiler, 1990). All of these texts offer nuts-and-bolts advice for building and developing WAC programs rooted in experience, knowledge of the field, and writing theory and research—but not theories of writing program administration or methodologies for creating sustainable programs. Extending the focus on the features of enduring WAC programs, William Condon and Carol Rutz (2012) introduced a taxonomy for categorizing WAC programs according to their characteristics, identifying four types: foundational, established, integrated, and institutional change agent. However, like the earlier literature on enduring programs, Condon and Rutz do not attempt to explain the underlying reasons why WAC programs at higher levels in this taxonomy outlast programs at the lower levels. Even WAC surveys over the years that have looked at the issue of program longevity (McLeod, 1997; Thaiss & Porter, 2008) have identified representative program features that may be replicated rather than offering a systematic understanding of why these traits lead to program persistence.

Barbara Walvoord's (1996) "The Future of WAC" departs from this largely descriptive body of literature as the first attempt to theorize the vulnerability and endurance of WAC programs. Walvoord draws on social movement theory to analyze why WAC programs and the field at large have been vulnerable to such a wide range of challenges. Exploring program variability, for instance, Walvoord argues that WAC has been largely decentralized, realized through the development of programs on individual campuses and spread through conferences and a group of "traveling workshop leaders" (p. 61), but never becoming a national movement through the development of a national WAC organization. Walvoord sees this decentralization as strengthening individual WAC programs because it allows them to form their own goals in relation to their individual contexts, but also as leaving them "vulnerable to cooptation, becoming special interest groups, settling for narrow goals and limited visions, or simply being wiped out by the next budget crunch or the next change of deans" (p. 62). Indeed, the loss of so many WAC programs as indicated by Thaiss and Porter's 2008 survey is evidence of this continuing vulnerability.

Walvoord uses social movement theory to distinguish between micro-level actions (such as "changing personal behavior") and macro-level actions (such as "changing structures and organizations") (p. 60). For instance, she argues that faculty workshops, long the "backbone of the WAC movement," are effective at the micro-level as they "generate high energy and enthusiasm" for teaching writing among those that attend (p. 63), but do not lead to changes at the macro-level because they do not affect the wider campus culture or university structures. She then turns to the future of WAC, drawing on strategies used by social movements to suggest approaches for strengthening WAC programs, such as coming to a deeper understanding of the wider campus and societal contexts within which WAC programs live, connecting to other institutional and national movements, and connecting to university missions and accrediting bodies' standards. Though Walvoord's article has been widely cited, we do not see scholars taking on her larger claims or more pointed insights about WAC.

Our approach builds on Walvoord's germinal work. We start with her premise, using theory to better understand WAC program development within the complex and dynamic contexts of higher education. Like her, we theorize practice by providing WAC directors with strategies to develop enduring WAC programs. Like Walvoord, we keep our focus on program administration rather than pedagogy. As WAC program directors, we understand and value the power of WAC pedagogy on faculty and have ourselves led many workshops, but we believe that WAC directors need to do more than train individual faculty. They should aim to transform a campus culture to create lasting change by approaching the problem of program sustainability systematically. Departing from Walvoord, we find social movement theory inadequate. While it provides a useful lens for considering program vulnerability and suggesting strategies, social movement theory cannot provide WAC directors with a comprehensive theoretical framework, methodology, and set of strategies for launching, revitalizing, and reviving WAC programs, as does the whole systems approach we develop here.

To introduce this theoretical framework, we return to the email that opens this article. The newly appointed WAC director of TAMUSA, Katherine Bridgman, contacted Jeff to consult on their nascent program at a moment when we were drafting material on the planning stages of WAC program development for the whole systems approach. Jeff spoke with Katherine several times to learn more about the situation. He learned that TAMUSA is a branch campus with about 5,500 students. About 60% of their population are first generation college students, 70% are Hispanic or Latinx, and 64% of their students are first generation (Texas A&M). At the time Jeff met the director in January of 2016, TAMUSA was making plans to transition from an upper division two-year college to a four-year institution for fall 2016. Prior to starting these changes, the institution established a four-semester set of mandatory one-hour student support courses and a university-wide e-portfolio. Further, he learned that TAMUSA planned to establish a WAC program that same fall, which would feature what the committee defined as a writing-intentional (W-I) program.

Like many new WAC directors, Katherine started by examining programs and practices at other universities as a way to conceptualize their own. She selected two WAC initiatives that proved effective on other campuses—student writing portfolios and writing-intensive requirements—and reached out to a WAC consultant for guidance on moving these initiatives forward. The primary problems with this approach are: (a) it looks outward, away from the institution, rather than inward to understand existing or previously existing writing initiatives; (b) it focuses primarily on isolated practices rather than a systematic process for integrating curricular change at a given institution; and (c) it concentrates on program initiation but not necessarily sustainability.

To address these problems, for TAMUSA and other new WAC programs, we need a theoretical model that can build from context and represent the complexity of large-scale reform. This model also needs to provide WAC directors and committees guidance on evaluating needs, setting goals, planning programs, implementing projects, assessing initiatives, and tracking sustainability. To create such a theoretical model, we turn to theories that provide tools for describing and introducing change to dynamic systems.

THEORIES THAT INFORM OUR WHOLE SYSTEMS APPROACH

Complexity theory, first used in computational and scientific fields to describe complex phenomena, provides an umbrella framework for our approach and offers ways to study the interactions among a large and diverse group of actors and organizations within a complex adaptive system. When scientists talk about such systems, they often refer to examples such as flocking birds, each of which makes minute adjustments in their flight in relationship only to the birds next to them. These decentralized decisions among individual birds are driven by feedback loops that either magnify a small action across the system or keep it in check. A flock of starlings, for example, can appear in such numbers that they seem to fill the sky. As one watches these large flocks, one sees how the micro-relationships among individuals can result in a flowing mass that sometimes splinters off but often forms amoebic shapes. Complex systems science works to understand the emergence of these coordinated macro-behaviors, the local rule-following activity that leads to these behaviors, how the system (flock) remains identifiable, and how the system maintains its relative internal stability (Leon, 2014).

Some scholars have argued that universities are complex systems (Leon, 2014) with multiple levels of stakeholders (students, faculty, administrators, board members). If we imagine the university as a social ecosystem, we can better understand how adding stresses within the system can lead to behavioral adaptations until the stresses become too great and lead to program failure. While a WAC program is not a complex system itself, it might lead to adaptive behaviors within the system that both increase its complexity and contribute to collective pattern-forming processes of the larger complex system. The greater the diversity and connectivity of the individuals at the lowest levels of the system, the more complex the system becomes and the more likely emergent and adaptive behaviors will be introduced. Perhaps this is the reason why WAC lore has often emphasized the need for WAC programs to start by gathering grassroots support and create an advisory board early in its development. According to complexity theory, the more top-down the program, the fewer interactions among individual actors in the system, the weaker the feedback loops, and the less likely emergent behaviors will spread across the system. It also stands to reason that systemic transformational change may have roots in top-down decisions or strategic plans but cannot be realized unless those goals resonate at all scales within the system.

While complexity science provides ways to understand how complex systems work, it does not offer strategies for intervening within the systems it studies. As scholars began to extend complexity theory from natural systems to social networks like corporations, they desired theoretical frameworks that were not just descriptive, but also predictive and focused on intervention.

Systems theory focuses primarily at the macro-level, mapping the system to better understand the relationships that govern it. Systems theory encourages us to approach complex systems by focusing on relationship patterns and by "using the concept of wholeness to order our thoughts" (Checkland, 1981, p. 4). Systems practice begins with stakeholder discussions of relationships among system structures and processes to paint a rich picture of the whole. These actors also create a conceptual model that exposes ideologies structuring the system and defines their ideal vision of it. This focus on system mapping to direct change requires moving beyond "parochial boundaries" (in the case of a university, individual courses, departments, and colleges) and finding the points of leverage where "actions and changes in structures" can lead to "significant, enduring improvements" across the system (Senge, 1990, p. 114). Points of leverage are highly connected places where even a small change might have significant ripple effects for the entire system (for example, linking a student writing portfolio to a graduation requirement rather than a first-year writing requirement). These ripple effects are what Senge refers to as reinforcing processes, where a single intervention can have a snowball effect on students, faculty, and the campus culture of writing.

A WAC director applying a systems approach might begin not by choosing WAC initiatives to implement, but by taking the time to study the campus system to create a rich picture of writing across the university. In fact, this is the first activity that Jeff encouraged the WAC committee at TAMUSA to undertake, work that they did in preparation for his second consultation. Their goal was to map the different writing activities happening on campus and then identify the stakeholders that impact or are impacted by these writing activities.

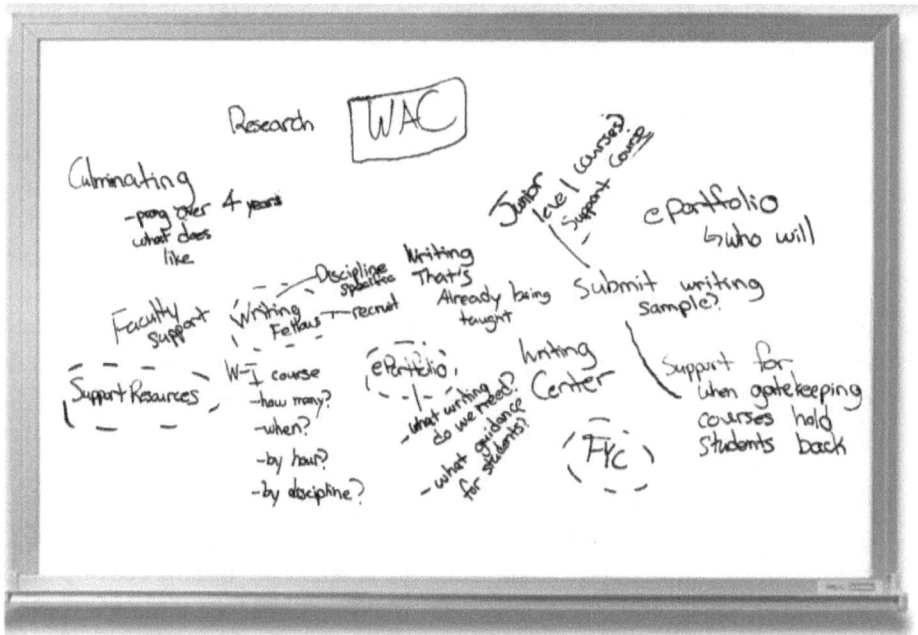

Figure 1: Photo of whiteboard program mapping completed by TAMUSA WAC committee.

This rough sketch provides a baseline understanding of a campus writing culture that stakeholders can use to consider their ideal goals for writing on campus and create alternative models of the system. The complexity of this rough sketch grows as the stakeholder group discusses lines of communication and interaction among each node, enabling them to identify points of leverage for introducing change to the university's curricular ecology.

Systems theory—and especially the more recent approach of "critical systems theory"—also recognizes that disparities of power exist in all human systems; changes to a system can affect different groups within the system differently; and when introducing change to a system we need to be particularly cognizant of those groups with less power, less of a voice, and less visibility in the system (see, for example, Flood, 1990; Jackson, 1985; Midgley, 1996). In the WAC literature, two groups of marginalized faculty and students have emerged as a focus: contingent labor and multilingual student writers (see, for example, Cox & Zawacki, 2011; LaFrance, 2015; Johns, 1991; Zawacki & Cox, 2014). Systems theory reminds us that it is important to consider potential unintended ripple effects in a system early in WAC program planning.

While systems theory provides a framework for considering the macro-level, to focus more on the micro-level, we draw on **social network theory**. This theory originated as a way to understand how ties among individuals impact social networks, beliefs, and behaviors, and it considers a group of people (e.g. faculty and staff) as an interconnected system of nodes with a wide range of ties, or links, to others. These connections can be visually mapped to examine the lines of communication, patterns of interaction, and distribution of knowledge within that system. Mapping communication pathways along a network of nodes can help to identify individuals who serve as conduits or bottlenecks. This theory prioritizes "the relationships and ties with other actors within the network" (Marsden, 2005, p. 8) rather than attributes of individual actors. For example, when considering the effectiveness of a WAC director, it is more important to examine the web of relationships that a WAC director establishes with others on campus than to focus on the director's personality traits.

Albert Lazlo Barabasi (2002) argues that interactivity with network hubs is key for innovative programs (such as WAC) since in complex networks, failures predominantly affect the smallest nodes first. Barabasi also points out that there is a critical threshold (the tipping point) where the number of links an innovation connects to begins to increase exponentially, and conversely, if an innovation fails to reach a threshold number of nodes, it is bound to fail. Finding points of interactivity in the university system is also key because of the network analysis concept of *preferential attachment*: actors are more likely to link to nodes that are already well connected and popular than to more isolated and less popular nodes.

The methodology that emerges from this theory is typically called social network analysis or organizational network analysis (ONA). Typically, ONA practitioners survey every member of the targeted group to uncover a specific set of organizational patterns within the group. Once the data is collected, the individual actors are visually mapped as a set of nodes in a three-dimensional network that provides links among actors in the form of lines connecting individuals, subsets, and larger groups. Such a detailed and comprehensive survey would not be practical or even necessary for most WAC programs. However, simply mapping the relationships among stakeholders could prove useful. At TAMUSA, this map would identify several sets of actors connecting the director to WAC committee members and each of those members to their respective departments. Katherine would also be connected to the writing center, which she directs, and the newly forming FYC program. Also included would be links to individuals in the library, faculty who will receive training, managers of e-portfolios, and curriculum committee members that will review course proposals across the institution.

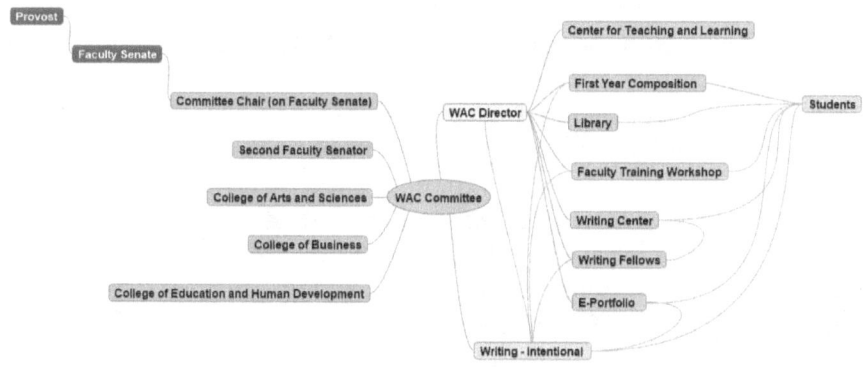

Figure 2: Early network map of TAMUSA's WAC program constructed by Jeff in consultation with Katherine Bridgman.

The more a stakeholder group can visualize the nodes, hubs, and links within the network, the easier it becomes to identify bottlenecks such as the "gatekeeping courses" mentioned in the institutional map, as well as conduits of change.

Complexity, systems, and social network theories offer approaches for describing, visualizing, and analyzing a complex system. To consider the effects of change on a system, we turn to resilience theory and sustainable development theory.

Resilience theory helps us understand how systems handle stresses yet maintain a relatively stable state. Resilience theory was first introduced to help understand the "capacity of ecosystems to handle challenges or changes to the system while maintaining a relative balanced state or to shift to an alternative, potentially transformative, state" (Folke et al., 2010, para. 3). For example, an ecosystem with an existing dam that has been in place for many years tends to reach a relatively stable state. As certain factors change over time, that same system can cross a threshold and reach an alternative stable state, which may or may not be as desirable as the previous state. For example, if the dam breaks and is not repaired, the system will settle into an alternative transformed state. The key to understanding these system changes are the feedback loops that "determine their overall dynamics" (Folke et al., 2010, para. 6). In the example of the dam, changes in the relatively stable state may be much less dramatic than a break, but lead nonetheless to equally significant shifts in the homeostatic state that the system reaches over time. Over-farming upstream could release enough phosphates into the lake to eventually result in a massive blue-green algae bloom that causes a mass fish kill. Resilience theory has implications for WAC program adaptation and longevity in relation to the curricular ecology—the relationship between social and curricular practices—of an institution. At TAMUSA, the introduction of downward expansion, e-portfolios, and a writing-intentional program all at once would put too much strain on faculty and curriculum committees to create a stable writing culture, so slowing down the development of the W-I initiative to ensure resilience became crucial. This shift enabled the WAC committee to propose a four-year timeframe for implementation so faculty could develop W-I courses and get them approved in sufficient numbers to avoid course bottlenecks for students taking these required courses.

Resilience theory reminds us that resilience and adaptability are dynamic processes that require constant monitoring and intervention. That initial stable state is going to shift over time as practices are tested and revised, as personnel come and go, and as program elements shift in purpose or function. To promote program resilience, the TAMUSA WAC committee established a system for re-certifying their W-I courses every three years and planned for the WAC committee to conduct an "annual program assessment using work that students include in their writing portfolios along with other documents from the program" (Texas A&M, 2017). Building in such monitoring is needed since interventions like the development of writing-intensive courses can easily shift away from their original intent with changes in the faculty who teach the course.

Compared to the other theories we've presented, **sustainable development theory** is significantly more project-focused and action-oriented, as it emerged to solve serious global challenges. Broadly defined, sustainable development is "development that meets the needs of the present without compromising the ability of future generations to meet their own needs" (United Nations World Commission, p. 43). This same UN report, referred to as the Brundtland Report, laid out the goal of building a future "that is more prosperous, more just, and more secure" (para. 3). This ambitious political agenda requires buy-in from stakeholders at every level of the system as well as clear guidelines for building consensus and introducing and assessing change. This theory thus provides a practical whole systems methodology for introducing change into a system by grounding program development in discrete projects that work through cycles of planning, doing, checking, and improving (Environment Canada, 2013) and for monitoring progress through sustainability indicators (Bell and Morse, 2008), further discussed below.

Sustainability serves as a core value and outcome of any significant curricular initiative, which is as important as the guiding vision of the curricular reform itself. No institution would undertake a potentially paradigmatic shift in its mission, with the time, money, and resources it takes to do so, without a desire for these changes to persist. Thus, in creating our whole systems approach for WAC program development, we've borrowed heavily from sustainable development theory. Inspired by a report on sustainability indicators that emerged from a sustainable development conference in 1996 in Bellagio, Italy (referred to as the Bellagio Report), we've developed a set of principles for sustainable WAC program development, while integrating insights from across the theories we introduce here. From sustainable development theory, we reconceptualized WAC programs and interventions (i.e. writing-intensive requirements, writing fellows programs, and faculty development institutes) as projects—each with their own cycles of development and assessment. And we've borrowed the idea of using sustainability indicators to guide program and project assessment. Below, we list the guiding principles we derived from the Bellagio Report and the five theoretical frameworks introduced above for developing WAC programs and then describe a methodology—also inspired by sustainable development theory—for putting these principles into action.

Principles for a Whole Systems Approach for WAC Program Development

The following principles represent a synthesis of our theoretical framework. They are interrelated and meant to be used as a full set, rather than piecemeal.

1. **Wholeness**: understanding a WAC program as a significant intervention within a complex system with competing ideologies and many levels, actors, and practices.
2. **Broad participation**: engaging stakeholders from all levels of the institution to help plan, approve, implement, and assess program goals, outcomes, and projects.
3. **Transformative change**: identifying points of leverage for introducing change to the university system at multiple levels, including changes in ideologies and practices as they relate to writing culture.
4. **Equity**: working to minimize disparities in current and future generations of WAC faculty and student writers.
5. **Resilience**: adapting to program challenges, maintaining self-organizing practices, and increasing the capacity for learning and adaptation to sustain desirable pathways for development.
6. **Leadership**: identifying leadership that can serve as the hub for the program, with the authority on campus to lead a cohesive effort of planning, launching, developing, and assessing WAC.
7. **Systematic development**: building a WAC program incrementally over time with a clear mission and prioritized goals.
8. **Integration**: building program components that synchronize with national and local mandates, integrate into existing structures and practices, and facilitate collaborative campus relationships.
9. **Visibility**: ensuring that program development, assessment, and change are transparent, regular, and public as well as promoting program events and successes through multiple means of reporting.
10. **Feedback:** identifying indicators and repeated measures to reveal trends, stimulate recursive and adaptive change, promote collective learning and feedback for decision-making, and determine whether a WAC program is in balance and whether individual WAC projects are sustainable and achieving their goal.

These principles underlie our methodology and strategies, which we describe below.

Whole Systems Methodology

Our whole systems methodology creates an iterative and participatory cycle to establish institutional change that integrates ongoing assessment of sustainability. It is designed for developing entire WAC programs as well as particular WAC projects (i.e. WI programs, faculty seminars, etc.) and tracks sustainability through the use of sustainability indicators (SIs) (see figure 3). We developed this methodology from two models used in sustainable development: Canada's Federal Sustainable Development Strategy (FSDS) (Environment Canada, 2013) and Bell and Morse's (2008) Imagine approach. The FSDS model was developed to implement a national strategy for sustainable development in Canada through a "plan, do, check, and improve" multi-stage approach. Like the FSDS model, Bell and Morse's Imagine model is project-based and cyclical, with stages of understanding context, imagining alternative scenarios, and publicizing projects. However, Bell and Morse's Imagine model places more focus on the participatory process of developing and using sustainability indicators to track and predict project sustainability.

SIs are the most significant distinguishing feature of sustainable development methodology. Emerging from the idea of indicator species, an SI may be understood as "a quantitative tool that analyzes changes, while measuring and communicating progress towards the sustainable use and management of economic, social, institutional, and environmental resources" (Olsson et al., 2004, p. 8). Rather than look at a single indicator, SIs "aim to develop a framework that tries to bring the economic, social and environmental aspects of society together, emphasizing the links between them" (Olsson et al., 2004, p. 9). For example, when considering the sustainability of a natural resource, one would not only focus on availability of the resource (say, coal), but also on environmental aspects (such as the impacts of extracting and burning coal on air and water quality and the release of toxic materials into the soil), economic aspects (such as the number of related jobs, impact on other industries in the area), and social aspects (such as the working conditions of coal miners and health risks to the local community). And each of these indicators must be clearly defined, reproducible, unambiguous, understandable, and practical. It should be possible to deduce from a set of chosen indicators the viability and sustainability of the given system being studied in comparison to alternate development paths, in this case, coal mining within a specific local ecology.

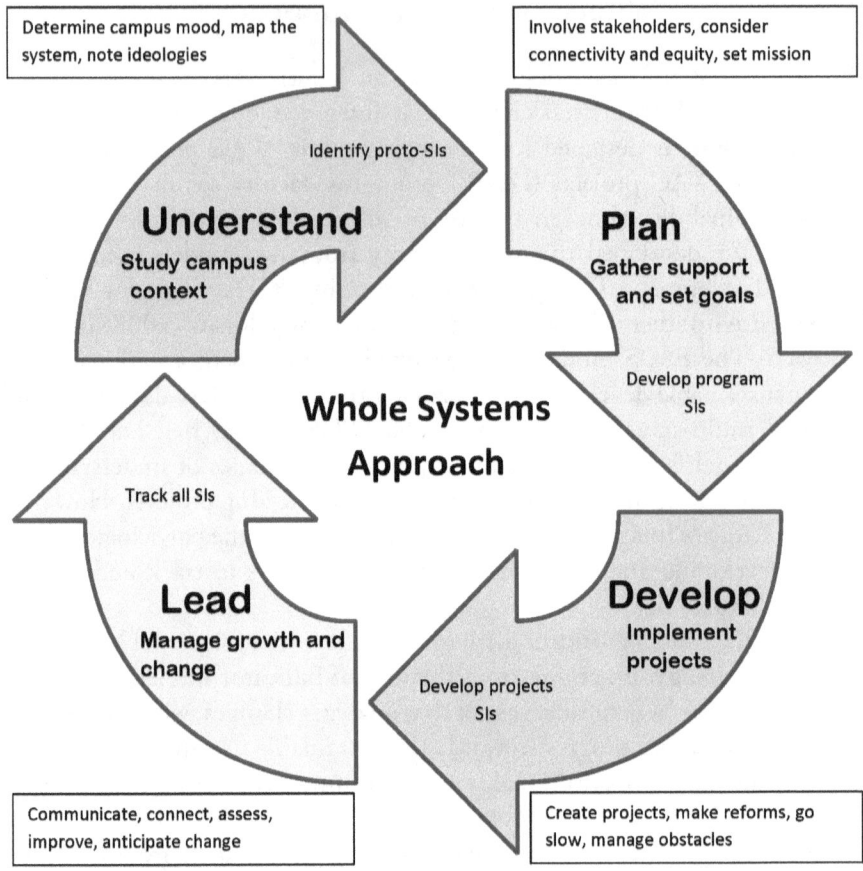

Figure 3. The whole systems methodology for transformative change.

To aid WAC directors in identifying SIs, we turn to a model introduced by Hardi and Zdan (1997) and extended by Bossel (1999). Their model focuses on three major systems, two of which include subsystems: the human system (comprised of individual development, the social system, and the government system); the support system (comprised of the economic system and infrastructure system); and natural system. These systems are outlined in figure 6, which Jeff adapted from Bossel (1999, p. 18) to reflect WAC concerns.

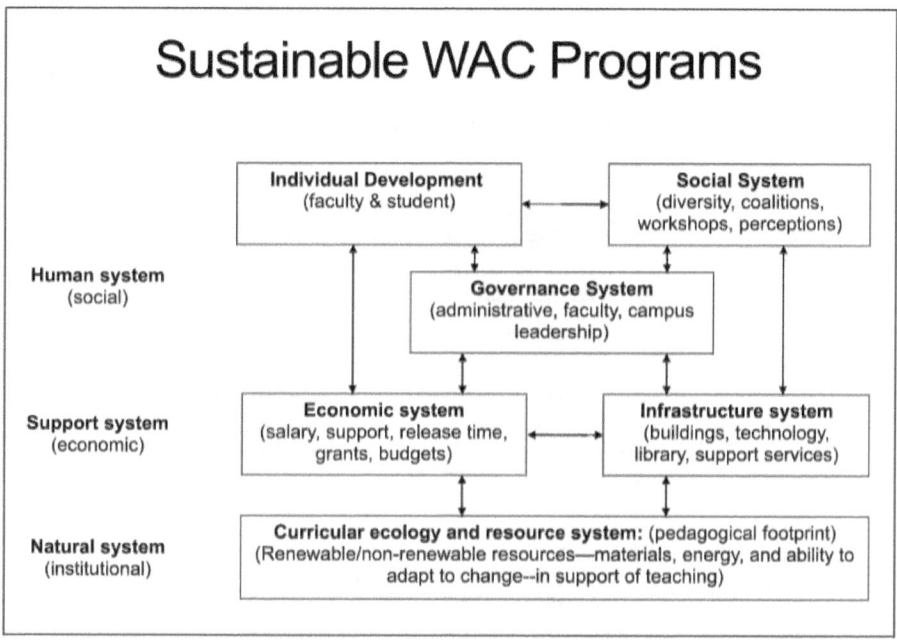

Figure 6: The six major systems of the anthrosphere and their major relationships. Reprinted from Galin, Jeffrey R. (2010), Improving rather than proving: Self-administered sustainability mapping of WAC programs. Council of Writing Program Administrators Conference, Minneapolis, MN.

These six systems of the WAC anthrosphere may serve as a heuristic for identifying SIs, particularly indicators of distress. Table 1 below demonstrates how TAMUSA might apply this heuristic to develop SIs for their W-I program:

Table 1

Example Indicators of Distress for TAMUSA

Level	Example indicators of distress
Individual	Director's time commitment increasing for WAC management without commensurate release time or compensation Compliance of W-I syllabi dropping significantly Student or faculty perceptions of WAC shifting negatively
Social	Membership of WAC committee decreasing or shifting so that it is no longer representative across campus Increase in administrative obstacles to program management or growth
Governance	Increasing class sizes resulting from university policy changes Dynamic program director leading too many faculty workshops to focus on other program development Decrease in writing quality in e-portfolios resulting from new statewide outcomes
Financial	Diminishing budget resulting from increased pressure from competing units Budget threshold overrun resulting from new costs and/or projects without commensurate budget increases
University Curricular Ecology	Fall in departmental participation resulting from merging or fracturing of college departments or divisions Insufficient classroom, office, or meeting space resulting from substantial changes in allocated space

Tracking SIs is so integral to sustainable development that we have included them in every stage of our methodology. The SIs themselves, however, are only the means of assessing the visibility and sustainability of a given program or project. Each of the four stages of the whole systems methodology—understanding, planning, developing, and leading—is scaffolded by a set of strategies that enable sustainable program development and growth.

Understanding, a stage we borrowed from the Imagine approach, involves examining the campus context, including the structures and network of relationships of the system.

Strategy 1: Determine the campus mood. "Campus mood" refers to the overall readiness of an institution for increased commitment to student writing. Determining the campus mood is a mix of collecting data, talking to stakeholders, reflecting on current writing practices across university contexts, identifying points of conflict and agreement about possible WAC program models, and identifying the current state of writing and teaching of writing on campus. This understanding will allow the WAC director to establish proto-SIs that mark the pre-implementation status of a WAC program. Determining the campus mood will also help program leaders facilitate an overall approach to program initiation, development, and timing. For example, if upper administration wants a WAC program but will not provide funds for a dedicated director, faculty support, or assessment processes, the mood for WAC might be judged somewhat hostile. Such a context would warrant a slower development, broader outreach, and possibly pilot projects that can be evaluated and then reported back to upper administration.

Strategy 2: Understand the system in order to focus on points of interactivity and leverage. Institutions of higher education are complex entities that not only foster connectivity through nodes and hubs (such as academic senates and centers for teaching), but also segregation and isolation (the siloed structure of departments and colleges). Creating rich visual maps of the places where writing occurs, the requirements involving writing, hubs of writing instruction, and the units and stakeholders impacting writing will help WAC directors choose interventions that will have leverage to make significant and sustainable change.

Strategy 3: Understand the ideologies that inform the campus culture of writing. The ideologies that define campus writing will inevitably shape the behavior of individual faculty and administrators. Understanding these ideologies helps to locate reinforcing processes that amplify problematic attitudes or behaviors. For example, an institution that is focused on timed writing tests is informed by a theory of writing as a product and creates an ideology and a process that reinforces that writing tasks can be completed and assessed in a single draft. Shifting from timed writing to portfolio assessment would not only change the theory of writing under which the system operates, but also could reinforce positive changes to students' conception of writing processes and teachers' writing pedagogies.

Planning involves gathering support, such as a WAC advisory board, and working with this group to determine program goals and the sustainability indicators that will guide program development.

Strategy 4: Involve multiple stakeholders in the system. Building WAC programs that have a high level of connectivity and influence requires the involvement of multiple stakeholders across the system and across scales, from individual faculty to department chairs to academic senate committees to deans and provosts. These stakeholders are crucial for building a

WAC program through participatory processes, including collaborating to map the system, setting the mission and goals, determining and operationalizing program sustainability indicators, and setting the agenda for program development.

Strategy 5: Work towards positioning the WAC program so that it has greater interconnectivity and leverage in the institution. WAC programs that do not fully integrate into existing institutional structures and do not move beyond a small core group are rarely sustainable. From their inception, every WAC program should aim to be a hub within its institutional network and not just a node. Furthermore, it is more effective to locate a WAC program in existing hubs that are connected across disciplines preferentially, like writing centers, centers for teaching, and independent writing departments, than a less connected node like a traditional English department. WAC directors can also link to highly connected institutional structures such as the faculty senate, libraries, academic assessment, or the office of institutional diversity. Connecting the WAC program in these ways also increases program stability by not being perceived as marginal or temporary, but integral to the institution.

Strategy 6: Consider the impact of WAC on faculty and student equity. A whole systems approach acknowledges that disparities of power exist in all human systems, that changes to a system typically affect different groups unevenly, and that when systems change, particular attention should be paid to groups with less power and visibility. For instance, the creation of WAC curriculum such as first-year writing seminars could unintentionally increase reliance on non-tenure track faculty or workload for junior faculty (LaFrance, 2015). The creation of a timed writing assessment could lead to inequitable conditions for multilingual students (Janopoulos, 1995). How WAC affects the faculty it involves and the students it serves should be considered in the early stages of program development and tracked with one or two SIs.

Strategy 7: Set mission, goals, and sustainability indicators. While WAC programs often develop organically and even opportunistically, those that set a mission statement, goals, and sustainability indicators in the development phase are more likely to have a system-wide impact, since they will be more coherent and goal-driven. These goals and indicators should be shaped by a group of stakeholders from across the networked system, such as a WAC advisory board. The mission, goals, and program outcomes then serve as a foundation for systematic program development and assessment.

Developing uses a systematic approach to fulfil mission and goals through project development and assessment.

Strategy 8: Maximize program sustainability through project-based program development. Translating program outcomes into action requires an intentional project-based approach. WAC projects such as writing-intensive initiatives or faculty development retreats are self-contained to a large degree, each targeting a specific problem/outcome and moving through a full set of stages from inception to implementation and assessment. SIs are developed in the initial stages of the project and evaluated regularly to establish threshold boundaries within which each project can be expected to function successfully. Taken together, a set of projects is used systematically to fulfill the program mission and goals. Using a project-based approach enables WAC leaders to prioritize which programs should be developed, in what order, and on what timeline to most impact the system.

Strategy 9: Make reforms at both the micro-level and the systems-level. In WAC programs, working at the micro-level (i.e. consulting with individual faculty, giving classroom presentations) and working at the systems-level (i.e. working with a department to create a departmental writing assessment plan, instituting a writing-intensive requirement) go hand in hand. Typically, when WAC programs start, the director focuses on the micro-level. This work is rewarding and can help the director establish relationships with faculty, create credibility, and build critical mass. However, if directors spend most of their time at the micro-level, then they can't spend much of their time at the systems-level, which is necessary for making enduring changes to the campus culture of writing.

Strategy 10: Plan for gradual rather than rapid reforms to the system. Academic institutions are complex organizations that do not change course easily. WAC programs seek to shift the culture of writing at the institution, and this kind of change happens incrementally. From established WAC programs, we know it can take many years to transform the writing culture a campus. Even specific projects can take years to develop fully. For example, a shift to building a writing-enriched curriculum model that involves departments making multi-year commitments to curriculum analysis and change might take several years to gain footing. Quick change can end in disaster, as quick changes do not allow time for cross-institutional buy-in or an understanding of the potential impact on other parts of the system.

Leading focuses on promoting program sustainability through program guidance and management.

Strategy 11: Deal with obstacles to program or project development systematically. The resiliency of a WAC program depends on its ability to overcome challenges and obstacles, which will inevitably arise throughout its development. A systems process for resolving conflicts necessitates a broad understanding of an obstacle, which includes collecting necessary data, considering the scope of its reach, coordinating with relevant stakeholders, balancing concerns that need to be considered, compromising, and proposing clear models or simulations to help predict the system's performance before the changes are implemented. For example, a dean who appeared supportive of WAC suddenly decides that a writing-intensive program cannot work because so many departments have large section courses. Rather than taking personal offense and confronting the dean, an approach might be to bring an external visitor to campus who made such a program work at another institution or encouraging use of breakout sections with TAs for the writing in these courses.

Strategy 12: Communicate regularly and at all levels of the system to keep the program visible. For WAC programs to be perceived as integral to the institution, they need to stay visible through good PR, partnering with popular campus hubs, and reminding other units of the program's relevance. This maintenance of visibility can take many forms—through WAC websites, newsletters, and event announcements—but also through such activities as preparing annual reports, attending campus meetings, joining university committees related to teaching and learning, and publishing results of WAC initiatives both locally and nationally. Creating visibility can also be about branding signature events like faculty retreats or student recognition ceremonies. Tracking visibility through SIs ensures that the program remains visible to faculty and administrators while not over inundating them with messages and events.

Strategy 13: Be aware of systems beyond your institution and connect to those that are beneficial to the WAC program. Changes in systems beyond your institution may affect the campus culture of writing. Some of these effects may be negative, such as a state government slashing funds for basic writing programs, and some may be positive, such as disciplinary accrediting bodies like IEEE, ABET, or CCNE increasing emphasis on written communication. Still other systems—such as the CCCC WAC Standing Group, the WAC Clearinghouse, IWAC conference, the WAC Summer Institute, NCTE, the Association for Writing Across the Curriculum, and the AACU—may provide a WAC leader with important resources, such as access to mentors, scholarship, and position statements. Tapping into such resources will assist WAC leaders as they seek to create change on their campuses.

Strategy 14: Assess and revise the WAC program. Systems tend toward segregation and stagnation, and comprehensive writing programs are susceptible to becoming static rather than dynamic if assessment feedback loops are not built into them. For example, a writing-intensive requirement without oversight or regular faculty development will most likely face dwindling enthusiasm and less coherence as a program. Ideally, WAC directors should identify a set of questions based on organizational and program maps (i.e. which departments are contributing WI courses?); identify the necessary but sufficient set of indicators to track program sustainability (i.e., what balance of WI course instructor rank would indicate a sustainable WI initiative?); develop an assessment model that keeps track of the full picture; and revisit the pool of questions and indicators as programs grow and change.

Strategy 15: Create a plan for sustainable leadership. There are many tales from WAC lore of vibrant WAC programs that crumbled when the leader stepped down or left for another institution. Distributed leadership models can help guard against this reliance on a single individual's energy or career choices. From a systems perspective, leadership that is located at only one point in the system and that comes from only one perspective is not as effective as leadership that is collective and disbursed throughout the system. Tactics include developing a critical mass of individual teacher-leaders across disciplines, working with a WAC advisory board or committee, creating graduation writing requirements that are overseen by cross-disciplinary committees, and developing an assistant director position.

THE WHOLE SYSTEMS APPROACH AT TAMUSA

When Katherine first reached out to Jeff, she described WAC as on the brink of the *developing* phase. Jeff convinced her and the WAC committee to take more time in the *understanding* and *planning* phases before moving forward. In his first meeting with the WAC committee, Jeff introduced four key points about program development, including the need to: (a) map visually how the program they were imagining would tie into existing initiatives on campus; (b) establish a clear mission statement and goals; (c) develop a set of sustainability indicators to track the emergence, growth, and sustainability of their WAC program; and (d) operationalize each SI by determining their bands of equilibrium with measurable thresholds of success and distress. This six-member committee had broad participation, with members from each college and the WAC director. It also had leverage to make change, since it was a subcommittee of the faculty senate and also had a direct line of communication to the provost.

Originally, the committee was going to propose only a single writing-intensive course requirement, but in an email to Katherine, Jeff prompted the committee to think about the larger goal of system-wide change:

> I would encourage you to think of WAC as the introduction of transformative change for the curriculum on your campus. If you

> can get [the committee] to think about more than just adding writing, but changing the way that writing is taught and perceived at the institution, then you have room to think of WAC as a shift in the whole curricular system, even if it is only starting with a few WI designated courses and some faculty support. If the committee can realize that a sustainable WAC program at most universities is much larger than a single WI initiative, they can set criteria for WI that situates it in this larger context. (Jeff Galin, personal communication, March 18, 2016)

The committee was persuaded by Jeff's argument that WAC should be thought of as a transformative intervention into the system, and they decided to aim for a more expansive four-course WI requirement. They slowed down the implementation process, established pilot courses to test out strategies, developed W-I criteria, extended the period for course development and faculty training to four years, and formulated an assessment plan.

During this process, the committee thought about project sustainability by considering the number of courses that need to be certified W-I (sufficient sections across the majors prevent bottlenecks for student progress), number of faculty trained (all faculty teaching W-I courses need to participate in WAC workshops), and sufficient funding (WAC director release time, faculty workshop stipends, assessment raters, departmental grants, additional faculty as course size drops). These parameters could all easily be translated into SIs. For example, they decided to cap W-I class sizes at twenty students. To establish an SI related to course size, they could set the band of equilibrium between fifteen students per course (a sign of distress, as it might indicate that students are putting off the requirement) and twenty-five students per course (another sign of distress, as it may mean that not enough sections are being offered). Indicating the band of equilibrium within which each SI remains sustainable can help WAC directors monitor initiatives and make arguments for appropriate funding and support.

When the new provost arrived mid-summer, he supported the committee's desire to slow down the implementation process from fall 2016 to fall of 2021. He also supported the committee's recommendation to shift from writing-intensive to "writing-intentional" courses and enabled one course to be piloted. The shift to W-I reflects a desire to focus on quality over quantity and an emphasis on high impact practices as defined by the AACU (Katherine Bridgeman, personal communication, April 18, 2017). A small group of instructors are now planning to pilot W-I courses in fall 2017 after participating in a six-week required training course and working with the WAC director. By 2021, all entering students will be required to take four

W-I courses, thus increasing the chances for transforming the institutional culture of literacy.

The careful and strategic process that the WAC committee engaged in reflects a whole systems approach that values incremental but sustainable reform over quick and easy reforms that often fail due to lack of buy-in or lack of influence on and leverage within the system.

BUILDING SUSTAINABLE WAC: FROM THE CAMPUS TO THE FIELD AT LARGE

Our principles and methodology provide the coherent and theorized approach that has been missing from the WAC lore, while still taking into consideration the highly specific contexts of an institutional landscape, comprised of curricular histories and politics, changing faculty and student demographics, and evolving missions and goals. Furthermore, our approach provides justification for moving slowly and systematically, positioning WAC programs within institutional hubs, and supporting WAC leaders with adequate resources for making the kinds of transformative changes to campus writing culture that we know WAC can generate and sustain.

This focus on transformative change, and the theoretical and methodological sophistication needed to develop sustainable WAC programs, may seem intimidating at first. However, we feel that the typical process to starting a WAC program is more intimidating. Many new WAC directors jump right into program implementation and then become overwhelmed, as they have not laid the groundwork, coordinated with stakeholders, or created a strategic plan. This accelerated startup leads quickly to director burn-out. This may have been the path that TAMUSA took if they had not taken up Jeff's suggestions to slow down, think systematically and strategically, and pilot a program before full implementation. Furthermore, our approach provided justification to upper administration for a slower roll-out, more institutional resources, and more stakeholder collaboration, which may lead to more buy-in across campus.

WAC leaders have always stressed that WAC is not a quick fix to a "problem" with student writing but has the larger goal of transforming a campus culture of writing. Until now, WAC has not had a theoretically-based framework, methodology, principles, and strategies for enacting this goal. We hope our whole systems approach provides this. We are also hopeful that the whole systems approach can begin to address the larger concerns that Walvoord expressed about the sustainability of WAC as a field. Walvoord argued that the lack of a coherent theory for WAC, as well as the field's focus on how WAC plays out on individual campuses, has prevented WAC from achieving the status of a national movement. In our larger project, we explore the implications of this framework for better understanding the vulnerabilities of the field at large and creating structures that promote sustainability, such as an umbrella organization for WAC.

References

Barabasi, A. L. (2002). *Linked: The new science of networks*. Cambridge, MA: Perseus.

Bell, S., & Morse, S. (2008). *Sustainability indicators: Measuring the immeasurable? 2nd ed.* Sterling, VA: Earthscan. Retrieved from https://www.u-cursos.cl/ciencias/2015/2/CS06067/1/material_docente/bajar?id_material=1210909

Bossel, H. (1999). *Indicators for sustainable development: Theories, methods, applications*. Winnipeg, Canada: International Institute for Sustainable Development.

Checkland, P. (1981). *Systems thinking, systems practice*. New York: Wiley and Sons.

Condon, W., & Rutz, C. (2012). A taxonomy of writing across the curriculum programs: Evolving to serve broader agendas. *College Composition and Communication, 64*(2), 357–82.

Cox, M., Galin, J., & Melzer, D. (2018). Sustainable WAC: A whole systems approach to launching and developing WAC programs. Urbana, IL: NCTE.

Cox, M., & Zawacki, T. M. (Eds.). (2011). WAC and second language writing: Cross-field research, theory, and program development [Special Issue]. *Across the Disciplines, 8*(4).

Environment Canada. (2013). Planning for a sustainable future: A federal sustainable development strategy for Canada 2013–2016. Retrieved from https://www.ec.gc.ca/dd-sd/default.asp?lang=En&n=A22718BA-1

Flood, R. L. (1990). Liberating systems theory: Toward critical systems thinking. *Human Relations, 43*(1), 49–75.

Folke, C., Carpenter, S. R., Walker, B., Scheffer, M., Chapin, T., & Rockström, J. (2010). Resilience thinking: Integrating resilience, adaptability, and transformability. *Ecology and Society, 15*(4), art. 20.

Fulwiler, T., & Young, A. (Eds.). (1990). *Programs that work: Models and methods for writing across the curriculum*. Portsmouth, NH: Boynton/Cook.

Hardi, P., & Zdan, T. (1997). *Assessing sustainable development: Principles and Practice*. Canada: The International Institute for Sustainable Development. Retrieved from https://www.iisd.org/pdf/bellagio.pdf

International Network of WAC Programs. (2014). Statement of WAC principles and practices. The WAC Clearinghouse. Retrieved from wac.colostate.edu/principles/

Jackson, M. (1985). Social systems theory and practice: The need for a critical approach. *International Journal of General Systems, 10*(2), 135–51.

Janopoulos, M. (1995). Writing across the curriculum, writing proficiency exams, and the NNES college student. *Journal of Second Language Writing, 4* (1) 43–50.

Johns, A. M. (1991). Interpreting an English competency exam: The frustrations of an ESL science student. Written Communication, 8, 379–401.
LaFrance, M. (2015). Making visible labor issues in writing across the curriculum: A call for research. *Forum: Issues about Part-Time and Contingent Faculty, 18*(3), A13–A17.
Leon, J. (2014). *Complexity science 2: Complexity theory* [YouTube Video]. Retrieved from www.youtube.com/watch?v=P00A9IZ7Pog
Marsden, P. (2005). Recent developments in network measurement. In P. J. Carrington, J. Scott, & S. Wasserman (Eds.), *Models and methods in social network analysis* (pp. 8–30). New York, NY: Cambridge University Press.
McLeod, S. (Ed.). (1988). Strengthening programs for writing across the curriculum. San Francisco: Jossey-Bass, 1988. Reprinted by the WAC Clearinghouse, 2002. Retrieved from http://wac.colostate.edu/books/mcleod_programs/
McLeod, S., Miraglia, E., Soven, M., & Thaiss, C. (Eds.). (2011). *WAC for the new millennium: Strategies for continuing writing-across-the-curriculum programs*. Urbana, IL: NCTE, 2011.
McLeod, S., & Shirley, S. (1988). Appendix: National survey of writing across the curriculum programs. In S. McLeod (Ed.), *Strengthening programs for writing across the curriculum* (pp. 103–30). San Francisco: Jossey-Bass.
McLeod, S. & Soven, M. (1991). What do you need to start—and sustain—a writing-across-the-curriculum program? *WPA: Writing Program Administration, 15*(1–2), 25–33.
McLeod, S., & Soven, M. (Eds.). (1992). Writing across the curriculum: A guide to developing programs. Newbury Park, CA: Sage Publications. Reprinted by the WAC Clearinghouse, 2000. Retrieved from http://wac.colostate.edu/books/mcleod_soven/
Midgley, G. (1996). What is this thing called CST? In R. Flood & N. Romm (Eds.), *Critical systems thinking: Current research and practice* (pp. 11–24). New York: Plenum Press.
Miraglia, E. & McLeod, S. (1997). Whither WAC? Interpreting the stories /histories of enduring WAC programs. *WPA: Writing Program Administration, 20*(3) 46–65.
Monroe, J. (2006). *Local knowledges, Local practices: Writing in the disciplines at Cornell*. Pittsburgh, PA: University of Pittsburgh Press.
Olsson, J. A., Hilding-Rydevik, T., Aalbu, H., & Bradley, K. (2004). *European regional network on sustainable development: Indicators for sustainable development*. Cardiff: Nordic Centre for Spatial Development.
Russell, D. R. (2002). *Writing in the academic disciplines: A curricular history*. Carbondale, IL: Southern Illinois University Press.
Segall, M., & Smart, R. (2005). *Direct from the disciplines: Writing across the Curriculum*. Portsmouth, NH: Heinemann.
Senge, P. (1990). *The fifth discipline: The art and practice of the learning organization*. New York: Doubleday.
Texas A&M - San Antonio. (2017). Writing-Intentional Course Requirement Proposal.

Thaiss, C. (2001). Theory in WAC: Where are we going, where have we been? In S. McLeod, E. Miraglia, M. Soven, & C. Thaiss (Eds.), *WAC for the new millennium: Strategies for continuing writing-across-the-curriculum programs* (pp. 299–325). Urbana, IL: NCTE.

Thaiss, C., Bräuer, G., Carlino, P., Ganobcsik-Williams, L. & Sinha, A. (Eds.). (2012). *Writing programs worldwide: Profiles of academic writing in many places.* The WAC Clearinghouse and Parlor Press.

Thaiss, C. & Porter, T. (2010). The state of WAC/WID in 2010: Methods and results of the U.S. survey of the International WAC/WID Mapping Project. *College Composition and Communication, 61*(3), 534–70.

Townsend, M. (2008). WAC program vulnerability and what to do about it: An update and brief bibliographic essay. *The WAC Journal, 19,* 45–61.

United Nations World Commission on Environment and Development. Report of the world commission on environment and development: Our common future. Retrieved from www.un-documents.net/our-common-future.pdf

Walvoord, B. (1996). The future of WAC. *College English, 58*(1), 58–74.

Wasserman, S., & Faust, K. (1994). *Social network analysis: Methods and applications.* Cambridge, MA: Cambridge University Press.

Young, A., & Fulwiler, T. (1990). The enemies of writing across the curriculum. In T. Fulwiler & A. Young (Eds.), *Programs that work: Models and methods for writing across the curriculum* (pp. 287–94). Portsmouth, NH: Boynton/Cook.

Zawacki, T. M. & Cox, M. (Eds.). (2014). *WAC and second-language writers: Research towards linguistically and culturally inclusive programs and practices.* The WAC Clearinghouse and Parlor Press.

Michelle Cox directs the English Language Support Office in the Knight Institute for Writing in the Disciplines at Cornell University. She chairs the CCCC WAC Standing Group and the Association for Writing Across the Curriculum. Her scholarship focuses WAC program administration, graduate student writing, and second language writing.

Jeffrey R. Galin is Associate Professor in the Department of English at Florida Atlantic University. He teaches academic and multimedia writing and is founding director of FAU's University Center for Excellence in Writing, WAC program, and Community Center for Excellence in Writing. His most recent co-authored book is *Sustainable WAC: A Whole Systems Approach to Launching and Developing Writing Across the Curriculum Program.*

Dan Melzer is an associate professor at the University of California, Davis, where he serves as the director of the first-year composition program. He has published the book *Assignments Across the Curriculum* and, with the authors of this article, *Sustainable WAC*. His articles have appeared in *College Composition and Communication*, *WPA*, and the *WAC Journal*.

Supplemental Material

"Building Sustainable WAC Programs: A Whole Systems Approach"

Michelle Cox, Jeffrey Galin, and Dan Melzer

Part I: Reflection on the Origins of the Article

This work began from two concerns by the authors: the need for a guide for building WAC programs that addresses current and complex contexts in higher education, and the concern that WAC programs fail at an alarming rate. The authors originally intended to write a kind of "how to" book for building WAC programs, but as we reviewed the literature we realized that what was missing in WAC was a robust theory and methodology for developing programs. Much of the guidance for developing WAC programs was based on lore, and there was a lot of wise and helpful advice, but it wasn't necessarily informed by a coherent theory or methodology, with the exception of Barbara Walvoord's article "The Future of WAC," which draws on social movement theory. We found inspiration for our theory and methodology as we read various complexity theories. Each theory of complexity we integrated provided a different affordance: systems theory helped us think about the macro level of WAC work and ways to transform institutional cultures of writing, social network theory provided methods for analyzing more micro relationships within systems, resilience theory helped us understand how WAC programs can manage stress and function within sustainable ranges over time, and sustainable development theory helped us conceive of a WAC program as a series of projects that aim for sustainable growth. Sustainable development theory also provided us with models for our "understand, plan, development, lead" methodology, the concept of sustainability indicators, and principles for sustainable growth that we revised and adopted for the purposes of WAC program building. Our project evolved from a simple "how to" guide to a complex process of theory-building and synthesis.

Part II: Description of Research Methods, Findings, and/or Pedagogical Impact

Our research methods focused primarily on synthesis. The various theoretical and methodological approaches to complexity that we included are not often explicitly in conversation with each other, so one goal was to make connections among these various complexity theories as well as to show how they can complement each other for the purposes of program development. There was also a great deal of translation of these theories for WAC program development. Complexity theories grew out of engineering, computer science, and environmental and social science, and although education scholars have considered the relevance of complexity theories for educational institutions, these theories had not been applied to WAC programs. Another aspect of our research method was theory building. As we synthesized the various complexity theories, we also consciously developed principles, strategies, and a methodology for building sustainable WAC programs that we hope provide a new theoretical approach, albeit one grounded in prior theories of complexity. Despite all this emphasis on theory, we also wanted to make the connection between theory and practice, so we put out a national call for vignettes from WAC directors and integrated these vignettes throughout our book *Sustainable WAC*. Although there was not room to include WAC program vignettes in this article, they inform our thinking about concrete strategies.

Our research has had a significant impact on our work as program directors. We have found ourselves acting more slowly and deliberately as we develop our programs and consider new projects, dwelling on the "understanding" stage and trying to understand the full context before we act. We have also become more deliberate about working across institutional stakeholders and finding ways to gather stakeholders across the institution in our programs and in our decision-making. We have become more strategic in our approaches to program development, and we are more focused on developing projects that have both impact and potential for sustainability. We are also more aware of how much time we are spending at the micro and macro levels of institutions. And at least two of us have begun to analyze our own programs for sustainability indicators.

We have also applied the WSA in positions as leaders in WAC as a field. As co-chairs (with Anne Ellen Geller) of the International Network of Writing Across the Curriculum Programs, we instigated a discussion at CCCC and IWAC of the potential of a national organization for WAC. Our primary goal was to help WAC's sustainability as the founders of the WAC movement retire. We see a connection between our research for this article and our book *Sustainable WAC* and the initial conversations that led to the formation of the CCCC WAC Standing Group and the Association for Writing Across the Curriculum.

Part III: Discussion Questions

1. How does the WSA differ from other approaches to writing program development and administration?

2. What types of WAC initiatives would you prioritize at your current institution for greatest impact and sustainability?

3. How can the WSA principles be applied to other types of writing programs (FYC, writing centers, independent writing programs, graduate writing support programs, etc.)?

4. What is the main challenge confronting your WAC program? How might you draw on the WSA methodology or strategies to address this challenge?

WLN: A JOURNAL OF WRITING CENTER SCHOLARSHIP

WLN: A Journal of Writing Center Scholarship is on the Web at https://wlnjournal.org/

WLN: A Journal of Writing Center Scholarship (previous title: *Writing Lab Newsletter*), a peer-reviewed publication with five issues per academic year, provides a forum for exchanging narrative and research-based studies of writing centers in high schools, colleges, and universities and addresses questions of the theoretical, pedagogical, and administrative work of writing centers. Articles illustrate how writing centers operate at the intersection of theory and practice, at once shaped by and producing innovative methods and scholarship. Authors reporting on research also describe programmatic models that can be adapted to other contexts. WLN aims to inform newcomers to the field as well as extend the thinking of those who are more knowledgeable and experienced. Authors are asked to keep their writing highly readable, useful, and brief (limited to 3000 words or less) and to keep our intended range of readers in mind. Issues of WLN regularly include a Tutors' Column of essays by and for tutors, essays that are often used in tutor training courses and discussed at staff meetings.

The Role of New Media Expertise in Shaping Consultations[1]

Drawing on the success of her own training program, Clements details how an assignment that challenged her tutors to learn how to use new media resulted in helping them gain confidence in their ability to work with students writing multimodal documents. Clements' article is aimed at many writing center directors who acknowledge that tutors should be equipped to meet with students who are using new media in their writing but are seeking guidance in providing training. Clements offers pragmatic suggestions for preparing to work with multimodal projects that could be valuable for both tutors and writing teachers who feel that they should offer more multimodal opportunities. As such, this article offers needed information both for newcomers and more experienced writing center professionals who read WLN. It speaks to experienced directors, who tend to help tutors become skilled users of multiple types of software and proposes instead a different goal when training tutors—to help them build a sense of confidence that they can work effectively with writers using various types of software and apps. For newcomers, Clements offers a lengthy series of practical suggestions, resources, and strategies and does so in clear, easily accessible prose, a goal of *WLN*.

---

1. *WLN: A Journal of Writing Center Scholarship*, vol. 43, no. 9–10. © 2019 by WLN.

The Role of New Media Expertise in Shaping Consultations

Jessica Clements

It is easy to say that digital technologies are changing contemporary communication—less easy to say *how* writing center practitioners should address this change. To explore the latter, I replicated Sue Dinitz and Susanmarie Harrington's study "The Role of Disciplinary Expertise in Shaping Writing Tutorials" to better understand how a tutor's new media expertise might affect a tutorial's overall effectiveness and what implications that might hold for how we best educate our tutors to address technology-rich writing assignments. My findings suggest that tutors' *confidence* may impact effectiveness more than their *expertise* with new media; therefore, this article includes practical suggestions for building new media composing confidence within existing tutor education programs.

CONTEXT: WRITING CENTERS AND "NEW MEDIA" EXPERTISE

Global Response: "New media" can be understood in a variety of ways but largely comprises textual production that transcends traditional word-based, print-based writing forms. When we think of new media, we often think of composing projects that use digital technologies, but new media texts do not have to be digital. Rather, multimodal texts—texts that utilize some combination of linguistic, visual, aural, gestural, and spatial modes of communication (words, photos, color, layout, etc.)— comprise the essence of new media composition. In other words, new media can be defined as interactive forms of communication technologies (Arola, et al. 4; Lee and Carpenter xviii).

Writing centers have tended to respond to new media in one of three ways (Lee and Carpenter xix):

1. *Hire tutors with little to no pre-existing new media-specific knowledge.* Most writing centers already carry the weight of helping writers across a plethora of disciplines and academic ranks. Writing center professionals may be reticent to add another dimension of assistance if we are uncertain of our own expertise in that regard (Grutsch McKinney 255).

2. *Require tutors to have a working knowledge of new media composition.* If writing tutors are already trained to respond to the rhetorical principles underlying a piece of writing, then why can't that knowledge be extended to improve new media compositions as well? "We don't need to be, say, filmmakers to respond to video in new media composition. However, we do need to be able, at a minimum, to respond to how the video relates to the whole of the text" (Grutsch McKinney 251).

3. *Require tutors to possess (or acquire) expertise in new media technology and software.* We must be careful not to conflate "expertise" with "mastery" and to note that this expertise is often practically enacted by a handful of specialist tutors within larger generalist organizations—much like Writing in the Disciplines tutors facilitate writing tutoring with disciplinary familiarity within larger writing programs.

Local Practice: I educate my small liberal arts college (primarily undergraduate) tutors by targeting the middle ground: cultivating a working knowledge of new media composition. Tutors apply and are interviewed in the fall. Selected tutors take a mandatory writing center theory and practice preparation course in the spring. In the preparation course, I require prospective tutors to complete a "Visual Rhetoric in Practice" assignment that I modified from Tammy Conard-Salvo's. This assignment asks them to "support an argument through advertising" or to craft a message primarily through visual means. To ground the assignment, I invite them to use our center's mission as the subject of their ad. I also ask them to complete a three-to four-page word-based reflection to explain how meaning was built in their visual message. We study contrast, repetition, alignment, and proximity (C.R.A.P), color theory, and the essentials of typography, and I introduce Adobe InDesign as a composing option. We spend significant time locating resources and discussing strategies for troubleshooting new media composing challenges.

Students have been both creative and critical of the work they produce for this assignment and excel at identifying individual rhetorical choices at work in their compositions—but *is that enough?* Will this foundational journey into the basic principles of visual rhetoric afford tutors sufficient expertise to help writers with the disparate multimodal projects that will cross their tutoring tables?

Study Design: In order to test the efficacy of my approach to new media tutor education, I replicated the methods of Dinitz and Harrington's study "The Role of Disciplinary Expertise in Shaping Writing Tutorials," one of the first empirical inquiries into the generalist versus specialist tutor debate. Replicating their methods (videotapes and coded transcripts of tutorial sessions) proved an apropos fit for my study given our shared goals of close and objective analysis of "how tutor expertise actually affects tutoring sessions" (74). I video-recorded writing center sessions involving multimodal projects (defined as any project transcending traditional word-based, print-based media) in Spring 2016, ultimately garnering fifteen willing participant tutor-writer pairs. To understand the role of new media expertise in shaping writing consultations, I considered whether each session was effective, overall, in "its likelihood in resulting in successful revision" (Dinitz and Harrington 79). An effective session was characterized by a tutor's ability to address global issues, to evaluate and—when necessary—challenge a writer's point of view, to ask questions to productively extend conversation, and to afford general lessons for the writer's development (85).

Results: Having Confidence Matters: Three patterns emerged from the videotaped and transcribed new media tutorials.

First, each tutorial presented a strikingly similar session structure—similar to one another and similar to what one might expect of a traditional word-based, print-based text tutoring session: agenda-setting and early session consulting focused on global issues, mid-session consulting focused on investment in more specific local issues, and end-of-session consulting that revisited global issues. Some sessions were more productively iterative than others, but tutors were clearly confident in opening sessions focused on global issues. Tutors asked adept questions about audience, purpose, and context when situating the work that needed to be done on their writers' new media compositions, primarily comprising whether the chosen media was appropriate for the communicative task at hand.

Second, in discussing local issues—such as particular font or color choices—most tutors were able to articulate the effectiveness of local media-specific choices related to audience and purpose. A few tutors devolved into less-than-productive like/dislike responses, which often tell us more about the unique and sometimes quirky predilections of an individual reader and less about the rhetorical response the author will likely garner from the target audience. However, this problematic response was offered less prevalently than tutors recalling and applying productive multimodal composing language, such as discussing the basic design principle of alignment and how alignment choices would impact what the author wants to "tell" their audience. Surprisingly, those same tutors opted to subsequently undercut their authority with phrases like "I'm not an expert in design . . ." While it can be helpful for a tutor to qualify their response "as a reader" (suggesting there are other viable composing choices available and that the author is ultimately responsible for making that choice), leaving a statement such as "I'm not an expert in design" without qualification—without pointing the writer to additional resources that could confirm or challenge the tutor's reading—might leave the writer questioning the effectiveness of the advice that was offered. This type of move is likely to undercut the success of the tutor's evaluation and credibility in challenging writers' points of view when necessary.

Third, when writers offered a working knowledge of new media composing, tutors felt confident in extending the writer's knowledge with their own working knowledge; however, when working with writers new to new media composition, only tutors with more "expert" knowledge of new media composing (or at least *more regular practice*) were able to project confidence. I determined sessions as more successful when (A) the *writer* already had strong ideas regarding the nature of what they wanted to compose, in what media, and through which software, and/or (B) when the *tutor* expressed additional confidence garnered through regular engagement with multimodal projects and software outside of tutor education and regularly scheduled tutoring hours (a confidence they may or may not have garnered through their disciplinary coursework).

In general, the study results speak to a productive level of engagement and improvement in each of the multimodal composing tutorials; writers were afforded sound advice that could improve the quality of the new media project at hand from tutors with working knowledge of new media composing strategies. Yet two prevalent patterns emerged from the transcript data that suggest generalist tutors' new media composing advice was clouded by a lack of confidence in that working knowledge, which has the potential to undermine or otherwise negatively impact the overall effectiveness of individual tutoring sessions. Even when tutors structure sessions productively, those sessions may be adversely affected if they feel compelled to (1) undercut the credibility of their new media composing advice or (2) wait for the writer to forward new media composing ideas if the tutor has no disciplinary resources or recent practice of their own from which to draw. While working knowledge may afford potential or temporary successes, tutors may need more than "working confidence" to create and *sustain* a tutoring environment in which new media composing strategies can be productively imparted and effectively retained to make writers better writers.

SUGGESTIONS AND RESOURCES FOR NEW MEDIA TUTOR EDUCATION

What can writing center practitioners do to build tutors' new media composing confidence? In this section, I offer practical suggestions for implementing new media education into existing writing tutoring programs—resources I have turned to in the past as well as strategies I intend to employ in the future based on the results of this study and on my continued scholarly engagement with the larger field of rhetoric, technology, and digital writing. I offer both small-scale and larger time- and money-intensive investments to support writing centers in a variety of institutional contexts. Suggestions and resources span the following five areas: promotion, formal education, individualized learning, tutors helping tutors, and hiring. Extended discussion of these pedagogical possibilities can be accessed in my chapter in the digital collection, *How We Teach Writing Tutors*.

Promotion: An intuitive way to get tutors more practice with new media composing is to funnel more multimodal project traffic into the writing center. I recently asked my tutors to serve as "Department Ambassadors," sitting in on department meetings to inquire about each department's relationship with the writing center. When it came time to pitch writing center services, we found that most weren't cognizant of the multimodal services we offered but that they would be enthused to assign more multimodal composing projects knowing this support was in place.

Formal Education: To support a culture of sustained, critical engagement with multimodal composing, in the Fall of 2018 I implemented a one-credit practicum that all employed tutors were required to take. Increasing tutors' confidence in consulting technology-rich assignments requires narrowing the scope of such a follow-up practicum to suit new media-specific needs: offering a curriculum scaffolded to address making invisible modal choices visible, facilitating meaningful access (see Banks), and, most importantly, engaging in a *series* of multimodal composing assignments. Ultimately, I advocate the need for follow-up reflection, a concerted effort on the part of participating tutors to actively and explicitly process and build upon their growing multimodal composing expertise.

Individualized Learning: At institutions where time and money are scarce, practitioners can point their tutors to multimodal composing resources freely available on the web, such as the Adobe Education Exchange, where you can "download free tutorials, projects, and lessons to teach digital media." These self-paced and online community-supported tutorials can be undertaken by tutors or practitioners as a part of required or voluntary professionalization. Some other multimodal composing resources I continue to utilize to productive ends in that regard include the following:

- **C.R.A.P.** *The Non-Designer's Design Book* (now in its fourth edition) has long been praised for its clear and careful explication of the four basic principles of design: contrast, repetition, alignment, and proximity (Chapters 2-6).
- **Typography.** The Purdue Online Writing Lab is a helpful starting point for discussing "Using Fonts with Purpose." Font personality, or why we wouldn't compose a professional email in Curlz MT, for example, is well illustrated in College Humor's "Font Conference" video. I would also recommend *The Non- Designer's Design Book*'s "The Essentials of Typography" for a more advanced understanding of things like sans/serif fonts, kerning, leading, etc. Finally, "WhattheFont" is a helpful tool that writers at any stage of multimodal expertise can use to identify fonts instantly.
- **Color.** There are many resources that introduce color theory, including the Purdue OWL and *The Non-Designer's Design Book*. Lesser-known and equally compelling resources include Claudia Cortés's *Color in Motion*, described as "an animated and interactive experience of color communication and color symbolism." There is also Adobe Color CC where writers can "Create" color schemes according to various color "rules."
- **Copyright and Creative Commons**. "A Fair(y) Use Tale" is an accessible Disney-parody explanation of copyright law and fair use. I would also suggest that tutors and the writers they work with be introduced to Creative Commons, a site that offers composers alternative licensing to copyright so that works may be circulated under "generous, standardized terms."
- **Software**. Not all writers will have privileged access to industry-leading composing software such as Adobe InDesign. That is why I make a point to introduce my tutors to open- source alternatives (Lynch), such as Canva or Scribus.

Tutors Helping Tutors: Concern about practitioner new media expertise is valid and can be ameliorated by taking advantage of what writing centers are best known for: peer-led learning. I implemented a task force model in my writing center to organize research and development among tutors. Tutors pursue task force work during downtime and have been required to engage their peers in directed education at staff meetings. Practitioners might also consider facilitating formalized peer mentor relationships— pairing tutors with contrasting levels of new media composing expertise—with the goal of jointly increasing tutor mentors' and mentees' new media composing confidence.

Hiring: Whether you operate a generalist, specialist, or hybrid generalist/specialist writing center, you have the opportunity to inventory and assess your potential tutors' new media proficiencies through recruitment, application, and/or interview processes. My center's writing tutor application, for example, asks applicants to speak to the following question: "Any specialized areas of expertise (i.e., ELL, business/technical writing, creative writing, multimodal writing, etc.)?" Such an inventory allows tutors to take ownership of existing new media expertise as well as identify areas for growth and development.

Conclusion

What I have learned from this study is that a working knowledge of new media composing is productive—desirable, even. And a single tutor education course assignment such as Visual Rhetoric in Practice can successfully foster that working knowledge; however, if we are looking for our tutors to consistently use that working knowledge with optimum effectiveness in a variety of multimodal composing situations, then we must also attend to *confidence*. That is, heeding Grutsch McKinney's and others' calls to embrace the evolution of technology-rich twenty-first century writing and to attend to new media composition as a significant— if not inherent—component of our contemporary writing center support praxis requires fashioning tutor education that does not prompt generalist tutors to consistently hedge their multimodal composing advice. We need to better support writing tutors who are not already embedded in disciplines invested in multimodal composing practices, tutors who may feel at a loss for ideas when it comes to working with writers on projects like infographics, research posters, or scholarly web texts. The results of this study suggest that tutors with working knowledge of new media composing have valuable advice to offer the writers they consult with; they just don't always feel confident in delivering that advice. So, if we want to decrease opportunities for writers to doubt the authority of tutors' (constructive!) new media composing advice, and if we want tutors to feel as confident in the resources they have for tutoring white paper design as they are confident in tutoring first-year composition rhetorical analyses, then we must provide *sustained engagement* with new media composing in our tutor education practices.

Works Cited

Adobe Systems. *Adobe Color CC*, 2016, color.adobe.com.

—. *Adobe Education Exchange*, 2017, edex.adobe.com.

Arola, Kristin L, et al. *Writer/Designer: A Guide to Making Multimodal Projects.* Bedford, 2014.

Banks, Adam. *Race, Rhetoric, and Technology.* Lawrence Erlbaum, 2006.

Clements, Jessica. "The Role of New Media Expertise in Shaping Writing Consultations." *How We Teach Writing Tutors: A* WLN *Digital Edited Collection*, edited by Karen G. Johnson and Ted Roggenbuck, 2019, wlnjournal.org/ digitaleditedcollection1/Clements.html.

Conard-Salvo, Tammy. *English 390-A01: Tutoring Practicum in Writing for First Year Composition.* Fall 2016. web.ics.purdue.edu/~tcsalvo/English390A/ syllabusfall2016.pdf.

Cortés, Claudia. *Color in Motion*, vimeo.com/129112056.

Creative Commons. "About the Licenses." *Creative Commons*, Creative Commons, 7 Nov. 2017, creativecommons.org/licenses/.

Dinitz, Sue, and Susanmarie Harrington. "The Role of Disciplinary Expertise in Shaping Writing Tutorials." *The Writing Center Journal*, vol. 33, no. 2, 2014, pp. 73-98.

"A Fair(y) Use Tale." *YouTube*, uploaded by Jas A, 18 May 2007, www.youtube.com/watch?v=CJn_jC4FNDo.

"Font Conference." *YouTube*, uploaded by CollegeHumor, 28 July 2008, www.youtube.com/watch?v=i3k5oY9AHHM.

Grutsch McKinney, Jackie. "New Media Matters: Tutoring in the Late Age of Print." *Writing Centers and New Media*, edited by Sohui Lee and Russell Carpenter, Routledge, 2014, pp. 242-56.

Lynch, Ryan. "5 of the Best Free Adobe InDesign Alternatives." *Make Tech Easier*, Uqnic Network Pte, 6 Mar. 2018, www.maketecheasier.com/ free-adobe- indesign-alternatives.

MyFonts. "WhatTheFont Mobile App." *MyFonts*, 1999-2018. www. myfonts.com/ WhatTheFont/mobile.

OWL at Purdue University. "Using Fonts with Purpose." *The Purdue OWL*, Purdue U Writing Lab, 17 Apr. 2010, owl.purdue.edu/owl/general_writing/visual_ rhetoric/ using_fonts_with_purpose/index.html.

Williams, Robin. *The Non-Designer's Design Book.* 4th ed., Peachpit, 2015.

Jessica Clements is Assistant Professor of English and Director of the Composition Commons at Whitworth University. She has served as Style Editor for *Present Tense* since 2012. Her scholarship centers on ethos and the role of human and object-oriented actors in contemporary multimodal communication.

Supplemental Material

"The Role of New Media Expertise in Shaping Consultations"
Jessica Celements

Part I: Reflection on the Origins of the Article

Fresh out of graduate school, I was hell-bent on ensuring those around me understood that writing no longer exclusively comprises word-based, print-based genres, that effective twenty-first century communication, in fact, is predicated on one's facility with connecting to networked assemblages of diverse audiences through adept multimodal composing choices. As a new assistant professor I was given the opportunity to reinvent the writing center at my small liberal arts college in the Pacific Northwest, and I, naively, assumed the students would already be "with me" in this regard. They *were* "with me" in the sense that they responded well to visual rhetoric education; they could well articulate how compositional design choices worked through visual hierarchy to communicate a rhetorical message to an audience. They even qualified exploring multimodal forms of communication as a valuable, eye-opening experience, one that created empathy for clients who might struggle to engage with a particular type or kind of academic writing. What I wasn't prepared for, however, was the metaphorical backchannel of resistance to multimodal consulting in practice. Consultants would engage with the occasional writer who brought a PowerPoint presentation or InDesign poster to the Commons, but I could see the fear in their eyes whenever I asked who was ready to lead the next Composing with Adobe InDesign workshop. They did not desire ownership of their roles as technology-rich writing experts. I desired to explore this conundrum in a systematic way.

Blessed with a richly rigorous rhetorical education from Purdue University, I knew I would need to design research that was replicable, aggregable, and data-driven if I wanted it to be taken seriously by the field as a whole. Turning to Dinitz and Harrington's "The Role of Disciplinary Expertise in Shaping Writing Tutorials" was an easy choice given how neatly multimodal composing fits into the continua of generalist vs. specialist writing tutor theory the authors were exploring; multimodal composing is, indeed, a "special" form of composing. I enlisted the help of my consultants in the data gathering and transcribing phases and am grateful for their open and honest reflections along the way. When the theme of "confidence" arose through careful data analysis, it was a lightbulb moment for me. I had found something specific to focus on when addressing this theory to practice disparity in future professionalization opportunities with my consultants. Finally, I have always had a passion for pedagogy, so practical applications were a "must" for fleshing out this article, which went through at least 7 rounds of revision. I am proud to have the results published in not only the May/June 2019 special issue of *WLN* but also the *How We Teach Writing Tutors* digital edited collection, https://wlnjournal.org/digitaleditedcollection1/Clements.html, an exceptional resource that all writing center practitioners should check out.

Part II: Description of Research Methods, Findings, and/or Pedagogical Impact

Navigating this research project helped me to actualize a growing desire for formalized ongoing professionalization opportunities for my writing center consultants. EL 421: Writing Center II (a one-credit practicum required of all currently employed writing tutors) now exists at my institution. I am fortunate to have this opportunity to meet weekly with my consultants to discuss pressing topics affecting their daily work in the Composition Commons, such as working effectively with writers engaging in multimodal composing. Since the Fall 2018 inception of EL 421, we have tackled the "Visual Rhetoric in Practice" (VRP) project versions 2-5: VRP remix, Adobe InDesign instruction set, writing center social media memes, and consultant manual revision (well-designed edition).

Outside of directly impacting my praxis in this way, the project sparked a string of scholarly projects focused directly on writing center pedagogy. My colleague, librarian and Director of Instructional Services Marianne Stowell Bracke, and I penned "It Takes a Village: Assembling Meaningful Access to Information Literacy through Library-Writing Center Partnerships." The chapter, which is forthcoming in *Advances in Library Practices in Higher Education: International Perspectives on Improving Student Engagement*, details our case study in which we jointly introduced writing center consultants to the ACRL Information Literacy Framework, how information is created, and strategies to help writing center clients with source evaluation; in this chapter, we forward our theory that assembling meaningful access to information literacy involves integrating the expertise of a wide variety of stakeholders, each tasked with facilitating a more pointed look at a smaller piece of the information literacy puzzle to an audience with whom they can best relate. I also recently finished final edits on "The Quest for Intersectional Awareness: Educating Tutors through Gaming Ethnography," a chapter which is forthcoming in Unlimited Players: The Intersections of Writing Center and Game Studies. In this chapter, I investigate the affordances of intersectional tutor education as effectively accomplished through game studies methodology: a gamer's autoethnography.

I, of course, have not completely solved the conundrum of waning confidence in multimodal composition consultation. At the March 2019 IWCA Collaborative in Pittsburgh, I presented a project-in-progress titled "Affective Bridges: Emotional Overload and the Professionalization of the Undergraduate Writing Tutor." In this presentation, I explored how continued education, writ large, was perceived by consultants to require too much—too much time, energy, and intellectual/emotional investment—prompting the following research questions: How/does the emotional labor of daily consulting affect undergraduate tutors' willingness to engage in extra-consulting endeavors? And, how should a director respond to such consultant exacerbation given emotionally dissonant feelings? I hope to continue to explore these questions in future research as well as to dive into how interdisciplinary approaches to documentation and assessment might reveal more productive means to probing such writing center phenomena.

Part III: Discussion Questions

1. How can generalist and specialist writing consultants best support multimodal composition in diverse writing center contexts, including a/synchronous virtual consulting?

2. What are readily accessible resources for facilitating multimodal composition tutor education as technology, and technology-rich forms of composing, continue to evolve?

3. How might writing center directors combat their own hesitancies toward technology-rich composition or lack of confidence in multimodal composition expertise to facilitate writing center professionalization opportunities surrounding new media more efficiently?

4. What intersectional variables may be influencing consultant and client engagement with multimodal composition in addition to expertise and confidence?

5. How might documentation and assessment strategies be interrogated in order to assist a writing center in productively moving forward with multimodal composition support?

www.ingramcontent.com/pod-product-compliance
Lightning Source LLC
Chambersburg PA
CBHW032141230426
43672CB00011B/2415